The Northern Ireland experience of conflict and agreement

MANCHESTER
1824

Manchester University Press

The Northern Ireland experience of conflict and agreement

A model for export?

Robin Wilson

Manchester University Press
Manchester and New York
*distributed in the United States exclusively
by Palgrave Macmillan*

Published by Manchester University Press
Oxford Road, Manchester M13 9NR, UK
and Room 400, 175 Fifth Avenue, New York, NY 10010, USA
www.manchesteruniversitypress.co.uk

Distributed in the United States exclusively by
Palgrave Macmillan, 175 Fifth Avenue, New York,
NY 10010, USA

Distributed in Canada exclusively by
UBC Press, University of British Columbia, 2029 West Mall,
Vancouver, BC, Canada V6T 1Z2

British Library Cataloguing-in-Publication Data
A catalogue record for this book is available from the British Library

Library of Congress Cataloging-in-Publication Data applied for

ISBN   978 0 7190 8289 4   hardback

First published 2010

Edited and typeset
by Frances Hackeson Freelance Publishing Services, Brinscall, Lancs
Printed in Great Britain
by CPI Antony Rowe Ltd, Chippenham, Wiltshire

Contents

List of figures and tables

Figures

Tables

Foreword

The 'troubles' in Northern Ireland are doubtlessly among the most widely covered and analysed conflicts. They have been featured in popular film, fiction and music, in electronic and print media, in reports by think tanks and NGOs, and in the academic literature on conflict and conflict settlement. For more than three decades, the questions asked were about the causes and consequences of the conflicts in, and over, Northern Ireland and how best to address them. Settlement initiatives were proposed and regularly failed to make a lasting impact. Peace seemed as elusive in Northern Ireland as in the Middle East, Cyprus or Kashmir.

All this changed fundamentally in the course of the 1990s. Initiatives by the British and Irish governments were followed by ceasefires announced by the main paramilitary organisations – republican and loyalist alike. Eventually, a complex institutional bargain for power-sharing in Northern Ireland, cooperation between the governments in Belfast and Dublin, and arrangements for the whole of the British Isles was negotiated among the local political parties and the two governments, aided significantly by the skilled, sustained, and high-level commitment of the Clinton administration. The agreement of 1998 led to two of its principal architects – John Hume and David Trimble – winning the Nobel Peace Prize. Referendums north and south of the border overwhelmingly endorsed the agreement.

Yet, not all was well. Implementation of the agreement was slow and stalled frequently over a myriad of issues, which in their majority were related to the decommissioning of the IRA's deadly arsenal of weapons. As Northern Ireland went off the news headlines and radar screens of policy-makers, the institutions established under the 1998 agreement were suspended frequently and for increasingly longer periods. Alleged 'hard-liners' became ever more powerful in electoral terms, and while nobody seriously considered a resurgence of large-scale violence to result from this, Northern Ireland had lost much of its glamour as an 'example' of successful conflict settlement.

More change, and this time for the better, was under way, though. In 2006 the leaders of Sinn Féin and the Democratic Unionist Party, by then the dominant political forces in their respective communities, and the two governments in London and Dublin reached an agreement at St Andrews that enabled a restoration of the power-sharing institutions in Northern Ireland, albeit with significant modifications. This new agreement ushered in a period of unprecedented political stability and progress in Northern Ireland. While not everything may be perfect and flawless, there was still a well-founded sense of real achievement, especially among those political elites intimately tied to the St Andrews Agreement in Belfast, London and Dublin.

This sense of success after so many failures has given rise to a trend to see Northern Ireland as a hallmark of successful conflict settlement, a model for export to other troubled regions. However, is this enthusiasm justified? Robin Wilson's study *The Northern Ireland Experience of Conflict and Agreement* asks precisely this all-important question, focusing on its two crucial aspects – the process of achieving agreement and the institutional 'content' of the compromise that the parties agreed. These are hard and necessary questions to consider if political science is to have an impact on the 'real world' of policy formulation and implementation in the area of conflict settlement. Too often lessons are learned selectively and out of context, applied elsewhere without the necessary sensitivity to specific conditions and often without consideration of the likely consequences of, and possible alternatives to, a specific set of institutions designed to help manage conflict by peaceful and democratic means.

Drawing on his own extensive experience in Northern Ireland, Wilson considers international efforts in the western Balkans as well – another laboratory of international conflict management. He engages thoroughly with the theory and practice of power-sharing, acknowledging its usefulness and shortcomings, and draws important conclusions that inform this most enduring debate in the field of conflict resolution. This leads him to a set of far-reaching proposals as to how Northern Ireland might be able to move from the uneasy peace established since the late 1990s to genuine reconciliation between the communities and the political elites that lead them. Once this has been comprehensively achieved, the peace process in Northern Ireland and its negotiated outcome(s) may truly be a model for export.

Stefan Wolff

Stefan Wolff is Professor of Political Science at the University of Nottingham where he also directs the Centre for International Crisis Management and Conflict Resolution. He has widely written on ethnic conflict and conflict resolution, and is frequently advising governments and international organisations in peace negotiations and on questions of institutional design.

Preface

Northern Ireland is no longer the relentless headline-maker in the global media it once was, when multiple killings and bombings provided a daily diet of depressing news and images. But the sequence of political moments in its recent past, pronounced by government leaders in London, Dublin and Washington to be 'historic' – the 1994 paramilitary ceasefires, the 1998 Belfast agreement, the establishment of power-sharing institutions in 1999 and their renewal in 2007 – have embedded in states across the globe a hazy but widely shared notion that this is a remarkable success story of a transformation from irrational sectarian violence to peace and reconciliation. This superficial grasp of a far more complex historical trajectory has opened up a disconnection between the Panglossian international perception and objective reality on the ground, rendering inexplicable such events as the recrudescence of lethal violence in 2009.

I have been engaged with the Northern Ireland conflict all my adult life: I still recall the shock of the TV images of police officers batoning civil-rights demonstrators in Derry on 5 October 1968 (two days before my fourteenth birthday) and digesting on the morning of 31 January 1972 the polarised newspaper coverage of Bloody Sunday, trying to make sense of it all. In a box under my bed I have a sixth-form essay supporting power-sharing as a political solution.

Over succeeding decades, as a journalist and think tank director I have worried away at the theme broached in that exercise book. This book – hopefully something of an advance on that jejune thinking – is the product of a Ph.D. on which I was able to focus after becoming an independent researcher in 2006. By bringing a broader intellectual and comparative perspective to bear (including via the privilege of being at the heart of the debate in the Council of Europe on intercultural dialogue in the mid to late 2000s), by trawling the archives in London and Dublin on the 1970s power-sharing experiment and by interviewing many of those involved with the more recent protracted effort to establish stable power-sharing, I have tried to present a more sophisticated, if more sobering, perspective than the conventional portrayal of the 'peace process'.

As a long-term supporter of the slogan favoured by Antonio Gramsci, 'pessimism of the intelligence, optimism of the will', I have also, however, concluded with positive proposals as to how Northern Ireland can yet make the political step-change required to achieve the normality its long-suffering citizens deserve. These draw on the work of the research team which since 1999 has monitored the outworking of devolution in the region (part of a wider project coordinated by the Constitution Unit at University College London), led by Professor Rick Wilford of Queen's University Belfast, who also supervised my thesis, and myself. I am obviously entirely responsible for my conclusions.

Many people deserve copious thanks for their generous assistance. My interviewees, including very senior officials, were often willing to give inordinate amounts of their time and Alison Gray diligently transcribed their responses. My friends Quentin, Lorna and Neil in London and Theresa and Gerry in Dublin were unfailingly hospitable during my work in the National Archives. Above all Professor Wilford was a constant source of help, criticism and advice. I am also indebted to Tony Mason at Manchester University Press for taking this project on board and making the book a reality.

Robin Wilson

1

Introduction

On his first full day in office as US President in January 2009, Barack Obama appointed the chair of the talks leading to the 1998 Belfast agreement,[1] George Mitchell, as his Middle East envoy. Anticipating the decision, the *Washington Post* reported that the former Senate majority leader was 'highly regarded as a negotiator for his work in the successful Northern Ireland peace process'.[2] Accepting the appointment, Mitchell referred to this experience – 'There recently, long-time enemies came together to form a powersharing government to bring to an end the ancient conflict known as the Troubles' – to suggest perseverance in the Middle East could win out.[3]

In fact, as the seasoned Northern Ireland journalist Ed Moloney pointed out in the *Jerusalem Post*, Mitchell had played a marginal role in the preparation of the agreement. The governments in London and Dublin had done the drafting – not, as we shall see, perfectly – and the two premiers, Tony Blair and Bertie Ahern, had presided over the negotiations in the days before Good Friday 1998 which turned their officials' work into the final text.[4]

Obama quickly tried to reinvigorate the moribund Middle East 'peace process' with his much-flagged Cairo speech in June 2009.[5] But, while pressurised into accepting the principle of a (demilitarised) Palestinian state, the right-wing Israeli premier, Binyamin Netanyahu, insisted Israel had to be recognised as a Jewish state with all of Jerusalem under its control. He thereby dismissed Palestinian aspirations for refugee return and for east Jerusalem to be the new state's capital – with Jewish settlement there creating contrary 'facts on the ground' – while failing to address the second-class citizenship to which Israel's 20 per cent Arab minority were condemned. Nor would he be diverted from his agenda of confrontation with the other religiously defined state in the region – Iran.[6]

The Israeli State had pre-empted Obama's inauguration with the invasion of Gaza – committing war crimes, echoed by its enemy Hamas, according to a 575-page report for the United Nations Human Rights Council by a distinguished team led by Justice Richard Goldstone.[7] The displacement on the Palestinian side of the secular (but corrupt) Fatah by the fundamentalist Hamas had been part of the same long-running process of polarisation which had undermined the moderate 'peace camp' in Israel and made a settlement even more difficult. Yet a parallel was widely drawn between the IRA and Hamas, with the implication, as the former US special envoy to Northern Ireland Richard Haass put it, that policy towards Hamas should now be 'to gradually bring them into the tent'.[8] And Hamas welcomed Mitchell's appointment, partly because of what it perceived to have been his role in brokering peace between the British State and the IRA.[9]

Blair's former 'chief of staff', Jonathan Powell (2008: 321–2), claims the key lesson from Northern Ireland is 'the importance of having a functioning process and keeping it going regardless of the difficulties'. Perseverant Mitchell certainly was, but any progress depended on the US moving from seeing Israel as its 'unbreakable' ally, as Obama put it, to a position of impartial broker, using its global power to insist on an end to the occupation in support of the 'two-state solution'. Mitchell accordingly failed to secure the settlement freeze identified as a prerequisite of renewed Israeli–Palestinian talks, his diplomacy proving 'fruitless'.[10]

The Belfast agreement, as will become apparent, nearly did not happen and the resultant fitful institutions collapsed in 2002. Emboldened by the re-establishment of devolved government in May 2007 however, the Deputy First Minster, Martin McGuinness, for decades a leading figure in the 'republican movement' of the IRA and Sinn Féin, became involved in an initiative to end violence in Iraq. 'Huge strides' had been made, he claimed, after a 'Helsinki agreement' was concluded in talks he chaired with Iraqi politicians in September.[11] This was modelled on the 'Mitchell principles' of non-violence which had led to the negotiation of the new polity.

Yet looking at Iraq through a Northern Ireland lens failed to recognise that, following the US-led invasion, the State there had already been reconstituted – with a breathtaking absence of planning, owing to the neo-conservative expectation that the 'liberating' forces would be met by 'garlands and flowers'. The resulting Shia domination and failure to resolve the position of Kirkuk, contested by Kurdish autonomists, inevitably fuelled continuing Sunni fundamentalist violence, including the loss of around 100 lives in a single day of attacks in August 2009.[12]

No more successful was the mission by McGuinness to Sri Lanka, where he sought to persuade Colombo and the Tamil Tigers to come to 'the negotiating table'.[13] In April and May 2009, the State elected instead to destroy the LTTE in a military offensive – from which, as in Gaza, the international media were barred – claiming the lives of more than 20,000 Tamil civilians and detaining hundreds of thousands more in camps.

The 'republican movement' has long sought to promote negotiations in the Basque Country involving the political wing of the separatist group ETA, as for example in a trip by McGuinness's leadership colleague, Gerry Adams, in June 2006.[15] Yet an ETA bomb at Madrid six months later was perceived by the Socialist Government as spurning dialogue and the elections in March 2009 for the Basque Parliament led to a coalition of the Socialist Party and the Popular Party in the region, leaving ETA (and even the moderate-nationalist PNV) in the cold. ETA responded with defiant attacks to mark its fiftieth anniversary but the organisation faced steady attrition by police arrests and appeared increasingly anachronistic in twenty-first-century Europe,[16] though the outlawing of its political wing sustained a niche of youthful fundamentalist support.[17]

Despite such contrary evidence, the Northern Ireland 'peace process' has been routinely offered as a model for ethnic troublespots around the globe. A month after devolution was restored, the then Northern Ireland Secretary, Peter Hain, gave a speech at Chatham House, 'Peace-making in Northern Ireland: a model for conflict resolution',[18] in which he described 'dialogue' as arguably the 'ultimate objective' and constitutional arrangements as 'secondary'. But as James Hughes (2009: 291) comments, 'this grossly underestimates the importance of the institutional and other outcomes of conflict settlement'.

Yet this chimes with the instinctive approach which the predominant state actors who comprise the 'international community', led by the US, have pursued to manage contemporary ethnic conflicts. This has been characterised by a *Realpolitik* which is the obverse of the suppression of non-state paramilitaries through overwhelming force pursued by Israel and Sri Lanka in 2009 – and, indeed, by the British State in the early period of the 'troubles' – with the associated egregious denials of human rights.

Concluding that a 'military solution' is impossible, or shying away from the large-scale and sustained international intervention required to impose the rule of law – as in Bosnia-Herzegovina (B-H) for example – this superficial approach has been driven by a stereotyped perception of the identity of domestic 'communities' and an associated focus on trading with those, however unsavoury, who present themselves unproblematically as their mouthpieces. Pursuing an end to violent threats to the State has been privileged over embedding universal norms and securing interethnic reconciliation – even where the former are symptoms of the absence of the latter. Thus, as the former president of the International Criminal Tribunal for former Yugoslavia complained, the US administration interpreted the Goldstone report – scrupulously framed by international standards of human rights and humanitarian law – as an obstacle to, rather than foundation for, progress on the Israeli–Palestinian conflict.[19]

It was notable that Richard Holbrooke, chief architect of the Dayton accords concluded at the close of the war in B-H, was appointed that same day in Washington by Obama, to a brief covering Pakistan and Afghanistan. In the Swat valley, a disastrous deal in April 2009 by the Pakistan Government with the Taliban, legitimising 'sharia' law despite an horrendous case of a young woman being flogged,[20] was quickly rescinded after its exploitation by the movement for military advance. Yet as British losses in Helmand mounted, the Foreign Minister, David Miliband, called for 'an inclusive political settlement in Afghanistan, which draws away conservative Pashtun nationalists – separating those who want Islamic rule locally from those committed to violent jihad globally'.[21]

This failed to address the root problem that, in the wake of the US destruction of the Taliban regime after the World Trade Center al-Qaida attacks, the Northern Alliance had been allowed to secure an ethnic-Tajik appropriation of the Afghan State via the Bonn conference on future governance in December 2001.[22] Nor did it appreciate that the very accommodations of local warlords by the installed Pashtun frontman, the Afghan President, Hamid Karzai,[23] had by further corroding State legitimacy eased the Taliban revival – problems which were to be compounded by the contested presidential election of August 2009, with Karzai the focus of widespread ballot-stuffing allegations in Pashtun-dominated areas where turn-out was heavily diminished by Taliban intimidation.[24]

The *Guardian* reported: 'Significantly, and as if to counter public aversion to talks with the Taliban, ministers and military commanders alike compared the current campaign in southern Afghanistan to anti-terrorist operations in Northern Ireland.'[25] But later in the same paper a former head of policy for Oxfam argued: 'If deals are seen to reward violence, or empower thugs or criminals, we will simply be repeating the same mistakes that fuelled the fighting … [W]e must not retreat on basic human rights, already under threat.'[26]

Closer scrutiny of developments in Northern Ireland explains why the 'Irish model' may not travel. As this book will argue, *Realpolitik* is paradoxically not as 'realistic' as it seems. It is based on an essentialised conception of identity, discredited by theoretical and empirical work across the social sciences. The graph of violence in Northern Ireland has not followed the political engagement of paramilitaries in the benign downward manner assumed. Nor, even, was the purported requirement of such an 'inclusive' negotiating process the appropriate lesson to draw from the failure of power-sharing in 1974, as the material from the archives in London and

Dublin marshalled here, allied to memoirs and other sources, will demonstrate. I will show, via interviews with senior British and Irish officials and ministers, serving and former, as well as non-governmental reconciliation practitioners, how the moral hazard with which this ostensibly 'pragmatic' politics has been associated has left the gulf between the 'two communities' in Northern Ireland as wide as ever, as well as bequeathing governance arrangements by no means adequate by democratic standards.

In ethnic conflict as in so much else, prevention is better than cure. And where the 'international community' should look for models, I will contend, is not among the convalescing, often relapsing and sometimes chronic patients of this world. Instead, the gaze should turn to those relatively peaceful and tolerant regions – most obviously, most of western Europe since the Second World War – which came from bitter experience to appreciate that the vaccine against the virus of aggressive nationalism and xenophobia is commitment to the norms of democracy, human rights and the rule of law, where the individual citizen, rather than the ethnicised 'community', is the subject of politics. A comparative exploration in this book of power-sharing in ex-Yugoslavia shows how the influence of these norms via EU-led engagement led to a somewhat more benign outcome in Macedonia following the Ohrid agreement than in Northern Ireland, whereas, with the US playing the crucial role at Dayton, B-H remains a dysfunctional testimony to the effects of *Realpolitik*-inspired communalism (Ilievski and Taleski, 2009: 357).

This shifts the focus from who should or should not be included in a process of negotiations to the substance of the constitutional arrangements which need to be put in place by the 'international community' for the successful governance of cultural diversity, to ensure that individuals' complex identities are not hardened out by ethnopolitical entrepreneurs into one-dimensional communal markers – or, where this has eventuated, to allow such degeneration to be painstakingly reversed. As will be seen, a 'cosmopolitan' political architecture, defined by equal citizenship, reciprocal recognition and impartial treatment, meets this requirement, while the older 'consociationalist' power-sharing model, reflected in the Belfast agreement, is obsolete. In practical terms, for Northern Ireland this implies a more flexible power-sharing scheme, opening the road to a more normal, civic society.

Tolerant societies are in that sense all alike, whereas, as Tolstoy suggested of unhappy families, ethnically divided societies, with their particular historical trajectories, are each intolerant in their own way. As we shall see in the first substantive chapter, progress in Northern Ireland thus depends on a recognition that it has more to learn from the wider world than it has to teach.

Notes

1 I use this as a shorthand for *The Agreement: Agreement Reached in the Multi-party Negotiations* (Northern Ireland Office, 1998). I am conscious that Northern Ireland Catholics tend to prefer 'the Good Friday agreement'; I am also conscious that Protestants tend to prefer to call the region's second city 'Londonderry', whereas I refer to it as 'Derry'. I am not making a political point in either case, merely opting for the more concise version.

2 Michael D Shear and Karen DeYoung, 'On first full day, Obama will dive into foreign policy', *Washington Post* (20 January 2009).

3 Denis Staunton, 'Mitchell appointed as Middle East envoy', *Irish Times* (23 January 2009).

4 Ed Moloney, 'His wasn't the central role in the Northern Ireland peace deal', *Jerusalem Post* (4 February 2009).

5 'Text: Obama's speech in Cairo', *New York Times* (4 June 2009).

6 'A change of heart?', Economist.com (15 June 2009), www.economist.com/daily/news/displaystory.cfm?story_id=13813043 [accessed 15 June 2009].

7 Available at www2.ohchr.org/english/bodies/hrcouncil/specialsession/9/docs/UNFFMGC_Report.pdf [accessed 14 October 2009].

8 Sean Gannon, 'Resist the Irish model', *Jerusalem Post* (5 February 2009).

9 Ian Black, 'Hamas refuses to free Israeli soldier in return for lifting Gaza blockade', *Guardian* (20 February 2009).

10 BBC World Service news (20 September 2009).

11 'Ex-IRA chief hails Iraq peace talks', CNN.com (4 September 2007), http://edition.cnn.com/2007/WORLD/europe/09/04/iraq.finland/index.html?eref=rss_latest [accessed 20 August 2009].

12 Julian Borger, 'Bombers test Iraq's resolve to handle festering conflicts and resist goading from militants', *Guardian* (20 August 2009).

13 Andrew Whitehead, 'Ex-IRA men warns Sri Lanka's rivals', BBC news online (7 July 2008).

14 Catherine Philip, 'The hidden massacre: Sri Lanka's final offensive against Tamil Tigers', *The Times* (29 May 2009).

15 Richard McAuley, 'Adams calls for all-party talks in Basque Country', *An Phoblacht* (8 June 2006).

16 Jane Walker, 'Basque nationalists stand to lose power after poll', *Irish Times* (3 March 2009).

17 Guy Hedgecoe, 'ETA and the Basque labyrinth', Open Democracy (20 August 2009), http://www.opendemocracy.net/article/eta-and-the-basque-labyrinth [accessed 24 August 2009].

18 Speech by Peter Hain, Royal Institute for International Affairs, 12 June 2007, www.nio.gov.uk/nio_conflict_speech–2.pdf [accessed 20 September 2009].

19 Antonio Cassese, 'We must act on the findings of the UN report into Gaza', *Financial Times* (14 October 2009).

20 Declan Walsh, 'Pakistan bows to demand for sharia law in Taliban-controlled Swat valley', *Guardian* (14 April 2009).

21 Speech by David Miliband, 'Nato's mission in Afghanistan: the political strategy',

Nato headquarters, Brussels, 27 July 2009, www.fco.gov.uk/en/newsroom/latest-news/?view=Speech&id=20612884, [accessed 28 July 2009].

22　Patrick Smyth, 'Problems posed if Karzai is re-elected', *Irish Times* (22 August 2009).

23　'Afghans at the polls', *The Economist* (22 August 2009); Dexter Filkins and Carlotta Gall, 'Fake Afghan poll sites favoured Karzai, officials assert', *New York Times* (7 September 2009).

24　'More votes than voters', *The Economist* (29 August 2009).

25　Richard Norton-Taylor, 'Britain and US prepared to open talks with the Taliban', *Guardian* (28 July 2009).

26　Matt Waldman, 'These attempts to win hearts and minds are futile', *Guardian* (17 August 2009).

2

A new paradigm

A key question which underlies this book is this: why has the (relative) peace Northern Ireland enjoys not been accompanied by reconciliation? The political institutions established by the Belfast agreement of April 1998 have had a stop-start character, with delay in their establishment until December 1999, repeated suspensions and a prolonged collapse after October 2002. Their performance was poor then, by comparison with their Scottish and Welsh counterparts (Trench, 2004). And it was poorer still when they were renewed in May 2007, epitomised by a period of five months in 2008 when the power-sharing Executive was unable even to meet (Wilford and Wilson, 2009a). 'Orange and green' sectarian antagonism has continued to crowd out 'agonistic pluralism' (Mouffe, 2000) in politics, amid the proliferation of 'peace walls' on the ground (Community Relations Council, 2008).

More than forty years on from the fateful civil-rights march in Derry which forced Northern Ireland on to the agenda of the British State, the old communal inequalities have been eroded to near vanishing point, as a result of the outworking of the reforms won by the civil-rights movement (Purdie, 1990; Prince, 2007). But much deeper class inequalities (Borooah, McKee, Heaton et al., 1995) have yawned as a result of the Thatcherite economic interlude (McGregor and McKee, 1995; Hillyard et al., 2003), overlapping with a landscape of entrenched communal division (Jarman, 2004; Shirlow and Murtagh, 2006). Indeed, recent scholarship suggests that in 'dominance hierarchies' such inequality and incivility are mutually reinforcing (Wilkinson, 2005; Wilkinson and Pickett, 2009).

Beneath the surface of the alarums and excursions at Stormont, it was this polarisation which stretched to breaking-point the power-sharing arrangements during their first phase. And while in May 2007 devolution was eventually restored, it was only through the shoehorning together of the most polarised parties, whose relationship after a brief 'honeymoon period' betrayed the misanthropic characteristics of a shotgun marriage (Wilford and Wilson, 2007c).

In his 1990 survey of literature on the Northern Ireland conflict, John Whyte (1990: viii) suggested that, in proportion to its size, the region represented 'the most heavily researched area on earth', estimating that some 7,000 books and articles might have been written on it. Doubtless that total has since reached five figures. It might seem, therefore, that the prodigious academic effort to which Whyte referred had, ultimately, been in vain – and, indeed, this book will show that policy-makers took remarkably little notice of it. How could the intellectuals have had so little benign impact on the politicians?

The answer to the paradox may be that both inhabited a world of bounded rationality – a common enough constraint in the pursuit of 'evidence-based policy-making' (Nutley and Webb, 2000: 34–5). The intellectuals were too constrained by the habits of thought of the protagonists as to be able themselves to conceive of alternative discourses which could have taken Northern Ireland beyond sectarian antagonism. Indeed, the very reason Whyte was able to produce such a unique and authoritative review was his own distance from either set of ethnopolitical entrepreneurs.

M. L. R. Smith (1999) contradicted Whyte in suggesting Northern Ireland was one of the most *under*-studied conflicts in the world – not a reference to the quantity of the material but its range. In a nicely ironic comment, he said Northern Ireland had been 'intellectually interned', notably from his discipline of international relations. Citing Smith, Arthur Aughey (2005: 63–4) bemoaned the limited contribution made by political theory – apart from the consociationalist school of Arend Lijphart (1977), followed by Brendan O'Leary and John McGarry (O'Leary, 2001a; McGarry and O'Leary, 2004) – to analysis of the conflict, a vacuum which Aughey suggested had been filled by literary criticism, including the very valuable contribution of Edna Longley (e.g. Longley, 2001).

Indeed, there are three highly germane debates within, though not confined to, political theory which have largely passed Northern Ireland by, and to which the body of work on the conflict has, with important exceptions, in turn contributed little. Theories operate at different levels of abstraction and, beginning at the highest and moving to the most particular, these debates concern:

- what has come to be known as 'identity politics';
- the nature of nationalism;
- power-sharing models for divided societies.

These are linked by a still more abstract question within the social sciences in the round, which concerns the philosophical category of essentialism.

Each tends to pit those persuaded by the intellectually (and morally) compelling anti-essentialist case against those who would present an essentialist perspective as – essentially – more 'realistic'. Yet, in reality, essentialism as a 'common sense' conception of the world has had deleterious consequences for ethnic[1] conflict, as this book will demonstrate.

The remainder of this chapter reviews the literature on, first, essentialism and then in the three domains above. In each case, the implications for key aspects of the Northern Ireland problem are drawn out. What will emerge is a set of antimonies, represented in Table 2.1, and the case will be made that the right-hand column represents a new and more adequate paradigm.

Table 2.1 Old and new paradigms in conceptualising ethnic conflict

Theme	Old paradigm	New paradigm
Essentialism	Essentialist	Anti-essentialist
'Identity politics'	Multiculturalism	Interculturalism
'Nations'/Nationalism	Perennialist	Modernist
Power-sharing	Consociationalist	Integrative

The argument of this book, moving down the ladder of abstraction, is that conflicts such as that in Northern Ireland can only be adequately understood within a broader and more complex philosophical frame, freed of the appealing simplifications of essentialism. Transcending the associated stereotypes implies a move in the arena of 'identity politics' from multiculturalist to interculturalist approaches to the management of ethnic diversity, in which dialogue across communal divides is privileged, founded on universal norms. Where such management has failed, and ethnopolitical entrepreneurs pursue conflicting assimilationist/secessionist goals, reconciliation is only feasible if the categories of nationalism are understood in a labile, modernist fashion, as against the fatalism perennialist perspectives engender. And if power-sharing is essayed as the keystone in a process of reconciliation, then it should stimulate and incentivise interethnic coalition-building in an integrative manner, rather than perversely entrenching division behind ethnic vetoes.

Essentialism

Essentialism represents the reduction of the complexity of a concrete object of study – 'a rich totality of many determinations and relations', in the redolent phrase of Karl Marx (1973: 100) – to a single aspect, or essence, held to encapsulate its meaning. This serves to take for granted, or naturalise, and so eternise the phenomenon in question, rather than it being seen as subject to internal dynamics and external interactions, and thus having a complicated history and uncertain future.

An obvious example was how the wars of the Yugoslav succession were widely reduced to 'ancient hatreds', as the then British Prime Minister, John Major (Glenny, 1999: xxiv), and the US Secretary of State Warren Christopher (Allen and Eade, 1999: 12) put it. Indeed, US President Bill Clinton was reported to have concluded, having read a journalistic account in this vein, that any intervention in the Balkans was doomed (Kaufman, 2001: 5).

This could not explain how those who had lived for decades as neighbours nevertheless came to visit extreme communal violence on each other (Conces, 2005: 140) – and nor did it offer much of a guide to reconciliation. In reality, the disintegration of the state (Calic, 2003: 110–13; Woodward, 1995: 378) and the resulting 'Hobbesian fear' (Ignatieff, 1999: 7) produced 'ethnic fragmentation and war', and ensured paramilitaries played such a prominent role (Kaldor, 1999: 83–4). This was equally true of the twentieth-century explosions of violence in Ireland after 1912 (Townshend, 2005: 28) and 1968 (Bew, Gibbon and Patterson, 1995: 145), when the collapse of state authority saw political polarisation and the dramatic growth of competing paramilitary forces.

The former UK Prime Minister Margaret Thatcher (1995: 385) was to connect the two regions in her memoirs. She airily remarked: 'But what British politician will ever fully understand Northern Ireland? ... In the history of Ireland – both North and South – which I tried to read up when I could, especially in my early years of office, reality and myth from the seventeenth century to the 1920s take on an almost Balkan immediacy.' Her Conservative predecessor, Edward Heath (1998: 421), suggested in his autobiography: 'Those who have never visited the province cannot appreciate the bitter, tribal loathing between the hardline elements in the two communities, springing from an atavism which most of Europe discarded long ago.'

His Labour predecessor had taken just the same view, choosing to describe the outbreak of violence in August 1969 as 'the culmination of three centuries of atavistic intolerance' (Wilson, 1971: 692). Critically, this perception was shared too by Thatcher's eventual successor Tony Blair, who in the Commons in October 1997 urged the people of Northern Ireland to put aside their 'ancient hatreds' in the search for a lasting peace settlement.[2] It was a view shared also by Mitchell (1999: 13), who argued that 'for all its modernity and literacy, Northern Ireland has been divided, by a deep and ancient hatred, into two hostile communities, their enmities burnished by centuries of conflict'.

Such essentialism engenders the mixture of exasperation of understanding and denial of responsibility which has underpinned the approach of the British State to Northern Ireland since re-engagement was imposed upon it by the explosion of 1969. An illustration was a 1975 report by the Central Policy Review Staff (CPRS), the government's 'think tank':[3]

> Since 1969 the role of the United Kingdom Government has increasingly been to hold the ring between the two communities. It has been a thankless role. With the imposition of direct rule it has become easy for all parties in Northern Ireland to blame the ills of the Province on rule from London. As a result, an awareness has developed, in both communities, of a common interest as Ulstermen in recovering the right to govern themselves ... But this sense of common interest has so far shown little ability to transcend the ancient confessional hatreds and induce a readiness to compromise.

The report argued that Northern Ireland's continued UK membership was not in Britain's interest but concluded that 'there is no radical policy option which offers us an easy way out of the Northern Ireland quagmire'. Ken Heskin (1980: 17) characterised this mindset thus:

> For Britain, the Northern Ireland problem is that, because of the sense of duty of their government, they are unwillingly and unreasonably caught in the middle of a distasteful dispute between two groups of intransigent, belligerent Irishmen. The dispute is not of their making, except in some vague historical sense and yet they find themselves engaged in preserving as British a part of Ireland which, by the behaviour of its inhabitants, is demonstrably not British and of which they would dearly love to be rid.

This clearly has political consequences. Not only in Northern Ireland but also, as we shall see, in ex-Yugoslavia, the essentialist perspective engenders a reluctance to intervene sufficiently urgently and robustly to stem an emerging ethnic crisis. Amid the spiral to disaster in 1969–72, pusillanimity in London led to fruitless efforts to shore up the discredited unionist regime at the expense of ever-rising violence (Bew and Patterson, 1985: 20–1; Cunningham, 2001: 5–10; Dixon, 2001: 112–18). Moreover, essentialism lends itself to an excessive readiness, as we shall also see later, to hand over power to the very ethnopolitical entrepreneurs – taken to be merely the passive representatives of ethnic 'communities' – whose protagonism has driven the conflict itself.

Perhaps worst of all, essentialism rules out *ab initio* the most promising response to the challenges posed by divided societies – 'constitutional engineering' (Sartori, 1997), which incentivises the construction of inter-ethnic coalitions, allied to integration in the wider society, within a framework of universal norms. Such an approach, however intuitively attractive, is only conceivable in a paradigm in which 'communities' are seen as neither homogeneous nor mutually exclusive.

Conversely, the essentialist conception of the Northern Ireland 'problem' which has predominated within the British State dovetails neatly with the argument of those who would offer consociationalism as the appropriate political 'solution'. For it similarly treated Westminster as the constitutional reference point, against which Northern Ireland was defined as 'different'. And, despite the failures to establish a consociationalist arrangement in the region, its recurrent collapse when established and its sub-optimal character when functioning, the 'consistency and continuity in British policy ... constructed around the notion of Northern Ireland's "difference"' (Cunningham, 2001: 155) ensured its constant reapplication.

Essentialism has come under criticism right across the social sciences. The political philosopher Seyla Benhabib (2002a: 4) complains that it is based on 'faulty epistemic premises', notably that 'cultures are clearly delineable wholes' congruent with population groups. Modern anthropological thinking no longer accepts the essentialised notion of 'culture' that has entered political rhetoric (Cowan, Dembour and Wilson, 2001: 3) and almost all anthropologists 'would flatly reject the idea that ethnicities are discrete cultural entities' rather than social constructs (Allen and Eade, 1999: 13, 16). Within cultural studies, as Tony Bennett (2001: 53) presents the field, 'it is no longer adequate to think about the relations between cultures in a society in the form of their compartmentalised division into separate ways of life and identities'. He speaks instead of 'overlapping trajectories', building on the insight of the foundational figure in cultural studies Stuart Hall (1996a: 444) that *identification* should not be conceived 'as a simple process, structured around fixed "selves" which we either are or are not'.

From a social-psychological perspective, Xenia Chryssochoou (2004a: 45) worries that essentialised social categories can become negative stereotypes, which throw swathes of people 'outside the boundaries of humankind'. Indeed, as Amin Maalouf (2000: 6), a Lebanon-born writer living in France, has warned, this is precisely how 'murderers are made'. Conversely, the development economist Amartya Sen (2006: xiii–xiv) argues that we have 'inescapably plural' affiliations, which means that as individuals we are all 'diversely different'. Hence the role played by ethnopolitical entrepreneurs in precipitating conflict (Sen, 2006: xv): 'The art of constructing hatred takes the form of invoking the magical power of some allegedly predominant identity that drowns other affiliations, and in a conveniently bellicose form can also overpower any human sympathy or natural kindness that we may normally have.'

An expert on former Yugoslavia, Roberto Belloni (2007: 8–9), warns of the danger of external actors 'uncritically accepting and involuntarily reproducing the same categories of ethnic exclusivism that underpin the ethno-nationalist project', sharing the underlying assumption that particular definitions of identity are 'inescapable and mutually exclusive' rather than 'contingent and fluid'. Interventions on these premises may secure a certain peace – in the sense of absence of war – but do little 'to move the local political dialogue beyond antagonistic and irreconcilable identities', and so prevent future violence.

This is a weakness in the otherwise excellent work by Stefan Wolff, which embraces a rich empirical understanding of ethnic conflicts across the globe. Wolff (2004: 3) presents 'ethnic groups' as bounded, timeless, collective actors, who 'make demands'. Yet 'minorities' do not make demands: associations of individuals represent themselves *as if* they embodied (and equally and comprehensively embodied) such minorities, in the same moment as they constitutively define them.

In fairness, in a subsequent text Wolff (2006), while using the language of 'ethnic groups' throughout, does recognise that ethnicity is not the only aspect of an individual's identity and is only foregrounded when it becomes politically relevant. He appreciates that to define groups in terms of an 'us' versus 'them' relationship 'requires activists to define the in-group both in itself and as opposed to the out-group' (*ibid.*: 35) and that it is 'leaders of ethnic groups' who make claims, 'supposedly on their constituents' behalf' (*ibid.*: 37). He addresses the role of the political entrepreneur, like Slobodan Milošević, in 'utilizing and manipulating ethnic identity and the social splits that it can create as a powerful tool to mobilize people' in pursuit of power (*ibid.*: 83). And he recognises that it is misleading to assume that groups in conflict – he instances Serbs and Albanians in Kosovo – are 'homogeneous actors' (*ibid.*: 97).

Ethnic protagonists only succeed, achieve a sense of 'groupness' (Brubaker, 2002), if they can suppress individuality by condensing the complex determinants of identity into one simple definer, such as nationality, in which they can invest great significance and which they can represent as a boundary marker against the 'other' – represented via a similarly stereotypical and dehumanised enemy image. Thus, as Goran Janev (2003: 304) contends, identifying ethnic groups as 'solid blocks that aim at political consolidation ... does no good for decreasing dangerous confrontation between "imagined communities"'.

Michael Ignatieff (1999: 38) talked to a Serb gunman in a bunker in Krajina in 1993, asking how in such a short time this man had come to be at war with his former Croat neighbours:

[T]he kind of Serb this man believes himself to have been before the descent into war is not the kind of Serb he became after the war. Before the war, he might have thought of himself as a Yugoslav or a café manager or a husband rather than as a Serb. Now as he sits in this farmhouse bunker, there are men two hundred and fifty yards away who would kill him. For them he is only a Serb, not a neighbour, not a friend, not a Yugoslav, not a former teammate at the football club. And because he is only a Serb for his enemies, he has become only a Serb to himself.

Similarly, Aziz Al-Azmeh (2008: 208–10), concluding a volume on Islam in Europe, complains that 'we are being told repeatedly [that] Muslims, European or otherwise, are above all Muslims, and that by this token alone they are distinctive and must be treated as such', at the behest of 'nativist right-wing movements' on the one hand and Muslim organisations and 'state-sponsored multiculturalist vested interests' on the other. Ethnicity is in this sense a fundamentally relational phenomenon (Allen and Eade, 1999: 24–6; Eriksen, 1993: 9). Far from it being the case that 'difference' is a simple *datum,* as Thomas Hylland Eriksen (1993: 39) argues, 'It is only when they *make a difference* in interaction that cultural differences are important in the creation of ethnic boundaries.' Similarly, Paul Brass (1991: 13) asserts that 'the conversion of cultural differences into bases for political differentiation between peoples arises only under specific circumstances'.

What needs to be explained, according to Ignatieff (1999: 36), is 'how neighbours once ignorant of the very idea that they belong to opposed civilizations begin to think – and hate – in these terms; how they vilify and demonize people they once called friends; how, in short, the seeds of mutual paranoia are sown, grain by grain, on the soil of a common life'. And so, like Donald Akenson (1988), explaining ethnogenesis in nineteenth-century Ireland, Ignatieff (1999: 48–53) has found useful Sigmund Freud's concept of the 'narcissism of minor difference', illuminating as this does the disproportion between ethnic antagonism and any 'real' distinctions between groups of human beings so stereotypically constructed and counterposed. Intolerance, then, is characterised by an excessive self-regard, associated with – indeed dependent upon – aggression towards the ethnic 'other'.

Just how small these differences can be is demonstrated by a remarkable coincidence. To illustrate his claim, Ignatieff (1999: 36) describes how he asked the Serbian paramilitary in his bunker an apparently naive question: what distinguished him from his Croat 'enemy'? His interlocutor's answer was the cigarettes they smoked. To exemplify the same reference to Freud, the Cypriot psychologist Vamik Volkan (1997: 108–9) recalls how, during their evening strolls, Nicosians negotiated the rising ethnic tensions in the wake of independence by treating cigarette packets as a boundary marker: Greek Cypriots favoured blue and white packs, Turkish Cypriots red.

James Fearon and David Laitin (2000: 848) challenge the essentialist belief 'that particular social categories are fixed by human nature rather than by social convention and practice'. They argue that, in the context of *intra*-group divisions, provocation of violence by ethnopolitical entrepreneurs 'can construct groups in a more antagonistic manner – that is, alter the social content associated with being a member of each category – and in turn set in motion a spiral of violence'; such figures can 'sharply delineate identity boundaries that everyday interaction and moderates' political agendas threaten to blur' (*ibid.*: 865). For example, Ornit Shani (2007: 136) has criticised the perspective of 'two monolithic and coherent communities of Hindus and Muslims in India that are liable to be drawn into conflict with each other', showing how in Gujarat political struggles among Hindus, organised around categories of caste rather than class, have translated into communalist clashes.

Belloni (2007: 7) contends that 'no long-term political solution can emerge from local ethno-nationalists', as 'their proposed "solutions" perpetuate the problem'. International agencies should thus challenge ethnonationalism and promote participatory democracy and individual human rights, 'together with the active involvement and empowerment of domestic civil society groups'. Viewed through essentialist lenses, however, civic associations – based as these are on relationships of affinity rather than ascription – become invisible. Non-nationalist forces in Bosnia-Herzegovina were marginalised by the 'international community' (Kaldor, 1999: 61), yet civic associations, *as long as* they generate networks that cross communal divides, can be a powerful antidote to violence.

In India, Ashutosh Varshney (2002) has shown by comparing three pairs of cities – in each case one peaceful, the other prone to Hindu-Muslim violence – that there is nothing inexorable about intercommunal violence, in the wake of political 'shocks'. This is inexplicable within essentialist talk about an implicitly homogeneous 'Hindu community' or 'Muslim community'. Varshney demonstrated that business, trade-union or similar networks can act as buffers against what Anthony Giddens (1994: 245) calls the 'degenerate spirals of communication' through which intercommunal violence escalates. It is by such small intercultural acts as scotching lurid rumours that diverse human beings can live securely as neighbours.[4] A cross-community network of community activists in Derry played just such a role in the city (Wilson, 2006: 50), where violence effectively wound down before the formal paramilitary ceasefires.

John Keane (2003: 160–1) explains how civil-society organisations can play this role:

[T]he institutional rules and organisations of civil society presuppose the emotional willingness of actors to get involved with others, to talk with them, to form groups, to change loyalties. In a civil society, this propensity of women and men to associate freely and to interact with others is not linked to any one particular identity or group, whether based on blood, geography, tradition or religion. The capacity for free association also requires women and men to renounce ideological groups, movements and parties driven by nationalism or xenophobic racism.

The Northern Ireland 'peace process' has already been defined in journalistic accounts as emerging significantly with the 'Hume–Adams initiative' by the respective leaders of the Social Democratic and Labour Party and Sinn Féin, John Hume and Gerry Adams, made public (though nothing was published) in September 1993. Central was the construction of a 'nationalist consensus', to which Fianna Fáil, and in particular the then Taoiseach, Albert Reynolds, was to be midwife (O'Donnell, 2007: 95). In fact, the communal solidarity implied by the initiative instantly polarised society and in October that year issued in the worst month in terms of deaths, with 28 killings, for 17 years.[5]

The former SDLP figure Paddy Devlin was (typically) blunt about this development, even on reflection: 'Look at the behaviour of Hume and Adams[;] it's just the Catholics ganging up against the Protestants.'[6] The horrors of the 23 October Shankill Road bomb in Belfast, in which ten civilians were killed in an attempted IRA attack on an Ulster Defence Association meeting, and the Greysteel massacre near Derry a week later, where the UDA killed seven civilians in reprisal, perfectly illustrated the 'security dilemma' that such political polarisation creates and how paramilitaries filled it.

It was significant that 1976 had been the last year in which there had been such a surge of fatalities. For that was also the year of the Peace People, a movement which emerged spontaneously after three children had been killed in west Belfast by an out-of-control car whose driver had been shot dead by soldiers following sniper attacks. The movement, in which an aunt of the children, Mairead Corrigan, played a leading role, mobilised tens of thousands on the streets in a series of demonstrations (Bew and Gillespie, 1999: 114). While another key figure, Ciaran McKeown (1984: 170), was careful to say it was impossible to quantify the effect, he reflected eight years later that 'the descent into violence of an ever more sectarian kind [had been] halted and reversed'.

Following lunchtime protests on 3 November 1993, on 18 November the trade unions, supported by the business community, organised huge peace demonstrations in Belfast and 15 other towns across Northern Ireland, attracting tens of thousands of participants.[7] In Belfast, on behalf of the Irish Congress of Trade Unions, Jack Nash stressed repeatedly that what they sought was a 'unifying peace'.[8] Just one person was killed as a result of the 'troubles' in November 1993, and violence never returned to such a terrifying scale before the IRA declared its ceasefire in August 1994, followed weeks later by its 'loyalist' counterparts.

Yet far from encouraging such civic associations to play a more prominent role, the focus of the 'peace process' was to be on the political and paramilitary elites, taken as simple expressions of their respective 'communities' – their power to be consolidated in the consociationalist arrangements of the agreement. Over time, the effect was to marginalise civic society (Acheson and Milofsky, 2008; Guelke, 2003) and thus prevent it from dampening sectarian tensions and buffering the communal protagonists. The incidence of violence, principally stemming from 'loyalists' albeit less lethal than before, thus rose in the years after the ceasefires, and rose again (after an initial decline) in the years after the Belfast agreement. Indeed, it receded only in the years following the collapse of the institutions in 2002, as Figure 2.1 indicates.[9] The figure is derived from the data presented in Table 2.2.

Table 2.2 Shootings and bombings in Northern Ireland by year, 1995–2009

Year	Shootings	Bombings
1995–96	65	0
1996–97	140	50
1997–98	245	73
1998–99	187	123
1999–2000	131	66
2000–01	331	177
2001–02	358	318
2002–03	348	178
2003–04	207	71
2004–05	167	48
2005–06	156	81
2006–07	58	20
2007–08	42	23
2008–09	54	46

As the 'peace process' ground to a halt, the two governments were driven by their own ideology to anticipate rising violence unless their efforts to re-establish devolution were successful – yet a downward trend once more set in. In July 2001, in the run-up to the unsuccessful inter-party talks at

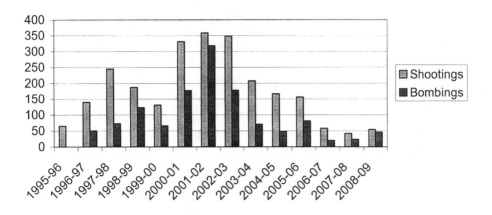

Figure 2.1 Shootings and bombings in Northern Ireland by year, 1995–2009

Weston Park after the resignation of the Northern Ireland First Minister (Ulster Unionist David Trimble), the Taoiseach, Bertie Ahern, said he feared a political vacuum, as 'if you get a vacuum people will get killed'.[10] In March 2003, after another round of failed negotiations at Hillsborough, Blair said of the Belfast agreement: 'It is either implemented or we don't have the peaceful future in Northern Ireland we want, and I want to see that peaceful future.'[11] In March 2004, after yet further unproductive talks at Hillsborough, Ahern contended that drift 'creates a vacuum' while a British representative warned of 'dangerous forces'.[12] Even as late as April 2008, Blair reflected: 'I knew above all else the importance of having a process. The talking had to go on, we had to keep it moving forward and prevent a vacuum developing that would have soon been filled by violence.'[13]

Far from sharing the governments' concern at the supposedly malevolent consequences of the absence of devolution, direct rule was accepted by a weary public anxious just to get on with their lives. Arguing against an Assembly election in autumn 2003, the moderate-unionist *Belfast Telegraph* detected 'no evidence that the people of Northern Ireland are clamouring for devolution to be restored'.[14] It was a view echoed by the moderate-nationalist *Irish News* when the election led to renewed deadlock and the review of the agreement. It editorialised: 'Many ordinary people have become increasingly bored or frustrated with the political process, and are prepared to accept an indefinite period of direct rule as the least worst [*sic*] option available.'[15] The leader-writers' view was confirmed by the 2003 Northern Ireland Life and Times (NILT) survey, which found that half the population didn't care if devolution was restored.[16]

After devolution was eventually re-established in 2007, and the jockeying for ethnic power with its associated insecurities was renewed, violence rose once again. The first half of 2009 saw four fatal 'dissident' republican attacks (Wilford and Wilson, 2009b: 9) and a brutal 'loyalist' slaying, against the backdrop of a resurgence of paramilitary 'punishment' shootings (*ibid.*: 13).

In the conventional discourse of the 'peace process', these incongruent trends between political events and violent incidents are counter-intuitive. And, following 'the DUP–Sinn Féin pact', McGarry and O'Leary (2009b: 369) prematurely declared: 'The downward trend in non-lethal violent acts has continued.' But in as far as the 'process' was about the ever-deeper embedding of essentialist, antagonistic categories, its unintended effects become easier to comprehend.

'Identity politics'

As Zygmunt Bauman (2004: 17) has put it, 'a few decades ago "identity" was nowhere near the centre of our thoughts', whereas today '"identity" is "the loudest talk in town"'. He quarantines 'identity' in inverted commas for a reason: the risk is the metaphorical distillation of multi-ethnic societies into mutually antagonistic camps for whom the legitimacy of the state is in contest – or, worse, the violence that beset ex-Yugoslavia in the 1990s (Silber and Little, 1995) or Northern Ireland during its 'troubles'. While the invasion of Iraq reminded us that inter-state wars are not entirely a thing of the past, 'new wars' (Kaldor, 1999) have in the main been intra- rather than inter-state, the *casus belli* 'identity' rather than conventional state interests, the protagonists often paramilitary rather than military, and the victims all too often civilian. As the annual Conflict Barometer generated by the Heidelberg Institute on International Conflict Research (2008: 2) indicates, while the international system organised around the United Nations since 1945 has virtually rendered inter-state wars obsolete, intra-state wars have risen relentlessly over that period, from fewer than ten at the end of the Second World War to between thirty and fifty in any one year in the 1990s and 2000s.

Ethnic protagonism in the name of identity came to be articulated in terms of the 'politics of recognition'. This became fashionable in the 1980s and 1990s largely on the back of the experience not of Europe but of North America and Australasia (Vincent, 2002: 160). Advocates of ethnicised blocs of African, Asian, Hispanic and native Americans sought collectivised political power in the US (Hollinger, 2005), where the weakening of the category class was counterpointed by the foregrounding of identity (Brubaker,

2004: 30). In Canada discussion focused on the contested place of Quebec, from which Charles Taylor (1994) and Will Kymlicka (1995) generalised to argue that rights to recognition attached to minorities as collectives, understood as embodying enduring 'societal cultures'.

In a survey of European policies on cultural diversity, Kevin Robins (2006: 12) detects in contrast a 'new discursive frame', which 'has taken the issue of difference and complexity in European culture beyond the simplistic "minority/majority" opposition'. But given the Anglo-American dominance of normative political philosophy, multiculturalist arguments received a ready audience where – particularly in Britain and the Netherlands – they chimed with a 'common sense' rooted in the 'otherisation' of colonial populations. Yasmin Khan (2007: 20) complains of the Indian colonial state that its 'inability to see the finely grained distinctions' within, and between, peoples, meant that 'all sorts of misguided imperial interventions on behalf of "communities" were put in place'.

Brubaker (2004: 219) contends that 'reified and groupist understandings of culture as a bounded and integral whole have been institutionalized in the ideology and practice of multiculturalism'. Premised on the 'community' as the unit of politics, multiculturalism flies in the face of much evidence of *individualisation* in contemporary societies characterised by 'reflexive modernisation' – in which the individual becomes '*actor, designer, juggler* and *stage director* of his own biography' (Beck, 1997: 11–19, 95, original emphasis). Against this, communitarianism – positing as it does a 'common moral good' which must trump individual rights (Mouffe, 1993: 31) – represents a retreat into a 'counter-modernity' of 'constructed certitude' (Beck, 1997: 62).

Multiculturalism flies in the face of the 'individualistic concept of society' which underpins the modern discourse of human rights from the Universal Declaration of 1945 (Bobbio, 1996a: x). It confuses damage to the dignity of individuals who have affinities to particular imagined communities with damage to the latter perceived as hypostasised groups, and it confuses the requirement that equality be substantive as well as formal with the suggestion that it must be difference-sensitive as well as difference-blind (Lægaard, 2008).

The establishment of British direct rule in Northern Ireland in 1972 was to import the multiculturalist conception into official discourse in the region. While a dramatic improvement on the assimilationism of the unionist *ancien régime*, its ill-thought-through consequences proved highly problematic. McGarry and O'Leary (2004: 20) see no difficulty in presenting Northern Ireland in straightforwardly communitarian terms: 'The two main communities have distinct national identities, not merely ethnic heritages.' But this needs unpacking.

The political philosopher Andrew Vincent (2002: 137–43) explores how 'community' emerged in the eighteenth and nineteenth centuries to convey a sense of a 'natural' order rather than an 'artificial' construction and he highlights its normative political connotations (*ibid.*: 141): 'This idea of being pre-established and unavailable to "reasoned alteration" is central to conservative thought.' In a warning at the close of the twentieth century about contemporary international over-indulgence of the 'claims of community', Fred Halliday (2001: 151) affirmed: 'The problem in Northern Ireland is not two conflicting traditions, it is tradition itself.' And from her survey of identities in the region, Máiréad Nic Craith (2002: 20) similarly contends that 'the two traditions paradigm' gives the impression of particular 'traditions' being attached to specific groups, preventing embrace of shared heritages or the rendering non-threatening of cultural diversity.

Ulrich Beck (2006: 67) puts it clearly:

> The strategy of multiculturalism presupposes collective notions of difference and takes its orientation from more or less homogeneous groups conceived as either similar to or different, but in any case clearly demarcated, from one another and as binding for individual members ... According to multiculturalism, there is no such thing as the individual. Individuals are merely epiphenomena of their cultures.

Multiculturalism thus perversely presents 'apartheid as a human right' and this '[t]alk of "identity" and "autonomy" ends in the principle of ghettoization' *(ibid.:* 115, 116). Deploying Frank de Zwart's notion of the 'dilemma of recognition' (de Zwart, 2005), which they insist is 'inherent in all forms of group rights', Jan Erk and Lawrence Anderson (2009: 192) assert: 'The paradox of collective representation is that it perpetuates the very divisions it aims to manage.'

More sharply still, Kristina Kausch and Isaías Barreñada (2005: 6) argue: 'Multiculturalists, who only want to build bridges, and only bridges, pave the way for the construction of walls.' By 2007, the Northern Ireland Office (NIO) was admitting officially to there being 46 'peace walls' across the region, mainly in Belfast.[17] Even this colossal figure turned out to be deceptive, as independent research demonstrated not only that around half of the 41 walls listed in Belfast had been built, extended or heightened since the paramilitary ceasefires of 1994 but a similar number had not been counted at all (Jarman, 2008). The nearest thing to a full tally was 88 barriers of one sort or another (Community Relations Council, 2008).

Eight years after the Belfast agreement, the *Irish Times* said it was 'a standing affront, surely, to all democrats that Irish and British citizens live on a part of this island in a near-apartheid state of separate track development'.[18]

And, unaffected by the renewal of devolution in 2007, three years later, in the wake of clashes in north Belfast around an Orange Order parade in July 2009, the Taoiseach, Brian Cowen, was still bemoaning the 'continued existence of sectarianism, of peace walls and of deep communal divisions in parts of the North' as 'an affront to democracy and to a civilised society'. He said: 'It defies belief that this is continuing in the year 2009.'[19]

Julie Mostov (2007: 137) points to the trouble this politics caused in ex-Yugoslavia (a point developed in Chapter 3): 'The trap in recognizing difference as a political identity is in not paying enough attention to the ways in which the institutionalization of difference can reproduce new sets of "natural" identities, binary oppositions, and hierarchies.' In a context in which individuals were dissolved into collective subjects, she writes, 'Rather than the possibility of shifting majorities based on interests, the politics of national identity produced the expectation of permanent majorities and minorities, so that one of the few things upon which everyone could agree in the former Yugoslavia was that no one wanted to be a "minority" in the "other's" ethno-national state.'

The argument of the politics of recognition is on the misplaced premiss that rights claims can only be universalist and individual (as in the international bill of rights or the European Convention on Human Rights) or difference-based and attaching to a putative group (Taylor, 1994: 37–8). In fact, the alternative embodied in the 1992 UN Declaration on the Rights of Persons Belonging to National or Ethnic, Religious and Linguistic Minorities (Eide, 1993: 4) and the 1995 Council of Europe Framework Convention for the Protection of National Minorities (Council of Europe, 1995)[20] retains the core human-rights notion that rights have as their subjects free and equal individuals. The distinction is between rights attaching to individuals *in the abstract* and those where the individual associates himself or herself with a national/ethnic/religious/linguistic minority.

While presenting itself as the antithesis of assimilation, in reality multiculturalism shares the same paradigm: it is the other side of the similarity/difference coin and it is wrong to 'confuse difference with diversity' (Chryssochoou, 2004b: 55). The contrast between both and an emergent *inter*culturalism is explained in the Council of Europe (2008) White Paper on Intercultural Dialogue.[21] The White Paper shifts the focus from the vertical relationship between the individual (assimilation) or 'community' (multiculturalism) and the state to the horizontal imperative of intercultural dialogue, defined as 'an open and respectful exchange of views' across ethnic fault-lines.

Such important distinctions get lost in the sprawling concept of 'identity' – a 'category of practice', like 'race' or 'nation', which should not be confused with a 'category of analysis', where much greater rigour is necessary (Brubaker, 2004: 31). As Siniša Malešević (2002: 212–13) puts it, '"Identity" is a fuzzy term for fuzzy times … no more than a common name for many different and distinct processes that simply need to be explained.'

The multiculturalist confusion has had unintended but potentially dangerous effects. It can fix 'cultures', which are never hermetically sealed from their environment and so otherwise evolve and change. Thus, Yash Ghai (2002: 169–70) argues:

> It is worthwhile to caution against reifying temporary or fluid identities, which are so much a mark of contemporary times. There is a danger of enforcing spurious claims of primordialism and promoting competition for resources along ethnic lines, thereby aggravating ethnic tensions … Constitutional recognition of cultures tends to sharpen differences between cultures … [W]e need more intercultural than multicultural enterprises.

Melita Richter Malabotta (2005: 117) writes that multiculturalism represents 'the *coexistence of non-communicating vases in the same shared space*' (original emphasis). Interculturalism, on the other hand, is 'based on the plural presence of individual subjects' and 'not only on the communities they belong to'. In this model, 'The meeting and exchange take place between the different elements within the public space ... and the society has a low ethnic conflict rate.'

This distinction between 'multicultural' and 'intercultural' is neatly encapsulated by Bauman (2002), as that between the perspective of a 'variety of cultures' and 'cultural variety' respectively. By the first, Bauman means an essentialist conception, in which 'cultures' are thought of as things – simple, separate and homogeneous wholes – for which individuals are cyphers. The second, by contrast, is premised on the individualistic concept of society and recognises that individuals have complex identities and occupy a range of overlapping networks of relationships. In this context, 'ethnicity cannot be used as a blunt instrument to classify widely varying and complicated beliefs and attitudes' (Bakke, Cao, O'Loughlin *et al.*, 2009: 247–8).

Christian Joppke and Steven Lukes (1999: 10) challenge superficial, collectivised readings of 'cultures':

> Cultures are not windowless boxes, each containing a discrete territory. And in any cultural group whatsoever in the modern world, there will be at least the following: identifiers, quasi-identifiers, semi-identifiers, non-identifiers, ex-identifiers, cross-identifiers, and anti-identifiers. A multicultural politics of identity is angled exclusively towards the concerns and interests of the first group.

Fiona Bloomer and Peter Weinreich (2003: 155–7) establish such a nuanced spectrum of identity in Northern Ireland – their five categories being 'in-group identified', 'mixed identified', 'conflicted', 'alienated' and 'cross-ethnically identified'. Their research with a sample of 145 young people found only 46 per cent were in-group identifiers, albeit 57 per cent of Catholics as against 33 per cent of Protestants; the remainder were spread across the other four categories – including 20 per cent of Protestants and 10 per cent of Catholics who were cross-identifiers.

The study also found that while respondents viewed members of the 'other' religious community reasonably positively, they were negatively disposed towards the unionist/nationalist political group from that side – unsurprisingly, given the ethnonationalist nature of the associated ideologies. Respondents 'did not simply stereotype Catholics and Protestants in terms of the views held by their political representatives' (*ibid.*: 154–5). This implies rather more potential support for a politics of intercommunal accommodation which is *not* perversely determined to hook this to antagonistic ideologies – a conclusion which would chime with research on the workplace (Hargie, Dickson and Nelson, 2003) whose results appeared in the same volume, showing strong public backing for a policy of neutrality, rather than symbolic expression of difference there.

If the 'community' (Bauman, 2001) of the multiculturalist is always an imagined one, the linked rights claims can only ever be pressed by an association which claims to speak on behalf of the collective. The supposedly ascriptive nature of such 'communities' (i.e. one's allocation to them by accident of birth) often means the democratic norms related to associations of affinity (a club one chooses to join) are absent (Hollinger, 2005). As Sen (2006: 158) puts it, while often based on a claim of 'cultural freedom', multiculturalism has 'the tyrannical implications of putting persons into rigid boxes of given "communities"'.

This bears down particularly heavily on women (Okin, 1999), as the notion of 'group voice' can 'in actuality collude with fundamentalist leaderships who claim to represent the true "essence" of their collectivity's culture and religion, and who have high on their agenda the control of women and their behaviour' (Yuval-Davis, 1998: 29). 'Culture' as a superficial portmanteau term can be the excuse for the 'generous betrayal' of the human rights of actually-existing individuals, as in documented cases in Norway of second-generation South Asian girls abducted for forced marriage (Wikan, 2002). It is for this reason that the modern minority-rights conventions enshrine a 'right of exit' in the principle that all individuals must be free from discrimination – whether because they choose to be associated with a minority or, conversely, because they do not.

The Council of Europe framework convention also enjoins states party to promote 'a spirit of tolerance and intercultural dialogue' – the meaning of which was fleshed out in the 2008 White Paper. For the most worrying aspect of multiculturalism is how claims for 'parity of esteem' between competing communalist representatives can even exacerbate, rather than assuage, intercommunal tensions. In a sobering address in March 1999 on 'Equality and the Good Friday Agreement', the then Northern Ireland Deputy First Minister, Séamus Mallon, said: 'We are still struggling to reach agreement on how to afford equal respect to our differing cultural identities. Our failure to do so degrades us all. As a country, we boast the finest poets and playwrights: Heaney, Hewitt and Friel. Yet we hurl sectarian abuse at each other.'[22]

The then Northern Ireland Secretary Peter Mandelson said in May 2000 that he wanted to 'build on, not suppress these traditions', fostering a society 'in which Orange and Green can live side by side in mutual respect, as keen to protect each other's rights as their own'.[23] The paradox, however, is that since the 'communities' are defined by their supposed differences from one another, it is as easy to compare apples and oranges as it is (say) to know when parity has been achieved between Orange and Green. Warning that 'parity of esteem' in Northern Ireland can 'cement the existing blocs' and become 'a charter for apartheid', Longley (2001: 7) ponders whether 'parity of *dis*esteem' might not be preferable.

At best this can only lead to what Ernesto Laclau (1996: 32) describes as a politics of 'negotiation' – a term which became repetitively familiar in the Northern Ireland 'peace process'. This he defines as 'a process of mutual pressures and concessions whose outcome depends only on the balance of power between antagonistic groups'. And he comments: 'It is obvious that no sense of community can be constructed through that type of negotiation. The relation between groups can only be one of potential war.'

Particularistic claims can by definition only be reconciled via the assertion of universal values (Laclau, 1994: 5). The Council of Europe White Paper stresses intercultural dialogue must be premised on universal norms of democracy, human rights and the rule of law. This bears out a simple but fundamental point by Vincent (2002: 187) in his critique of multiculturalism: 'Trust needs some overarching unity.'

If the politics of recognition fails to address relationships *between* reified ethnic groups and can endanger the liberties of individuals *within* them, the intercultural alternative supports a culture of tolerance (Habermas, 2004) that is in a sense *indifferent to difference* (Ignatieff, 1999) – where citizens do not even know 'who' is 'who' (Bakke *et al.*, 2009: 229) – so that a normal civic society becomes possible. The positive, interculturalist paradox is that the complexity and non-exclusive nature of identity means overlapping identities, and so a 'solidarity among strangers' (Habermas, 2001: 21) in the name of a common humanity, are possible. This is also, by the by, the only basis on which to address the widening gulf of *material* inequality that has accompanied the *symbolic* protagonism of 'identity politics' in recent decades (Barry, 2001: 3).

The multiculturalist suggestion that 'mere' tolerance is insufficient, as conveying only that its exponents will 'put up with' members of minority communities, misses the point that the tolerant among 'host' majorities are precisely those who feel an affinity with their minority counterparts, rather than an uneasiness – or worse – in their company. Conversely, requiring liberal members of majority communities to show 'respect' for conservative practices among minority communities only serves to push the tolerant into the intolerant camp – as the Dutch experience indicated with the Pim Fortuyn phenomenon, playing as this did on concerns that liberal values of sexual equality were not being adequately upheld within Muslim communities (Sniderman and Hagendoorn, 2007).

Tolerance thus stems not from an orientation to 'difference' – this can lead to a distancing exoticisation and stereotyping of the 'other' – but from empathy based on a sense of common humanity. It is no surprise, then, that Northern Ireland's 'respect' for sectarian 'difference' is part of a culture of *in*tolerance, manifested in a composite 'bigotry measure' – combining survey data on racism, xenophobia, Islamophobia, anti-Semitism and homophobia – higher than for all of eighteen comparator western democracies (Borooah and Mangan, 2007). As Ignatieff (1999: 70) puts it, 'without this fiction – that human similarity is primary and difference is secondary – we are sunk'. It is this, he says, which sustains liberal-democratic institutions:

> The essential task in teaching 'toleration' is to help people see themselves as individuals, and then to see others as such; that is, to make problematic that untaught, unexamined fusion of personal and group identity on which nationalist intolerance depends. For nationalist intolerance requires a process of abstraction in which actual, real individuals in all their specificity are depersonalised and turned into carriers of hated group characteristics.

Tolerance has its limit – in the *intolerance of intolerance*. Rights claims which differentiate minorities via rejection of universally applicable egalitarian ideals are not legitimate. As Jürgen Habermas (2004: 17–18) argues, this is not 'a *one-way street* to cultural self-assertion by groups with their own collective identities'. He goes on: 'The coexistence of different life forms as equals must not be allowed to prompt segregation. Instead, it requires the integration of all citizens – and their mutual recognition across cultural divisions as citizens – within the framework of a shared political culture.'

The notion of citizenship, as Habermas recognises, is key here: one can uphold the French ideal of civic equality, of *les droits de l'homme*, while recognising the diversity of individual citizens. Jeff Spinner-Halev (1999: 65) has explained why the concept of citizen must trump that of 'community', as elaborated in Chapter 3:

> A multiculturalism that tries to create a society with several distinctive cultures deeply threatens citizenship. In this kind of multicultural society, people are not interested in citizenship; they are not interested in making the state a better place for all; they care little about how public policies affect most people or about their fellow citizens. Even the term 'fellow citizen' might strike them as strange. What they have are fellow Jews, or fellow blacks, or fellow Muslims, or fellow Sikhs. Citizens, however, are not their fellows.

Beck (2005: 284) contrasts such communalism with the cosmopolitan alternative, which 'presupposes the existence of *individualization*, and reinforces and affirms it' (original emphasis). David Hollinger (2005: 3) agrees: 'Cosmopolitanism is more wary of traditional closures and favours voluntary affiliations.' While, according to Steve Vertovec and Robin Cohen (2002: 3), 'multiculturalism has received broad criticism for resting upon and reproducing rather rigid notions of culture and group belonging', in contrast 'cosmopolitanism is now increasingly invoked to avoid the pitfalls of essentialism or some kind of zero-sum, all-or-nothing understanding of identity issues within a nation-state framework'. Similarly, Gerard Delanty and Patrick O'Mahony (2002: 186) argue that cosmopolitanism 'is gaining credibility as a normative antidote to destructive nationalism'.

David Held, Anthony McGrew, David Goldblatt *et al.* (1999: 449) contend 'that in the millennium ahead each citizen of a state will have to learn to become a "cosmopolitan citizen" as well: that is, a person capable of mediating between national traditions, communities of fate and alternative forms of life'. If intolerance is characterised by the projection on to the 'other' of unintegrated, negative aspects of the self (Volkan, 1997), cosmopolitanism by contrast implies 'the inclusion of the other in one's own life' (Beck, 2009: 189).

Cosmopolitanism can be dismissed cheaply as 'the class consciousness of frequent travel[l]ers' (Calhoun, 2002) but this is a dated view. Beck (2009: 61) writes: 'Down through history, cosmopolitanism bore the taint of elitism, idealism, imperialism and capitalism. Today it has unexpectedly become an everyday affair.' With Chan Kwok-Bun (2002: 191) we can 'look to the unspectacular, practical, everyday life activities that allow movement beyond group identities to the business of simply living together and solving practical problems collectively'. Robins (2006) identifies how migrants and refugees can be vectors of enriching 'transcultural' identities.

Brubaker (2002) argues that actually-existing individuals, rather than seeing themselves as, say, mere cyphers for 'the Serbs' in a Manichaean struggle, will tend over time to succumb to quotidian demands. Indeed, in this context, there is a danger that those responsible for international intervention in a society beset by violence may claim success when what has happened is that an extreme situation, such as a devastated Bosnia at the end of the war – or indeed Northern Ireland at the conclusion of the 'troubles' – has subsequently gone through a 'regression to the mean' (Belloni, 2007: 9).

Just such day-to-day pressures were evidenced in the election in 2003 of Boris Tadic as president of Serbia, and his re-election facing strong nationalist opposition in 2008, reflecting a readiness on the part of a weary population to cooperate with the war crimes tribunal if that might offer hope of better times via further economic assistance and eventual European Union integration. Similarly, during the brief civil conflict in Macedonia, a Serb resident of mixed Kumanovo said: 'Why should we fight with our neighbours when we all have the same daily problems?'[24]

Keane (1998: 112) has painted an appealing picture of 'late modern cosmopolitans':

> These new civilians maintain that, in the contemporary world, identity is more a matter of politics and choice than fate. They have an allergic reaction to nationalism and deep empathy for people suffering discrimination or enforced exile from their cherished nations or territories. They are humble about their own national identity, interested in others, concerned for their well-being, and consequently unwilling to indulge the feelings of revenge and narcissistic satisfaction characteristic of nationalists.

Held (2003: 169) argues that cosmopolitanism is based on three principles: 'egalitarian individualism', where humankind is treated as belonging to a single moral realm; 'reciprocal recognition', in which this status of equal worth is recognised by all; and 'impartial treatment', where all claims arising are subject to rules that all can share. Beck (2005: 92) contends that the 'cosmopolitan state' is '*grounded in the principle of the state's neutrality towards nationality and allows national identities to exist side by side through the principle of constitutional tolerance*' (original emphasis). Just as it was to be eventually recognised after the religious wars in Europe that only the separation of church and state could guarantee freedom of conscience, so the nationalistic wars of the twentieth century have seen in the EU – within and between the member states – a peaceful regime associated with 'the separation of nation and state' (Beck and Grande, 2007: 65).

Bo Rothstein (2005) agrees. He identifies the danger that, in the absence of impartial public authority, a 'social trap' will prevent the resolution of collective-action dilemmas – particularly in ethnically divided societies, where a collective memory of mistrustful behaviour by the stereotyped 'other' can become a self-fulfilling prophecy. Thus the 2007 NILT survey found only 10.4 per cent who disagreed with the statement 'If you are not careful other people will take advantage of you'[25] and a survey of more than 3,500 people in Bosnia-Herzegovina (Oxford Research International, 2007: 14) found just 7.2 per cent who concurred that 'others can be trusted'. Universal welfare states provide strong impartial authority and in the World Values Survey question asking whether 'most people can be trusted' or 'you can't be too careful' two-thirds of Swedes consistently pick the former option (Rothstein, 2005: 89). Sweden emerged as the most tolerant society in the comparative study cited above (Borooah and Mangan, 2007).

Rothstein stresses the importance of getting institutional arrangements right – in particular integrated education and housing, and the rule of law. The failure of the British State to ensure that mass schooling in Ireland was integrated facilitated the hardening of sectarian boundaries during the nineteenth century (Akenson, 1988: 119–22), while the failure to defend the rule of law in the face of the unionist revolt against the third Home Rule Bill delivered much of the rest of Ireland into the hands of militant separatism during the twentieth century (Garvin, 2005: 142).

Lars Trägårdh (2007: 260) additionally argues that what makes for high social trust is 'a sense of participation and having a stake that is promoted by involving the institutions of civil society, and thus the citizens, in the making of law and policy'. A noteworthy feature of the implementation of the Belfast agreement was that the last associated institution to be established was the Civic Forum, and at time of writing it remained to be re-established. Social formations characterised by strong states and civil societies, in which markets are regulated and embedded rather than private interests prevailing without accountability, ensure public goods[26] are in strong supply.

This is of mostly unexplored relevance to Northern Ireland, where one of the abiding difficulties has been explaining the origins and significance of the civil-rights movement, as a campaign to transform the Northern Ireland state rather than destroy it. The conventional wisdom has been that it emerged from a 'Catholic middle class' engendered by post-war educational reforms, a class-reductionist explanation (Laclau and Mouffe, 1985) which lacks empirical foundation (Dixon, 2001: 92–3). Michael Morgan and Rupert Taylor argue that the movement was historically framed by the emergence of the UK welfare state, which via the 'principle of parity' was extended to Northern Ireland, thereby opening access to public goods to the Catholic community and issuing in a struggle over their discriminatory supply.[27] It was thus the strength of the post-war state in the region which came tantalisingly close to ending the battle over the legitimacy over its existence, three decades before the Belfast agreement.

The fate of two projects since the agreement shows just how relevant these arguments are to the clash of communally articulated identities in Northern Ireland. On the one hand has been a bill of rights for the region, on the other a policy framework to develop a culture of tolerance.

As to the first, the Belfast agreement (NIO, 1998: 17) specified that, over and above the incorporation of the European Convention on Human Rights into UK law with the Human Rights Act of 1998, a Northern Ireland bill of rights should contain 'additional rights to reflect the principles of mutual respect for the identity and ethos of both communities and parity of esteem'. Premised as the notion is on incomparable particularisms, it has proved impossible to elaborate a consensual definition of 'parity of esteem' (Hennessey and Wilson, 1997). And, despite considerable effort on the part of the Northern Ireland Human Rights Commission (2001, 2004, 2008) to prepare an acceptable bill, the mutual antagonism of the ethnonationalist parties has left the project stalemated. Ironically, a ruling by the Council of Europe's Venice Commission (European Commission for Democracy Through Law, 2002) on Belgium, to the effect that its consociational arrangements mean *neither* the 'co-dominant' Walloons nor Flemings should be considered a minority under the framework convention, suggests the similar arrangements for Northern Ireland in one aspect of the agreement nullified the bill of rights proposition in another (Oberschall and Palmer, 2005).

There was a more benign outcome under direct rule to the consultation initiated in January 2003, shortly after the collapse of the devolved institutions, on a 'community relations' policy framework – the power-sharing Executive Committee having failed even to discuss the report of the policy review it had commissioned (Wilford and Wilson, 2003: 100–1). The underpinning notion of 'a shared future' has acquired some currency, particularly among reconciliation practitioners. The aim of the new policy (OFMDFM, 2005: 8) was drafted to effect the three principles of cosmopolitanism enunciated by Held:[28] 'The establishment over time of a normal, civic society, in which all individuals are considered as equals, where differences are resolved through dialogue in the public sphere, and where all people are treated impartially.'

Had *A Shared Future* been properly implemented, it could have helped foster the more healthily autonomous public sphere in Northern Ireland which John Dryzek (2005) identifies as a necessary corrective to the colonisation of debate in the 1990s by the political leaderships, engaged in negotiations with London and Dublin over the sovereignty contest, and which Michael

Edwards (2004) sees more generally as a key component of 'civil society'. But when the devolved Assembly was restored in May 2007, an Alliance motion endorsing *A Shared Future* was amended merely to take note of it.[29] Research commissioned under direct rule on the costs – including the opportunity costs – of sectarian division, which remarkably estimated these at up to £1.5 billion per year, was suppressed by the Executive (Wilford and Wilson, 2008b: 59), which was unable by the time of writing to agree its own 'community relations' policy (Wilford and Wilson, 2009a: 18–19).

Yet the issue remains urgent. Five years after the agreement, a joint declaration promulgated by the British and Irish premiers, Blair and Ahern, admitted the unavoidable reality:[30] 'The two governments recognise that Northern Ireland remains a deeply divided society, with ingrained patterns of division that carry substantial human and financial costs.' Anxiety rippled more widely into the 'international community', reflected in September 2004 in a motion passed by the Parliamentary Assembly of the Council of Europe, which worried that 'society in Northern Ireland remains deeply divided along community lines'. The resolution urged not only resumption of inter-party dialogue but also respect for human rights and education for reconciliation.[31]

In a 2001 report for the Minority Rights Group, Ghai (2001: 19) had expressed prescient concerns about the architecture of the Belfast agreement, and in particular its mutual vetoes. He wrote:

> While the antecedents of this system are understandable, it may tend to entrench religious/political differences, at a time when a substantial proportion of the people of Northern Ireland are willing to drop communal differences. It would give power to those who are adept at manipulating religious differences and nationalist politics. This system unfortunately downgrades the votes of 'others', and thus is less favourable to those who work across communities.

Nationalism

'Nationalist politics' is indeed incurious at best about working 'across communities'. It represents a particular form of identity politics – and particularly virulent, as it implies that members of different ethnic 'communities' can only inhabit separate national spaces (through secession and/or partition) or that members of minority communities must be assimilated to a dominant official ethos.

The late nineteenth- and early twentieth-century rise to power of the 'nation-state' socialised newly enfranchised subordinate social classes, in an assimilationist manner, into political environments in which their rulers presented themselves as embodiments of a unified, national-popular, collective will (Hobsbawm, 1990). This had obvious implications for those who deemed themselves – or were so deemed by those in power – as outside the 'imagined community' of the 'nation' (Anderson, 1983), as evidenced by the 'factory of grievances' (Buckland, 1979) that Northern Ireland was to become after its foundation.

This presented real difficulties for contemporary political actors. As Eric Hobsbawm (1990: 13–14) puts it, 'from the 1880s on the debate about the "national question" becomes serious and intensive, especially among the socialists, because the political appeal of national slogans to masses of potential or actual voters or supporters of mass political movements was now a matter of real practical concern'.

Nowhere was this debate more developed than among the 'Austro-Marxists' Otto Bauer and Karl Renner. A rapidly expanding Vienna had become a multicultural city, with large immigrant populations drawn from a range of nationalities, and it was in this context that Bauer (2000) wrote *The Question of Nationalities and Social Democracy*.

If in the Ottoman empire the millet system essentially assigned people to separate groups, in the Austro-Marxist scheme for 'nonterritorial national autonomy', as Ephraim Nimni explains in his introduction to Bauer's text, 'the autonomous communities are organized democratically and are based on individual consent to belong and on internal democracy' (*ibid.*: xxv). This related to the individualist 'personality principle', which Renner advocated should be formalised as a decision by each citizen as to their nationality upon reaching voting age (*ibid.*: xxvii).

The foreword to Bauer points to the progressive character of this thinking (*ibid.*: xi):

> National identities are thus conceptualized in Bauer's study not as 'naturally given' and invariable, but as culturally changeable. Such an understanding would seem to represent a fundamental prerequisite for an approach to national conflicts that operates within a democratic framework and in a spirit of mutual tolerance, rather than in 'biologistic' terms.

This was, ironically, too radical for Vladimir Lenin, who commissioned Josef Stalin to write his wooden *Marxism and the National Question* in response. Stalin adopted instead the inherently collectivist approach of defining the 'nation' by a set of just such taken-for-granted common characteristics (such as language). It was partly for this reason that, after the end of the Cold War, authoritarian collectivism could so readily transmute into ethnic nationalism. By enshrining rights of voice and exit for individuals within the suggested national 'communities', the personality principle offered an alternative to captive clienteles established by ethnopolitical entrepreneurs.

The Habsburg empire collapsed in the furnace of the First World War, with the 'appeal of national slogans' all too evident across Europe as 'national' social-democratic parties fell largely in line with 'their' states. But the problem was hardly solved by the post-war Versailles formula of 'national self-determination'.

This has often been cast in liberal guise, yet as Hobsbawm rightly notes (1990: 40) it was advanced by Lenin as well as Woodrow Wilson. As Delanty (1995: 108) argues, 'The principle of "self-determination" amounted to the politicisation of ethnicity since mutually antagonistic groups were placed in the same state. The older principle of polyethnicity [in Europe] was rejected in favour of mono-ethnic states.' Wilson, the first US president from a southern state since the Civil War, brought the 'Jim Crow' system to Washington, and 'self-determination' abroad was of an ethnicised piece with his conception of a segregated America (Hollinger, 2005: 131–2). It thus missed the obvious difficulty posed by Wilson's appalled Secretary of State, Herbert Lansing: 'When the President talks of "self-determination" what [political] unit does he have in mind?' (Sluga, 2005). In Ireland, the legitimation of claims couched in the language of 'self-determination' merely emboldened the republican and unionist antagonists and made a conciliatory outcome even more difficult to secure (Stanbridge, 2005).

Instead of addressing the subtle challenge of how individuals of different national affiliations could coexist, as the Austro-Marxists had essayed, the self-determination formula proposed the blunt instrument of 'one people, one state', with its inevitable consequences of minority oppression, partition and secessionism. As Lansing, an international lawyer, prophetically warned (Moynihan, 1993: 83), 'The phrase is simply loaded with dynamite ... What misery it will cause!' Wilson was to rue the consequences, telling the Senate (Sharp, 1996: 23): 'When I gave utterance to those words ("that all nations had a right to self-determination"), I said them without the knowledge that nationalities existed, which are coming to us day after day ...' The formula was to be the downfall of the inter-war League of Nations, which could not satisfactorily address the consequent minority claims (Mazower, 1998: 51–63), and was to offer Adolf Hitler a slogan with which he could challenge Versailles by raising the plight of the Sudeten Germans in Czechoslovakia.

Eugenio Biagini (2007: 24–5) persuasively argues that once a notion of Irish 'exceptionalism', associated with a 'colonial paradigm', is replaced by a 'continental' perspective, the relevance of this to Ireland is evident: 'Until 1919 most European "small nationalities" were included in multinational empires, and unless we wish to describe the experience of, let us say, the Czechs and Slovenes – not to mention the Catalans – as "colonial", we need to devise broader and less Anglo-centric models of historical analysis for Ireland.'

During the partition of Ireland, the competing 'selves' managed to squeeze out the socialists in Ulster: Frank Wright points to the divisive role played by the 'Labour Unionists' created by the Unionist leadership in the expulsions of Catholics and 'rotten Prods' (socialists) from the shipyards, amid republican violence. In the infant Czechoslovakia, by contrast, the strength of the Social Democrats among Bohemian Germans played a restraining role in preventing the eruption of national conflict and ensuring the Czech majority took a liberal line (Wright, 1987: 81) – though, tragically, this accommodation was not to last.

The Second World War and the early post-war period were to be the high-point for Labour in Northern Ireland. It is easy to dismiss the efforts of the labour movement in the region, given sectarian labour-market inequalities and the manner in which the Northern Ireland Labour Party could be torn apart by an issue as insignificant as (in the 1960s!) whether playground swings should be untied on Sundays. But Terry Cradden (1993) has rescued the pragmatic efforts of many activists and leaders over the Stormont decades, in very difficult circumstances, to steer an accommodationist course – and not without success. It was pressure from labour in the round which brought the demise of two Unionist prime ministers: John Andrews, over his Blimpish failure to prosecute the war (Walker, 1985: 147); and Lord Brookeborough, over mass unemployment in the late 1950s and early 1960s (Bew, Gibbon and Patterson, 1995: 131–2).

With its 'troubles' renewed in the wake of the civil-rights movement, Northern Ireland was to be widely seen as a throwback to the wars of religion. But in many ways it was to foreshadow the resurgence of ethnic conflict in Europe after the fall of the Berlin Wall. As Hobsbawm (1994: 31) wryly put it, 'the old chickens of Versailles' were 'once again coming home to roost'. Yet, as Hurst Hannum (1992: 27) reflected, the meaning and content of the right to 'self-determination' remained 'as vague and imprecise as when they were enunciated'.

Academic debate on nationalism was meantime renewed in the 1980s, with key 'modernising' texts from Ernest Gellner (1983) and Benedict Anderson (1983) and 'traditionalist' alternatives from Anthony Smith (1983, 1986). On the side of the former, including prominently Hobsbawm (1990), the 'imagined' nature of the national 'community', the modern character of nationalism as an ideology and the importance of the state were to the fore. The alternative view conceived of 'nations' as substantial, with enduring roots in pre-modern ethnicities, and stressed the deeply affective responses nationalism could engender.

Alan Finlayson (1996) draws a reasonable conclusion to this debate, well summarised by Umut Özkırımlı (2000), building on Marx's famous comment in the *Eighteenth Brumaire* (Marx and Engels, 1968: 96): 'Men make their own history, but they do not make it just as they please; they do not make it under circumstances chosen by themselves, but under circumstances directly encountered, given and transmitted from the past.' Finlayson (1996: 79) echoes this, arguing: 'Nationalist myth is not constructed out of thin air but derives from determinate conditions which it then actively interprets and transforms.' He sees nationality as the content of nationalism, produced by 'sedimentation' over time, and nationalism as a form emergent from 'dislocation', especially that marking the transition from feudalism to capitalism (*ibid.*: 175, 105).

Özkırımlı (2005) similarly urges a critical stance towards nationalist claims, in contrast to the taken-for-grantedness of nationalist theorists. Nationalism does work on pre-modern cultural materials but it selects and appropriates these according to contemporary concerns. More, nationalism precedes, and constitutes, the 'nation', yet it covers its tracks, so to speak, presenting the latter as eternal.

Interestingly, anti-nationalism can be associated with such perennialist sentiments too. In Tuzla in ex-Yugoslavia (Katunaric, 2003: 9) and in Ballynafeigh in Belfast (Byrne, Hansson and Bell, 2006: 36) – each an enclave of peace in the violence of recent times – residents tended to describe this distinguishing state as a 'tradition' of the area. Yet in both cases determinate agencies (in the first case the municipality, in the second the community association and inter-church network) played key roles in securing and sustaining this 'tradition' (Wilson, 2007).

In his elegant, but tragic, account of how cosmopolitan Salonica became Hellenised, Mark Mazower (2004: 474) contends: 'The history of the nationalists is all about false continuities and convenient silences, the fictions necessary to tell the story of the rendez-vous of a chosen people with the land marked out for them by destiny.' Ignatieff (1999: 38) describes nationalism as a 'fiction' too, evidencing how for his Serb interlocutor to become *just* a nationalistic Serb required that he forget all the other aspects of his identity which made a sense of common humanity possible.

More positively, Markus Kornprobst (2005) has shown how 'Irishness' was subject to a twentieth-century reconstruction. He demonstrates on the basis of Dáil debates and associated newspaper editorials a shift from a 'colonial episteme' characterised by a conservative Anglophobia, pre-eminently associated with Eamon de Valera, to a modern European version, developed by Garret FitzGerald and Conor Cruise O'Brien but now widely accepted across the party spectrum. Paralleled by a shift 'from a communitarian to a more individualistic notion of citizenship in the 1970s' (Hayward, 2009: 195), the latter has been more conducive than the former – as evidenced by

De Valera's wartime prioritisation of Irish neutrality over unity (Patterson, 2006: 30) – to fostering reconciliation across the island as a whole.[32]

Those who conceive of the 'nation' as an object in the real world are inevitably drawn into defining a list of its characteristics. From Stalin to Smith (1983: 186), the problem has been that the diversity of actually-existing nationalisms and the states with which they engage, so well explored by Breuilly (1982), makes it inherently impossible to establish any list which is internally consistent and yet does not face insuperable problems of inclusion/exclusion. Montserrat Guibernau (2004: 127) shows how Smith's own list has thus become more dilute over time. This relates to the intractable practical problem of establishing the 'people' entitled to 'self-determination' where that is contested.

There is, moreover, an epistemological critique here, informed by 'critical realism' (Benton and Craib, 2001; Sayer, 2000), which recognises that science is a social activity but that real objects are independent of it. Critical realism distinguishes the real world from interpretive schemata and scripts utilised by social actors to comprehend it. As Brubaker (2004: 81) argues, 'race, ethnicity and nation are not entities in the world but ways of seeing the world' and so cannot be treated as scientific concepts. And Smith (2009: 1) accepts that his own 'ethno-symbolist' approach to nationalism, however sophisticated, is a 'perspective' rather than a 'scientific theory'.

While recognising that the substantiality of the 'nation' has seemed less certain in recent decades, Smith (1998: 77) nevertheless asserts that the 'nation' is 'a felt and lived community' which secures otherwise inexplicably powerful attachment. Nationalism works precisely by establishing an attachment 'felt and lived' by real individuals *as if* the latter were mere instantiations of an entity in the world greater than themselves, but that does not imply such an entity has a real existence – any more than the belief of members of a 'faith community' implies the existence of the particular omnipotent god they claim, with equally powerful attachment, to define their lives. To sustain his position, Smith perversely describes 'political or other institutions' as 'abstractions' no more real than 'communities', thereby giving the 'state' the same status as the 'nation'. Yet governments and parliaments, armies and police, along with schools and museums, churches and NGOs, all have real effects on framing what members of particular social groups at particular conjunctures think of as the 'nation'; the reverse claim would make no sense.

Smith's error of treating the 'nation' as if it were, like nationalism, an object in the real world is rooted in Emile Durkheim's similarly hypostasised notion of the *conscience collective* (Malešević, 2004: 584–5). For Durkheim (1972: 58), 'social facts' were to be treated unproblematically as things, this being what he called 'the very foundation of our method'. But Pietra Costa (2004: 214) contends that 'the idea that the "nation" involves a natural correspondence between "name" and "thing" is only an indication of the extraordinary success of nation-building'.

Smith recurrently brackets together 'nations and nationalism' as if they were equivalent concepts, but once that link is broken the argument falls away: if the issue is reduced to the modernity of *nationalism* rather than 'nations', there is no contest. As Smith (1998: 97) puts it straightforwardly, 'On one matter, practically all scholars agree. As an ideology and movement, nationalism is modern.'

The error is evidential as well as epistemological, as the migrations and meldings of populations in medieval Europe show. As Patrick Geary (2002: 37) presents the case, 'Congruence between early medieval and contemporary "peoples" is a myth ... The past, as has often been said, is a foreign country, and we will never find ourselves there.'

Emergent capitalism – not 'industrialisation', as Gellner (1983) put it, rather superficially and teleologically – provided a dynamic for nationalism. It engendered the separation of the sphere of 'civil society' from that of the state, the sovereign power following the 1648 Treaty of Westphalia. Within that sphere 'public opinion' came to be formed, with the assistance of the printing press (Anderson, 1983), leading to the notion of representative government as an alternative to absolutism. And so to the question, who was to be represented?, the answer was the imagined 'national community' (Delanty and O'Mahony, 2002: 32–3).

This approach not only allows the modernist/traditionalist debate to be transcended but also of a periodisation of nationalism *within the modern era itself*, and an articulation of variants of nationalism to economic trends and social forces. The new phase of globalisation has thus been associated with the 'decoupling' of the 'nation' as imagined community and the state (*ibid.*: 170). While opening the way to a project of constitutional tolerance, this has been marked by the proliferation of what came to be described (Connor, 1994) as conflicts of 'ethnonationalism', most evidently in the Balkans (Glenny, 1999). Given its negative normative connotations, it is interesting how rarely the 'ethnonationalist' label has been applied to Northern Ireland, by contrast with ex-Yugoslavia, with the notable exceptions of Hayes and McAllister (1999) and Wolff (2002).

As Kaldor (1999: 39) recognised, this was not just a revival: 'It was new in the sense that it was associated with the disintegration of the state in contrast to earlier "modern" nationalisms which aimed at state-building and that, unlike earlier nationalisms, it lacked a modernizing ideology.' Socially, it was to be a vehicle for those disenfranchised by a transformation from 'national' industrial capitalisms, with relatively stable relationships of class and social welfare, to a globalising *informational* capitalism (Castells, 1996), in which the 'classic industrial worker' found himself (as, when it came to nationalist protagonists, it usually was) unable to compete with empowered 'symbolic analysts' and struggling to survive in the service, informal or even criminal economies (Kaldor, 2004: 166).

This ethnonationalism of *late* modernity brought once more into play the putative distinction between 'civic' and 'ethnic' ideal types (Ignatieff, 1994). If nationalism had acquired a positive connotation in the anti-colonial era, it was now 'seen increasingly as fuelling the currency of ethno-national intolerance, rivalry, tribalism, xenophobia, and worse' (Cassese, 1995: 4). So 'liberal nationalists', like Kymlicka and Taylor, were anxious to save their 'good' (in this case *Québecois*) nationalism from the 'bad' strain.

But here, too, there are fundamental epistemological problems with such Weberian, ideal-typical constructs. They do not identify real objects as the 'rich totality of many determinations' (Marx, 1973: 100) but rather represent them as if they were impure embodiments of a quantity which only exists as such in thought. This is problematic enough, but any 'actually-existing' nationalism will then be a blend of the two antagonistic, putative types – somehow to mix, despite being like oil and water.

In any event, the concepts 'civic' and 'ethnic' are so volatile that they cannot be used to establish a stable classification or normative scheme (Brubaker, 2004: 136–44). Thomas Miley (2007) shows their inapplicability to a comparison of Catalan nationalism with its Basque counterpart (the former presented as 'civic', the latter 'ethnic'). Gellner (1993: 19) punchily describes nationalism *tout court* as 'the beast we all have to contain'. And Özkırımlı (2005) makes a convincing case that any variety of nationalism, in privileging a particular imagined community, contradicts the liberal principle of equality.

That principle is however sustained by the non-nationalist notion of 'constitutional patriotism' advanced by Habermas (2001), where civic allegiance is given to democratic institutions, rather than to the 'nation' – a notion as applicable at the transnational level of the European Union as the 'nation-state' and essential for multi-ethnic societies. For all the travails of politics in Northern Ireland, it shows how even in a divided society allegiance to (in this case regional) democratic institutions can become *de rigeur*: all parties, whatever their nationalistic predilections on either side, now pay lip-service to power-sharing devolution, to which only Alliance was committed before the Belfast agreement.

A feminist perspective also casts nationalism in a negative normative light. Fidelma Ashe (2006: 152–3) highlights its tendency to identify women with the 'national honour' to be upheld – with severe consequences for those perceived as having betrayed or defiled it. She instances how Bosnian women raped as an act of war became in turn 'symbols of the nation's shame'. Wendy Bracewell (2000) addresses how rape in Kosovo was described in just such terms. And she adduces the economic transition to explain the appeal of Slobodan Milošević's turn, over Kosovo, from Yugoslav Communist to Serbian nationalist (*ibid.*: 578):

> It is suggestive that the mainstay of Milošević's support came from the unemployed and those threatened by the economic and political reforms of the 1980s (including unskilled and semi-skilled workers, agricultural workers, and low-level officials). These were men whose experiences were in sharp and frustrating contrast to an ideal of masculinity based on dominance, power and economic self-sufficiency.

Explaining how men have come to dominate politics and paramilitarism in Northern Ireland, consigning women largely to the private sphere, Ashe (2006: 151) writes: 'Irish nationalism and Unionism are ideologies based on the glorification of hegemonic masculine virtues such as national pride, courage, physical strength and self-sacrifice.' She complains (*ibid.*: 161): 'Mainstream political commentary has tended to ignore this facet of the Northern Irish conflict.'

For nationalists of all stripes,[33] the notion of 'national sovereignty' is critical to the suturing of 'nation' and state into the 'nation-state' they idealise or defend. But it is increasingly problematic in today's post-Westphalian environment. Benhabib (2002b: 440) protests: 'We are in the midst of developments which challenge the territorially bounded state-centric model which was re-established in Europe and elsewhere in the world after the Second World War; yet claims of sovereign statehood over bounded territories are still the guiding normative and institutional principles in the international arena.' Interestingly, in September 1972, with the republic, and the UK, due to join the European Economic Community the following January, the then Taoiseach, Jack Lynch, told the German Chancellor, Willy Brandt, in Munich that 'EEC membership might help to solve the [Northern Ireland] problem, just as questions such as Alsace/Lorraine and the South Tyrol had been solved in Europe'.[34]

As recently as 1981 a volume was published in which it was suggested that one knew a sovereign state like one knew a camel or a chair (Sørenson, 1999: 590). Yet in an integrated Europe and a globalised world, heavily populated with transnational organisations, treaties and conventions – even tribunals and courts – as well as international non-governmental organisations, states no longer collide like billiard balls in a bilateral relationship of pure exteriority, but interpenetrate and interweave in complex relationships of multilateral interdependence (Held *et al.*, 1999). Even a 'cosmopolitan orientation' for global governance becomes conceivable, in which sovereignty is 'recast' (Held, 2004: 93, 137).

In Europe in particular, the idea of sovereignty as 'absolute and indivisible', which allows only of an 'either/or' outcome, is obsolete (Beck and Grande, 2007: 77). The architecture of European 'multi-level governance' (Moore, 2008: 531) shares sovereignty and delegates it to sub-state bodies, renders borders porous and offers an overarching affiliation – in sharp contrast with the nationalistic discourse of absolute sovereignty, exclusive identities, territorial integrity and military balance (Noutcheva, Tocci, Coppieters *et al.*, 2004: 9–10, 18).

Since the Universal Declaration of Human Rights of 1948, the presumption of 'non-interference' in international relations has been progressively eroded by 'a massive expansion of international human rights treaties, setting out the civil, cultural, economic, political and social rights to which all human beings are entitled, regardless of race, creed, gender or age' (Mepham, 2005: 134–5) – embedding an *ius humanitatis* transcending conventional notions of rights attaching only to 'nationals' of states, as *ius soli* or *ius sanguinis* (Papisca, 2007: 477). Within states, the increasing impossibility of omnicompetence in today's ever more complex and individuated societies has led to governance arrangements spreading well beyond the sphere of government, conventionally understood – not only to embrace regional devolution, on which the UK was a laggard among west-European large states (Laffan and O'Mahony, 2008: 217), but also some delegation of functions to non-governmental associations (Hirst, 2002) and even enrolment of individual citizens in the 'co-production' of public programmes (Coleman and Blumler, 2009: 180–1).

As Timothy Sisk (2004: 267) rhetorically asks, 'If sovereignty today means something so different from what it did in the past, is it still worth fighting for?' It becomes possible to finesse tensions between nationalisms and the state by the blurring of 'sovereignty', the advocacy of minority rights and the promotion of genuine cultural diversity (Wilson, 2001).

Remarkably, apart from annexes, only one page of the Belfast agreement (NIO, 1998: 3) is devoted to 'constitutional issues', the pith and substance of the violent conflict. The agreement reaffirmed the principle that 'it would be wrong to make any change in the status of Northern Ireland save with the consent of a majority of its people'. This had been accepted by London and Dublin ever since the Sunningdale agreement of 1973 (Bew and Gillespie, 1999: 72–5), and was implied in the provision in the Anglo-Irish Treaty of 1921 for the Parliament established under the Government of Ireland Act of

1920 to opt out of the new Free State (Garvin, 1996: 206–7).

The 'constitutional issues' section is actually a brief excursus on the procedure for constitutional *change*. In an ironic reprise of history, it ensures the recurrence of Winston Churchill's 'dreary steeples' of Fermanagh and Tyrone, by representing the constitutional choice for the future of Northern Ireland in just the same, binary terms as in the heyday of 'self-determination' in 1921. *Pace* the former Northern Ireland Secretary Mandelson, who declared with characteristic certitude that the agreement 'settled the constitutional issues once and for all',[35] it is thus no surprise that it has failed to undermine the 'integrity' of the unionist-nationalist 'quarrel'.

Sumantra Bose (2003: 173), who draws parallels between Northern Ireland and the equally 'complex situation' of Kashmir, warns that 'a plebiscitary approach is not just deeply simplistic and inadequate but, potentially, deeply destabilizing'. In 1993 the Fianna Fáil co-chair of the British-Irish Interparliamentary Body, Dermot Ahern, referring to the similar provision in article one of the 1985 Anglo-Irish Agreement, said that this was 'a fallacious article in that it states that the day there is 50 per cent plus one in favour of a United Ireland we will promote in both Houses of Parliament legislation to bring that about'. The future Minister for Foreign Affairs explained: 'I would not like to be around the day that that happens because the unionists, rather than being a majority in the Six Counties, will be, against their wishes, a minority on the island.'[36] He would not have been reassured had he read, in *The Economist* a week earlier, the comment by a 'friend' of the Prime Minister, John Major: 'If [the Northern Irish] voted 51 to 49 to join the republic, we'd be the first to cheer. So would practically every sane Englishman. Good riddance.'[37]

The difficulty was also recognised in retrospect by the former Fine Gael Taoiseach John Bruton (2006: 23), who held office from late 1994 until 1997 and so was steward from the republic's side for most of the 'peace process' between the paramilitary ceasefires and the Belfast agreement. He affirmed: 'The obsession on the part of both Nationalists and Unionists with territorial sovereignty, a nineteenth-century notion, continues to do its damage.' Borrowing a phrase from the 1993 Middle East Oslo accords, he concluded that the problem with the agreement, and its 1973–74 predecessor, was the absence of 'final-status negotiations'.

Oddly, Blair was to admit this very belatedly. In a speech in Washington in 2006, he suggested that resolving the problems of the Middle East should actually prove easier (a judgement that could be questioned) than settling Northern Ireland. This was because 'in the case of Israel and Palestine we do now have agreement about the basic nature of the settlement – two states'. In contrast, he said: 'The problem we have had in Northern Ireland is that there has never been agreement on the basic nature of the final outcome, one part wanting union with the United Kingdom, the other with the Republic of Ireland.'[38]

Katy Hayward (2006: 276) recognises the overhang effect of this *longue-durée* conception of the problem:

> Progress from the Agreement depended on the growth of moderation within unionism and nationalism, rather than the establishment of a middle ground between them. The Agreement is thus an attempt at consociationalism, setting up non-majoritarian power sharing between what are defined as two ethno-national groups. An inherent problem with this, however, is that the Agreement also constitutionalizes the condition of majority consent – by which the status of Northern Ireland will change should an absolute majority within it wish so. Thus, it is integral to the logic of the Agreement that citizens vote for parties that most strongly represent and defend what they see as their identity and interests (defined along British unionist or Irish nationalist lines).

This polarising logic has offset the potential for devolution to lead to a moderation of attitudes on the conventional, bipolar constitutional choice. Roger MacGinty (2003: 3) questions the applicability of referendums to ethnonational conflicts, given they are 'zero sum, creating winners and losers', and he echoes Bruton in identifying as a 'key problem' that the Belfast agreement 'is not regarded as a settlement document' (*ibid.*: 19). He notes that the devolution embodied in the agreement itself complicated 'the traditional either/or constitutional absolutes of a united Ireland or the Union' (*ibid.*: 9). And he points to data from the NILT survey revealing that 'public attitudes towards constitutional preferences are becoming more diffuse and less absolute' – notably showing more support for a devolved arrangement than for direct rule and a united Ireland put together (*ibid.*: 12).

Power-sharing

The ethnonationalist conflicts arising from the absence of a neat 'nation-state' suture can of course be 'solved' through secession and/or partition. But such 'solutions' may merely displace the majority/minority problem into a new arena (as historically in Ireland) or simply be impractical – without 'ethnic cleansing' (Horowitz, 1985: 589–91). The alternative to this (or, indeed, to cantonisation or repartition) is power-sharing. Here, the principal policy prescription since the 1970s has been consociationalism, which its intellectual pioneer, Arend Lijphart (1977, 2002), would identify with power-sharing itself. A key move is to define the only alternative to consociationalism, other than secession/partition, as assimilation, with its (justly) negative connotations.

Yet, in doing so, Lijphart (*ibid.*: 44) rules out definitionally the alternative of integration and intercultural dialogue, refusing any conceptualisation of 'plural societies' other than that premised on homogeneous cultures and associated political blocs. And he takes a sideswipe (*ibid.*: 47) at a perceived tendency in 'peace research' to 'frown on peace which is achieved by separating the potential enemies'. Consociationalism might thus be described as mental partition: it is premised on the autonomy of ethnic 'segments' and mutual-veto arrangements between elites, as well as proportionality in public employment and grand-coalition government.

Consociationalism, however, came under increasing challenge in the 1980s and 1990s. M. P. C. M. van Schendelen (1984) found Lijphart's concepts slippery, Sue Halpern (1986) showed his cases did not conform to the model, Adriano Pappalardo (1981) demonstrated that the factors he claimed favoured consociationalism were mostly causally and empirically dubious, and Matthijs Bogaards (1998) added that they had shifted over time. Brass (1991: 334) contested the implicit assumptions of the fixity of ethnic identities and absence of intraethnic cleavages, as well as the model's normatively unattractive elitism, the latter concern echoed by Paul Dixon (1997). It has been variously suggested that consociationalism only works where it is not necessary, and where it is (by Lijphart's lights) it can unintentionally entrench ethnic division (Sisk, 1996: 39).

Bogaards (2000) highlights a particular disjunction between Lijphart's normative and empirical claims which demonstrates the fragility of the edifice. Lijphart defines consociationalism as the polar opposite of majoritarianism, in turn considered as a 'Westminster type' democracy with a plurality electoral system and a one-party, winner-takes-all government – he has the UK and US in mind. But this normative counterposition does not work empirically, as the counterpart of his consociationalist democracies in this regard should be those which Lijphart defines as 'centrifugal democracies' in the wider Europe. These are 'plural' societies, by his lights, yet critically have adversarial elites.

On the very first page of *Democracy in Plural Societies*, Lijphart (1977: 1) declared: 'In a consociational democracy, the centrifugal tendencies inherent in a plural society are counteracted by the cooperative attitudes and behaviour of the leaders of the different segments of the population.' This disjunction means, according to Bogaards (2000: 408), that 'the European centrifugal democracies do not present cases of the failure of majoritarian democracy and hence do not provide an argument against the recommendation of majoritarian democracy for plural societies'. And he claims Lijphart now essentially makes only normative claims for consociationalism, which leave it immune from empirical criticism. Vivien Schmidt (2006: 229) similarly argues that 'Lijphart's dichotomy implies that majoritarian democracies will always have confrontation and consensus ones the opposite. But in real life this is not the case.'

The empirical claim itself had always been vulnerable to the critical-realist argument that 'constant conjunctions' of events are not the same as 'causal laws' (Bhaskar, 1975: 34–5). In particular, the former do not establish the direction of any purported relationship of dependency. Specifically, Lijphart can not present a convincing answer to the charge by Brian Barry (1975) that instances of consociationalist grand coalition might be an epiphenomenon of a willingness to compromise rather than *vice versa* – in which case it would be unwise to export the elaborate institutional architecture to deeply divided societies. Lijphart does not help his case by referring (1977: 100) to a 'predemocratic historical tendency towards moderation and compromise' in the Netherlands and Switzerland.

Intuitively, the electoral dynamics of consociationalist regimes *discourage* cross-communal co-operation as they do not incentivise cross-ethnic appeals by members of ethnic elites, who tend to view each other in zero-sum terms, but favour gaming with mutual vetoes in a manner likely to lead to permanent stalemate (Belloni, 2007: 50–1). Lijphart (1977: 30–1) argues that such coalition arrangements minimise the risk of deception, or over-optimistic self-deception as to other parties' intent. Yet willingness to compromise is ultimately based on the idea that one can trust one's adversary not to *abuse* such willingness. If such trust is absent – as was all too evident in the 1999–2002 devolution experience in Northern Ireland, and became even more so after May 2007 – one will not credit accommodating behaviour from an adversary and may well be unduly pessimistic in this regard.

Lijphart's (2000) reaction to Bogaards' critique is, remarkably, to abandon the theoretical relationship between consociationalism and deeply divided societies altogether, by simply defining consociational democracy in terms of the four putative characteristics and excluding the fifth, 'plural society', aspect. Claiming little concern about normative versus empirical categorisations, he asserts that the concept is an ideal type and simultaneously an empirical category. But then one could normatively insist on the necessity of consociationalism even though the theoretical link to deep social division had been detached, and could contend that if it is not empirically instantiated anywhere it is because ideal types never fully are. Lijphart still insists on hegemonising the concept of power-sharing, dismissing Bogaards' claim that there are other models (*ibid.*: 427): 'This is not correct.'

Interestingly, Lijphart's (2000) defence has come to rest heavily on Northern Ireland. First, he stresses how the British government started

45

calling its 'consociational designs' there 'power-sharing' long before he did – though, as we shall see, even in 1998 the arrangements were *not* designed to implement a prior consociationalist schema. Secondly, when Bogaards argues that the disjunction between the empirical and the normative in Lijphart means he has no basis to make policy recommendations, he rhetorically asks if Bogaards really means power-sharing should not be recommended for Northern Ireland as an alternative to Westminsterist majoritarianism.

Lijphart also stresses in a footnote that, while he had become pessimistic about the possible application of consociationalism to Northern Ireland after the 1974 failure, he had said that recognition that it was the only alternative to repartition and consistent pressure by the British Government could lead to it being re-established – which he sees the Belfast agreement as realising (*ibid.*: 430). Indeed, the triumph of majority rule in South Africa, against Lijphart's prescription there, has left him very dependent on the Northern Ireland outcome.

Writing before the Belfast agreement, O'Leary (2004a: 98) similarly represented consociationalism as the alternative to 'the Westminster model of simple majoritarianism or minimum-winning coalitions, single-party governments, and a disproportional voting system which creates a governmental executive able to impose its will within a unitary state' – again without recognising its limited purview beyond the Anglo-American world. He presented as alternatives to consociationalism 'hegemonic control',[39] partition, 'cooperative internationalization', arbitration and 'integration'.

Significantly, O'Leary represented integration as entailing that one or other 'segment' collectively accepts that it will 'surrender its identity' or as requiring 'the creation of a transcendent identity' (*ibid.*: 100). But the first is assimilation, rather than integration, which is a two-sided process (Council of Europe, 2008: 11). And, even if one accepted the assumption of a one-to-one correspondence between 'segments' and collectivised 'identities', a Habermasian allegiance to shared democratic authority does not necessitate a new ethnic identity.

O'Leary (2004a: 111–12) rehearsed the conditions identified by Lijphart (1977: 54) as favouring consociationalism, including prior traditions of accommodation, a perception of a common external threat and 'society-wide loyalties, especially a sense of common national identity'. And he identified only two – small size and segmental autonomy – as present in Northern Ireland. As Lijphart had earlier done, he thus concluded (O'Leary, 2004a: 113) that, as regards 'voluntary' consociationalism, '[t]he implications are bleak'. So O'Leary argued for an even more conscious elite drive for consociation, premised on 'the stability of the subcultures', even in the absence of favourable social conditions – with the only alternative deemed 'another partition' (*ibid.*: 115, 131).

Rick Wilford (1992: 34–5) not only found consociationalism norma-tively unattractive but argued that a wiser reaction to the 1974 debacle (see Chapter 4) would be to recognise the need 'to generate sufficient grassroots support upon which amenable leaders could rely, rather than to depend upon elite accommodation atop mutually exclusive and distrustful communities'. At that time he detected, in late 1980s reforms in fair employment and edu-cation, 'more a bottom-up strategy' which he described as 'post-modern' or 'inverted consociationalism' (*ibid.*: 44): 'Instead of seeking to manufac-ture a fragile elite consensus which spans an inextricably divided society, they seem to represent attempts to erode the modernist and monolithic blocs within which the region's social segments are cast.'[40]

O'Leary (2004b) identifies the Belfast agreement as realising his vision but, as with Lijphart, developments since 2002 have provided mixed evi-dence. The volume of O'Leary's prior works – the above included – and those of his colleague McGarry published in 2004 appears like a retrospec-tive valedictory of a now completed line of inquiry, but the introduction (McGarry and O'Leary, 2004) is notably defensive in tone.

McGarry and O'Leary deny that the rise of SF and the DUP is indicative of growing extremism, claiming the former has moderated and the latter has adapted to the Belfast agreement. That they have triumphed by defeating more moderate rivals and that this would have predictable consequences for their ability to work together in government is however ignored. Yet in the watershed 2003 assembly election, as Karin Lutz and Christopher Farrington (2006: 728–9) have shown, DUP candidates were more con-servative on morality and religion than their UUP counterparts, while SF candidates were more nationalistic than SDLP runners. These results fore-shadowed the bible-based antagonism of DUP members (and now some ex-members) towards accommodating republicans in government after May 2007 and the willingness of SF to countenance that government being stymied. Farrington (2007) has confirmed by analysis of party manifestoes for the three Assembly elections a complex combination of moderation and polarisation on ethnic issues – the first explicable by post-'troubles' quotid-ian pressures, the second by the incentives of the political system.

McGarry and O'Leary (2004: 36) suggest that '*ceteris paribus*, an extended period of voluntary inter-group cooperation should reduce inter-community divisions rather than maintain or deepen them'. But the whole point of the application of the d'Hondt procedure to executive formation was to avoid any requirement for 'inter-group co-operation'. As Wolff (2005: 60) points out, 'by effectively guaranteeing the same four parties a place in government for the foreseeable future, sectarian divisions in the institutions, and by extension in society, have been entrenched rather than broken down, making compromise across the communal divide not only less necessary and desirable but in fact potentially dangerous in terms of compromising a party's electoral support'.

The tactical retreat of consociationalism, in the face of criticism, is also evident in O'Leary's work. He now defines it in such a way as to include only two of Lijphart's prerequisites: proportionality and segmental autonomy. He replaces grand coalition by the notion that power must be '*jointly shared*' and describes mutual veto as 'contingent' (O'Leary, 2006: xviii) – which would allow of more flexible power-sharing arrangements. He recognises the claims that grand coalitions entail absence of opposition and veto powers can have deadlocking effects, though he says the latter are exaggerated (*ibid.*: xxiv, xxx). Oddly, then, since proportionality in public employment was the least controversial of Lijphart's tools, all that is left for O'Leary to defend is segmental autonomy.

As with Lijphart, under pressure O'Leary simply excludes alternative viewpoints by definitional fiat. In one short text (*ibid.*: xx, xxi, xxxiv), he brackets together 'integration' and 'assimilation', and their advocates, three times. Yet, as indicated above, integration is defined by equality and mutuality, which can only succeed under neutral public authority, whereas assimilation is submission to a state marked by the prevailing ethos defined by members of an ethnic majority. Having evacuated the integrationist scenario, O'Leary can hold out only a dystopian prospect (*ibid.*: xxii, xxvi): 'Consociational politics is ... politics without "shared vision",' he writes, and – apparently unmindful of the echo of the infamous Plessy, 'separate but equal', US Supreme Court judgment – 'Equality with difference is the motto of this type of autonomy.'

McGarry and O'Leary (2009a) rehearse their position once more in an edited collection (Taylor, 2009) on their work on Northern Ireland. Their only innovative claim is to have transcended Lijphart in recognising the importance of the external political dimensions of such 'pluri-national' societies, though this looks suspiciously like generalising from their perspective on the Northern Ireland case. That potentially interesting theme is in any event captured within what Beck (2009: 167), would describe as a dated 'methodological nationalism' – in which 'the premise of the actors' normative-political nationalism is unreflectively adopted as the premise of the observer perspective of social science' – rather than in the cosmopolitan conceptualisation outlined in Chapter 2, with its recognition of '*ambivalence*', of '*contingency*' and '*transnational* spaces', which could be associated with a freeing up of sectarian identifications in Northern

Ireland (original emphasis).

Had they themselves conducted significant primary research on this theme, they could have developed a fuller and more nuanced account, but consociationalists seem generally incurious about subjecting their normative schemata to scrutiny as to empirical adequacy.[41] The response by McGarry and O'Leary (2009b) to a range of criticisms, assembled in the same volume, is recurrently dismissive and *ad hominem* – most notably towards those intellectuals living, and researching, in Northern Ireland.

Outside of Northern Ireland, even by Lijphart's (2002: 41) claims, only Belgium and Switzerland currently conform to his consociationalist model, though he suggests – accepting it is 'more controversial' – that India, despite the strictures of Brass (1991: 342–3), and, stubbornly, South Africa are also power-sharing examples. (He notably does not refer to Bosnia-Herzegovina, Lebanon or Macedonia.) Steven Wilkinson (2004: 97–136) shows that Lijphart is wrong to suggest that India under Congress rule was consociational, while demonstrating that coalition governments since the 1960s have become more consociational – a period which has seen a rise in intercommunal rioting.

Of Lijphart's cases, only Switzerland is governed by 'grand coalition', and even there the party system is not based on communal representation. Indeed, the Swiss *Sonderfall* is otherwise very much the opposite of the consociationalist approach – a grassroots democracy rather than an elite governance system (Rellstab, 2001). One of the features of Swiss politics – not unproblematic when it comes to issues touching on minority rights – is the role of referendums and citizens' initiatives.

Even at the federal level, the parties are organised on conventional, right–left lines. And while seats in government are distributed according to the 'magic formula', superficially similar to the operation of the d'Hondt rule in Northern Ireland, a key difference is that aspiring ministers must secure election from the United Federal Assembly, so that parties can only secure ministerial positions for candidates other parties can live with. Thus, even though the Swiss People's Party (SVP) has grown in strength – and secured an extra seat in Government through a modification of the formula – it withdrew from Government after the 2007 election because its leader and candidate for Justice Minister, Christoph Blocher, was rejected by the parliament following the party's overtly racist campaign.[42]

Lijphart (2004: 97–8) remains undeterred. He continues to insist that 'power-sharing' and 'consociational' democracy are identical and that 'very few critics have presented serious alternatives'. Yet most working interethnic democracies – most working democracies *being* interethnic democracies nowadays – are governed by more flexible arrangements, which may or may not explicitly represent power-sharing but certainly are unlikely to be manifestations of Lijphartian theory. Indeed, the declining academic interest in consociationalism (Lustick, 1997) has paralleled the atrophy of demonstrable instances in the real world. As Donald Horowitz (2002a: 23) concludes, 'Certainly, to conflate consociation with all of power-sharing is completely unwarranted.'

Consociationalism is premised on segmental autonomy – the notion that high fences make good neighbours (Guelke, 2003: 69). Yet this is to rule out the potential of public deliberation for reconciliation and, conversely, to risk further polarisation as narrowly intracommunal debates only reinforce prejudices (Dryzek, 2005). Ian O'Flynn (2006) highlights the odd compartmentalisation in political science in which work around deliberative democracy has proceeded in a separate sphere from work on divided societies.

And if persons with affinities to different ethnic 'communities' are best kept apart, why endorse power-sharing at all? Partition or repartition offers a real, not metaphorical, fence behind which to huddle. Conversely, if power-sharing really works, over time it will entail a blurring of communal divisions within civil society, as in Lijphart's disappeared Dutch case. The rarity of extant examples suggests that consociationalism is an unstable state between (re)partition and a less rigid governance scheme.

Reflecting on his four model cases, Lijphart (1977: 2) did then believe that communal divisions were 'declining', claiming consociationalism had been successful and thus represented 'a passing phase'. Unfortunately, this proved least true of the case which best embodied his four consociationalist elements, Belgium. As Kris Deschouwer's (2005) analysis of its shifting tectonic plates demonstrates, the country is drifting apart. The ethnopolitical elites tend to adopt more communalist stances than the public at large, they are only weakly accountable under consociationalist arrangements and there is no one to represent the *Belgian* interest at the recurrent rounds of constitutional negotiations (Cartritte, 2002). The prolonged hiatus after the 2007 Belgian election led to open discussion of a split.

Policy always lags best practice and intellectual renewal, however, owing to information deficits, ideology and inertia – perhaps particularly in 'intellectually interned' Northern Ireland. And a 'common-sense' consociationalism remains widespread among policy-makers dealing with divided societies, based on unquestioned acceptance of the essentialist conception of 'culture'. From his power-sharing survey – looking at Cyprus, Northern Ireland, South Africa, Fiji and Bosnia-Herzegovina – Ghai (2001: 21) notes that a particular difficulty of consociationalism is its assumption that 'groups are driven by primordial sentiments and have an unchanging identity'.

In his classic text, Lijphart (1977: 17) himself articulated this view, which he had gleaned from an earlier generation of anthropologists, that 'communal attachments' are 'primordial' and that in 'plural' societies people 'mix but do not combine'. He now accepts (Lijphart, 2001)[43] that such primordialism is obsolete, claiming however that his preference for 'self-determining' rather than 'pre-determined' communal 'segments' saves the theory. But this does not address the risk with consociationalist arrangements – however one deems the segments to be constituted – that they not only recognise but entrench communal divisions.

In his analysis of the Belfast agreement O'Leary (2004b: 284) argues: 'Unionists have recognized nationalists as nationalists, not simply as Catholics or the minority. Nationalists have recognized Unionists as Unionists, and not just as Protestants.' He adds that this would warm the heart of Charles Taylor. O'Leary appears unaware of the anti-essentialist criticisms of Taylor and oblivious to the fact that while it may be possible to craft well-functioning power-sharing arrangements between Protestants and Catholics, *qua* Protestants and Catholics, it makes it more rather than less difficult (as the attitudinal data rehearsed above indicate) if they are ideologically defined in terms set by ethnopolitical entrepreneurs.

As Wolff (2006: 55) makes clear, 'Different ethnic identities can, and in many cases do, peacefully coexist in the same state; different nationalisms cannot.' Their mutual antagonism is much more likely to lead to 'Balkanisation', the fate of the Belgian party system (de Winter, Swyngedouw and Dumont, 2006: 954), than stable adherence to common political arrangements. Yet in Northern Ireland the 'peace process' had a demonstrably polarising effect, by favouring a closer alignment between religion, national identity and state preference – as in 'Protestant'/'British'/ 'unionist' – in the public mind. It thus strengthened the 'strong pro-state' and 'strong counter-state' positions of the DUP and SF respectively, against their 'weak pro-state' UUP and 'weak counter-state' SDLP rivals (Hayes and McAllister, 1999: 33–6).

Rupert Taylor (2001: 38–9) draws attention to the perversity of this: 'It is neither obvious nor logical that ethno-nationalism can be cured by prescribing more of it through constitutional engineering.' He notes how consociationalists are not very interested in theoretical elaboration beyond what they take to be 'facts' and 'realities'. They are uninterested in probing levels of ethnonationalist consciousness, distinguishing more constitutional-patriotic manifestations or investigating change over time.

Taylor points out how the South African transition was possible because consociationalist prescriptions were rejected in favour of non-racialism. And for Northern Ireland he advocates 'a democratic, non-sectarian politics' for a project of 'social transformation' (*ibid.*: 47). While this is normatively attractive, it replaces the dispiriting determinism of consociationalism by a utopian call to human agency. Examples of progressive developments he rightly cites, such as the growth of integrated education and mixed marriages, are minoritarian and likely to remain so for some time.

Critics of arrangements derived from essentialist conceptions of identity must be able to offer realistic alternatives for divided societies. It is in the absence of a sense that these exist that Bose (2002: 247, 249) endorses consociationalism in Bosnia-Herzegovina, *faute de mieux*. While recognising the risk of entrenching communal identities, he nevertheless hopes that over time these will wither away, as indeed – equally counter-intuitively – do McGarry and O'Leary (2004: 36).

The trick is to recognise that the fear of ethnic domination which can lead to violence (Horowitz, 1985: 189) and to which consociationalism attends can be met without resorting to its standard responses of grand coalition and mutual veto, allied to proportionality in public employment and segmental autonomy. Bogaards (2000: 417) is right to stress that the consociationalist model falls 'at least one rung lower on the ladder of generality than the concept of power-sharing'.

On the composition of power-sharing government, once one takes account of intra-ethnic party competition – never mind non-ethnic or inter-ethnic parties – a coalition of the 'moderate middle' is actually *more* realistic than an inclusive executive. To expect all significant parties to cooperate in government in the wake of a power-sharing agreement is to expect that that they will simply put aside their divisions; more realistically, a new struggle over inclusion/exclusion ensues (Horowitz, 1994: 49), as has happened during both the periods of devolution in Northern Ireland since 1999. Hence the absence of durable examples, outside of the Swiss exception – and even there the relationship to government of the SVP has, as indicated, become a source of sharp controversy.

A particular concern with grand-coalition government, exacerbated by the consociationalist emphasis on politics as an elite activity, is that it makes it impossible for citizens to 'turf the scoundrels out'. This compounds the worrying tendency across western Europe towards the 'hollowing out' of democracy, as parties become less the representative voices of diverse sections of the citizenry and more vehicles for members of a detached political class to insert themselves in government (Mair, 2006). It can thus allow political entrepreneurs to represent themselves as the voice of the 'little man' against the 'establishment' parties. Combined with ethnic scapegoating, this contains rich potential for 'preachers of hate' (Roxburgh, 2002). And if one looks at the careers of Fortuyn, Filip de Winter, the late Jörg Haider and

Blocher in the Netherlands, Belgium, Austria and Switzerland respectively – Lijphart's four original cases – they have all stirred this political pot.

Giovanni Sartori (1997: 60) warns that in 'a polarised polity' coalitions are 'uncooperative, litigious and stalemate-prone', and further (*ibid.*: 71) that '[g]rand coalitions obscure responsibility to the utmost and are, as a rule, more heterogeneous and more easily gridlocked'. A better approach is thus to pursue incremental progress in reducing division, starting from a realisable coalition embracing the more moderate 'communal contenders', as against more militant 'ethno-nationalists' – to follow the distinction drawn by Asbjørn Eide (1993: 10). For if the former do recognise to varying degrees that persons affiliating to different ethnic communities have to rub along together in a shared polity, the latter operate on assimilationist assumptions, which can only be a recipe for an indefinite zero-sum conflict with their equal-and-opposite antagonists.

Failure to understand this distinction led Blair to assume ethnonationalist parties could be the basis of a viable power-sharing arrangement. Ten years after the agreement, with the devolved institutions having actually functioned for only some 40 months – a third – of the period, he wrote:[44]

> Today, unionists are still unionists. Republicans are still republicans. Each is still able to pursue what they want but within a framework that seems to them both equal and fair. The peace process made progress precisely because we never set out to turn unionists into republicans or republicans into unionists. We set out to make it possible for both to share power together.

A cross-communal but not all-party coalition will in itself be one guarantee against ethnic oppression, as the 'minority' component, if the 'majority' is divided by intra-ethnic tension and the ethnic outbidding party is not included in government, will be critical to government formation. In any event, arrangements for mutual vetoes are more likely to be used against the minority than in its favour, owing to the balance of power – as graphically demonstrated by the deadlocking behaviour by the DUP under Peter Robinson's stewardship from May 2008, effectively bringing the power-sharing executive in Northern Ireland to nought for several months (Wilford and Wilson, 2008d).

This can be supplanted by mechanisms that prevent ethnic subordination without reifying identities. International minority-rights declarations, such as those promulgated in the 1990s by the Council of Europe (1995), the Organisation for Security and Co-operation in Europe (Foundation on Inter-Ethnic Relations, 1996, 1998, 1999) and the United Nations (Eide, 1993), represent a supportive (if until incorporated into a bill of rights non-justiciable) set of external standards. If need be, power-sharing accords may additionally make provision for secular weighted-majority decision-making on controversial issues, without requirement for communal registration.

Proportional representation in public, and indeed private, employment should be the product of equal-opportunity legislation, including scope for affirmative action as required, in *any* society. But this should not normally involve quotas and should arise from objective recruitment procedures, rather than the operation of communal patronage systems. The latter are not only inefficient but in the case of Austria's *Proporz* system gave the Freedom Party an easy stick with which to beat the 'red-black' establishment on its political rise (Fallend, 2004).

Behind the focus on public employment is otherwise a lacuna in consociationalist theory, where the emphasis on the party system and political elites is at the expense of discussion of the state (Brass, 1991: 334). The answer to a party ethnocracy, like pre-1972 Northern Ireland, as the civil-rights movement recognised, is not an ethnic duopoly but the separation of party and state, and the promotion of impartial public authority, with all its trust-building potential. Wilkinson (2004) demonstrates the critical role played by partisan policing – and, in particular, non-policing – in fostering intercommunal violence in riot-prone Indian states like Gujarat, as well as the value of secular leadership in West Bengal and Kerala in preventing riots there.

As Hannum (1992: 455–6) argues, taking Northern Ireland as an exemplar, what distinguishes ethnic conflicts which escalate into violence from those which do not is commonly 'the violation of fundamental human rights'. Silke (2005: 243–5) similarly highlights the role of state authoritarianism in Northern Ireland in fostering, rather than defeating, the IRA in the early 1970s. The most serious rights violation was the introduction of internment in August 1971, and while 34 people had been killed in violence earlier that year fully 140 were to die in the remainder (Bew and Gillespie, 1999: 37).

Such violations (Boyle, Hadden and Hillyard, 1975, 1980) provided a series of *causes célèbres*, including the enduring horror of 'Bloody Sunday' in 1972 (Dawson, 2007), abusive police interrogation (Taylor, 1980) in the late 1970s and an apparent 'shoot-to-kill' policy by police (Stalker, 1988) and army (Urban, 1992) units in the early and later 1980s respectively. It was when this series exhausted itself, rather than as a result of 'tough' security policies, that paramilitary campaigns faltered.

This does not detract from the role of 'groupthink' and centrally imposed discipline in paramilitary organisations in perpetuating the conflict (Alonso, 2007) or the impact upon them of the decision in the early 1990s by human-rights organisations to turn the spotlight on their egregious violations of international humanitarian law (Amnesty International, 1994; Helsinki

Watch, 1991). These comments should be considered with the above discussion of the role of NGOs in dampening down paramilitary violence ahead of the 1994 ceasefires and the non-correspondence in subsequent years between consociationalist initiatives by London and Dublin and the recrudescence and decline of violence.

The absence of a written constitution, a product of the Westminsterist ideology of 'parliamentary sovereignty' (Morison and Livingstone, 1995: 24), and the associated failure until 1998 to incorporate the European Convention on Human Rights into domestic law – which led to many Northern Ireland cases being taken to Strasbourg – militated against recognition of how the behaviour of the British State breached universal norms. On the contrary, it was regularly claimed, as by a senior officer writing six months after Bloody Sunday: 'Probably no other army in the world could have "kept its cool" as well as the British Army has done in Ulster.'[45]

Yet only in the Basque country, and on a less violent scale, has any other European government faced such a protracted and powerful terrorist threat. As the editor of a collection on the 'root causes' of terrorism concludes (Bjørgo, 2005: 261), 'In counter-terrorism efforts, it is crucial to uphold democratic principles and maintain moral and ethical standards while fighting terrorism. Increased repression and coercion are likely to feed terrorism, rather than reducing it.' The Convention on the Prevention of Terrorism promulgated by the Council of Europe (2005) thus reaffirmed 'that all measures taken to prevent or suppress terrorist offences have to respect the rule of law and democratic values, human rights and fundamental freedoms'.

Finally, one accepts that in a divided society segmental autonomy is unavoidably the starting point for reconciliation. Yet high fences do not make good, but rather mistrustful, neighbours. A huge survey of 9,000 individuals living near interfaces in north and west Belfast revealed a deeply embedded culture of *méfiance*, which the authors linked to the validating of Northern Ireland's competing ethnonationalist positions, as if benign 'traditions', in the Belfast agreement (Shirlow and Murtagh, 2006: 34).

As ethnic violence is rooted in an internal politics based on manipulating ethnic symbols to generate strong hostile emotions, a stable peace requires not just a political settlement but also reconciliation. This requires mutual acknowledgement of responsibility and of the wounds of others, support for NGO and ecumenical initiatives, the *reconstruction* of nationalistic discourses to highlight conciliatory strands and the development of more co-operative social relationships (Kaufman, 2006).

Conversely, there is a large body of international social-psychological evidence showing that intercommunal contact in appropriate circumstances can lead to more positive attitudes to members of the 'out-group', particularly where individuals' affiliations are salient, partly through reducing anxiety and enhancing perspective-taking (Brown and Hewstone, 2005). Mario Cinalli (2005) rightly stresses the importance of horizontal relationships of interdependence within civil society if power-sharing arrangements are to go beyond ethnic pillarisation.

The Belfast agreement (Wilford, 2001) has often been described, particularly by officials in London and Dublin, as if it were the only possible accord. This reflects, however, a failure to recognise the lively international debate between the conventional consociationalist and emerging integrative perspectives on power-sharing (Sisk, 1996: 34–45). As a result, not only is the agreement an unconscious and contradictory combination of the two (Oberschall and Palmer, 2005), but the former was advanced at the expense of the latter during implementation.

Wolff (2007: 390) claims that elements of consociationalism and integrationism not only do but should combine in 'complex' power-sharing arrangements. He highlights as 'relatively stable' examples Belgium (including Brussels), Bosnia-Herzegovina, Crimea and South Tyrol. But the two paradigms have opposite implications, in as much as the former institutionalises ethnicity whereas the latter seeks to reduce its salience over time. Crimea and South Tyrol are in any event primarily instances of self-governance rather than power-sharing, and Belgium in the wake of the 2007 election and Bosnia-Herzegovina following the failure of constitutional-reform efforts there (see Chapter 3) illustrate the centrifugal tendencies consociationalism sustains.

Integrative elements of the Belfast agreement included the commitment, reflecting the influence of Alliance and the Women's Coalition, 'to facilitate and encourage integrated education and mixed housing' (NIO, 1998: 18). Yet there is an obvious collective-action dilemma: government must provide a lead for such initiatives to succeed. For the main Northern Ireland political parties to do so would strike a death-knell to the hermetically-sealed communal clienteles on which they depend.

The review of the agreement, which took place in 2004, was not the process of public deliberation the term implied but, rather, another private political arm-wrestle – Dublin, indeed, was unconcerned as to whether the 'review' was termed 'negotiation'.[46] This was unfortunate as, in advance of the review, 'government sources' there indicated a willingness to replace the communal-designation system in the Assembly by a secular weighted-majority protection and to address the absence of collective executive responsibility.[47]

Mitchell had never favoured either of the mutual-veto formulations to test 'cross-community support'. These were 'parallel consent, ie a majority of those present and voting, including a majority of the unionist and nationalist designations present and voting' and 'a weighted majority (60%) of members present and voting, including at least 40% of each of the nationalist and unionist designations present and voting' (NIO, 1998: 5). In practice, only the first, more strictly consociationalist, option has been used. The talks chair would have preferred a straightforward, two-thirds weighted-majority requirement (Horowitz, 2002c: 211).

When, in December 2004, Ahern and Blair did eventually present a post-review text (to which none of the parties had agreed), this 'comprehensive agreement' effectively filleted the Belfast agreement of its integrative aspects while strengthening the communal vetoes. That was to provide the basis for the St Andrews Agreement between the governments (though not the parties) of 2006, as a result of which devolution was restored in May 2007 – in a form more consociationalist than ever.

Conclusion

Whyte (1990: 258) concluded from his huge survey that – contrary to the claims of the ethnopolitical entrepreneurs – it had become established that the Northern Ireland conflict was primarily 'internal'. The implication was that the main *locus* of a settlement would be power-sharing institutions, on which Whyte had been one of the first to offer architectural proposals (New Ulster Movement, 1971). Unionist advocates, Whyte argued, were increasingly unable to represent the Republic of Ireland as an irredentist bogeyman – a conclusion borne out in the year *Interpreting Northern Ireland* was published by the election as President of the liberal Mary Robinson and reinforced by the subsequent painless withdrawal of the republic's territorial claim in 1999. Nationalist ideologues, by the same token, were increasingly hard pressed to sustain the category of 'British occupation'. Owen Dudley Edwards (1970: 320) had long argued that 'the Brits could hardly have been less occupied with Ireland' – a contention more diplomatically expressed in the disavowal by the then Prime Minister, Edward Heath, in a November 1971 speech at the Lord Mayor of London's banquet, of any British 'selfish interest' blocking reunification (Heath, 1998: 432).

And Whyte (1990: 258) offered a simple thought experiment: 'Though this conflict is influenced by the relations which Northern Ireland has with Britain on the one hand and the Republic on the other, those relations are not the heart of it. There would still be tensions between the two communities no matter what wider framework was adopted for the region.' This, too, is reinforced by the close relationships which have developed subsequently between London and Dublin: in 2005 the Taoiseach, Ahern, wrote of 'a new era of co-operation' and the Prime Minister, Blair, referred to a 'unique bond' (British Council Ireland, 2005: 4, 6).

The only significant intellectual challenge to Whyte's argument has come from Brendan O'Duffy (2007), whose definition of the problem in terms of the much less fraught London–Dublin axis can only be sustained by a synthetic argument that both states maintained a 'sovereignty claim' over Northern Ireland until 1998. This is only weakly credible, even on the side of the republic, given the disjunction between the *de jure* claim in *Bunreacht na hEireann* and its *de facto* limitation to a rhetorical anti-partitionism (O'Halloran, 1987). It is even less sustainable with regard to the British State, since article 75 of the Government of Ireland Act 1920 claiming sovereignty over both parts of Ireland was offset by the provisions for devolution to Northern Ireland – unwelcome to unionists – and a Council of Ireland, in tandem encapsulating a permissive attitude to reunification (Wilson, 1985). Repeal of the Government of Ireland Act on foot of the Belfast agreement was thus 'content-free', as a senior London official put it.[48]

Yet while Whyte's distillation of the accumulated wisdom, over decades, of the academic crowd has been largely uncontested, the political logic of the 'peace process' was based on quite another conceptualisation, which neglected this intellectual innovation. In effect, it defined the problem superficially as the 'men of violence', as paramilitaries came to be described in the early 1970s. While radical claims were often made that the process was based on a fundamental break with the past, in reality an earlier policy of repression of paramilitaries was replaced by one of propitiation (O'Donnell, 2007).

In both cases, this was associated with serious abrogations of universal norms, respectively of human rights and the rule of law. In both cases, it engendered an atmosphere of 'moral hazard', guaranteed to weaken further intercommunal trust. The outcome, unforeseen by those who championed the process, was a scenario best characterised not as 'peace and reconciliation' but a fragile peace *instead of* reconciliation.

Whyte (1990: 258–9) was sufficiently far-seeing to recognise that a new paradigm might replace the one he had designated. He speculated that this might involve a focus on sub-regional variation in Northern Ireland. Ironically, the new paradigm that can allow the region – and the *loci* of similar ethnonational conflicts – to progress towards the longed-for, but otherwise ever-receding status, of 'normality' entails a move in the opposite direction. The logic of the broader debates germane to Northern Ireland is that only a cosmopolitan perspective – in both the intellectual and the normative sense – offers a route to a future beyond perpetual sectarian antagonism, as the comparative analysis in the succeeding chapter will underscore.

Notes

1   The word 'ethnic' is used throughout in the widest sense, where language or reli-
     gion can be the boundary marker as well as skin colour.
2   Rachel Donnelly, 'Hume meets Blair on speeding up process', *Irish Times* (30
     October 1997).
3   National Archives, London (hereafter Kew), CAB 134/3921, report by Central
     Policy Review Staff, 'Northern Ireland policy', November 1975.
4   Steven Wilkinson (2004) contends that the critical differences in India are at the
     level of the state – where policing is controlled – rather than the city. Arguably,
     however, this complements rather than contradicts Varshney's thesis, as he offers
     little by way of data to challenge the latter's claims about the importance of the
     urban associational fabric, in allowing individuals from diverse communities to
     live together day to day without resort to public-order policing.
5   Jim Cusack, 'Worst month for casualties in at least 17 years', *Irish Times* (1
     November 1993).
6   David Sharrock, 'Blood, brothers and books', *Guardian* (20 November 1995).
7   Ruth O'Reilly, 'Peace demand on the march', *Irish News* (18 November 1993).
8   The author observed the Belfast demonstration.
9   Police Service of Northern Ireland statistics, available at www.psni.police.uk/
     security_related_incidents_fy.pdf [accessed 7 April 2009].
10 Frank Millar and Rachel Donnelly, 'Leaders seek early result in North talks', *Irish
     Times* (6 July 2001).
11 Gerry Moriarty, 'This is it. No deal, no peace, Blair insists', *Irish Times* (6 March
     2003).
12 Dan Keenan, 'Parties told political vacuum must end', *Irish Times* (24 March
     2004).
13 Tony Blair, 'Hard work came after the handshake – building trust', *Irish Times* (4
     April 2008).
14 'UUP's woes not the key problem', *Belfast Telegraph* (8 September 2003).
15 'Patience is the only strategy', *Irish News* (4 February 2004).
16 Data available at www.ark.ac.uk/nilt/2003/Political_Attitudes/NIAABOL.html
     [accessed 16 June 2009].
17 Sam Lister, 'Divided by 57 peace lines', *Belfast Telegraph* (26 April 2007).
18 'Eight years of the Belfast Agreement', *Irish Times* (10 April 2006).
19 Marie O'Halloran, 'Violence in NI a "challenge" to shared future, says Taoiseach',
     Irish Times (15 July 2009).
20 The convention was only a framework – i.e. non-justiciable – convention because
     four states, including the UK, were opposed to the proposal by senior Council of
     Europe officials for a legally binding protocol attached to the European Convention
     on Human Rights. See Andrew Marshall, 'Britain obstructs action on minority
     rights', Independent (13 July 1993).
21 The author was one of the drafters of the White Paper.
22 New Northern Ireland Assembly news release, 12 March 1999.
23 'Secretary of State's speech to the British Council conference', Northern Ireland
     Office news release, 8 May 2000.

24 Veton Latifi, 'Kumanovo holds together', *Balkan Crisis Report*, 268 (3 August 2001).

25 See www.ark.ac.uk/nilt/2007/Role_of_Government/TRUSTNON.html [accessed 16 June 2009].

26 These are defined by economists as being non-rival and non-exclusive, though their scope is a matter of legitimate political debate.

27 Michael Morgan and Rupert Taylor, 'Forget the myths: here's the real story', *Fortnight*, 266 (October 1988).

28 The author was involved in the drafting in liaison with officials in the Office of the First Minister and Deputy First Minister.

29 Northern Ireland Assembly, *Official Report*, 4 June 2007.

30 'Joint declaration by the British and Irish governments', *Irish Times* (2 May 2003).

31 'The Council of Europe and the Conflict in Northern Ireland', resolution 1389 (2004), adopted 7 September 2004, http://assembly.coe.int/Mainf.asp?link=/ Documents/AdoptedText/ta04/ERES1389.htm [accessed 16 June 2008].

32 This also puts in perspective the historic, and retrograde, significance of the no vote on the Lisbon treaty in the republic in 2008, as FitzGerald stressed repeatedly in his Irish Times column, and the inevitable political scramble to reverse it in 2009.

33 This of course means that 'unionism' should just be seen as another form of nationalism.

34 National Archives, Bishop Street, Dublin (hereafter Bishop St), TAOIS 2003/16/466, note of meeting between Brandt and Lynch in Munich, 8 September 1972.

35 Mark Brennock, 'Ministers "optimistic" of progress in review', *Irish Times* (20 October 1999).

36 Joe Carroll, 'We're all for democracy, but what does it mean?', *Irish Times* (13 November 1993).

37 'Bagehot', 'A far off country', *The Economist* (6 November 1993).

38 Frank Millar, 'Do DUP modernisers have say?', *Irish Times* (29 June 2006).

39 By hegemony he really means domination, whereas the concept was elaborated by Gramsci (1971) to connote a more subtle process of intellectual and moral leadership, able to engender a degree of consent, however contested, from subaltern social strata.

40 Coincidentally, this was confirmed by a contemporaneous conversation between the author and the NIO minister responsible for political development, Brian Mawhinney, who insisted – contrary to my suggested interpretation – that this raft of reforms was not a substitute for another effort at devolution but a complement to it.

41 I am indebted to Cillian McGrattan for this insight.

42 Derek Scally, 'Ousted politician leads party into Swiss opposition', *Irish Times* (14 December 2007).

43 I am indebted to Donald Horowitz for this reference.

44 Tony Blair, 'Hard work came after the handshake – building trust', *Irish Times* (4 April 2008).

45 Major-General J. Lunt, 'Soldiers should not be policemen', *Sunday Times* (30 July 1972).

46 Dan Keenan, 'Governments say NI accord "fundamentals" not for review', *Irish Times* (3 December 2003).

47 Mark Hennessy, 'Ahern hints changes possible for institutions', *Irish Times* (1 December 2003).

48 Author interview, 27 February 2008. While the former or serving elected politicians (five) and reconciliation practitioners (five) interviewed for this book have been named, the former or serving civil servants and diplomats, working for the UK Government (five), the Irish Government (nine) or members of the Northern Ireland civil service (three), have been anonymised. This is partly because they were expressing views which might or might not accord with official positions of governments they serve(d) and partly because (in two cases) they insisted upon it. As shorthand, I have referred to these latter sources as 'London', 'Dublin' and 'Belfast' officials.

3
Balkan lessons

Introduction

Because of their contemporaneity in a time of globalised media – not to mention the apparent partisan advantage they offered to political calculators – in the early 1990s the South African transition, the Oslo accords and the Northern Ireland 'peace process' became objects of political as well as academic comparison (Guelke, 2000).

The South African situation offered little by way of a model for Northern Ireland: it was a 'ranked' ethnic conflict (Horowitz, 1985: 22) with a vengeance, whereas in Northern Ireland intercommunal inequalities had been progressively diminished since the civil-rights movement and its communal blocs were thus vertically counterposed rather than horizontally superimposed. And in South Africa 'majority rule' was the solution, not the problem. Nor did Israel/Palestine: the deferral of key issues, such as 'final status', postponed by Oslo, foreshadowed the failure of the accords after the second *intifada*. And entrenched, 'two-state' partition was again seen as the solution, not the problem. Highlighting these contrasts and noting Northern Ireland's 'fundamental dispute on sovereignty', as a devolved government was finally formed in December 1999, *The Economist* editorialised: 'The Good Friday Agreement does not resolve this argument. It merely changes the rules of engagement.'[1]

The obvious Northern Ireland parallel – the ethnonationalist conflicts in former Yugoslavia – had little purchase by comparison, doubtless because the 'international community' saw nationalism (on all sides) there as the problem, not the solution. None of Northern Ireland's political figures would have had their mantle of 'statesmanship' enhanced by association with Slobodan Milošević or Franjo Tudjman. Yet echoes of and parallels to events in nineteenth- and twentieth-century Ulster can readily be found in east and central Europe, as two of the most insightful contextualisations of the Northern Ireland conflict attest (Bardon, 1992; Wright, 1987).

One of the most refreshing books about Northern Ireland (Prince, 2007: 52) recognises that the region's 'minority problem' does not set it apart, as the conventional counterposition to the particularity of Westminsterist governance assumes. On the contrary, against the broader European canvas of a 'maddening mosaic' of ethnic affiliations sedimented over centuries – for many of which only 'inhuman solutions' were found by Hitler and Stalin in the twentieth – Northern Ireland appears by no means unusual.

So the outworking of the ethnonationalist conflicts in former Yugoslavia, and in particular developments in Bosnia-Herzegovina and Macedonia, can provide valuable lessons, positive and negative. These cases, along with Northern Ireland and Lebanon, comprise the instances in recent times where the 'international community' has sought to (re-)establish ethnically shared governance arrangements via an accord at the conclusion of a violent conflict:

- the *National Reconciliation Accord*, or Ta'if agreement, of 1989 (Lebanon), reproduced in Russell (2004);
- the *Dayton Peace Accords* of 1995 (US State Department, 1995);
- *The Agreement: Agreement Reached in the Multi-Party Negotiations*, or Belfast agreement, of 1998 (NIO, 1998); and
- the *Framework Agreement*, or Ohrid agreement, of 2001 (Macedonia) (Council of Europe, 2001).

In terms of the degree to which power is genuinely shared and the resilience of the administration in the face of political shocks, from a Balkan comparison Macedonia emerges – at least until the stalemate with Greece over the name of the country – as somewhat more successful than Northern Ireland, with continuous power-sharing post-Ohrid rather than suffering repeated suspensions, while B-H represents a failed state. A closer look at the constitutional engineering shows that power-sharing has consolidated and conflicting ethnonationalist claims have diminished to the degree that accords are premised on the healing as against the acceptance – even entrenchment – of communal division, as Dave Russell (2004) shows in his comparative study of power-sharing in Northern Ireland and Lebanon (written, of course, before the hugely destabilising 2006 Israeli invasion).

At first blush, it would seem obvious that policy-makers should seek the former goal. Florian Bieber (2006: 120) has demonstrated why equal political representation for 'commmunities' in government does not address the problems arising from subordination of members of minorities. First, it does not attend to cooperation *between* political representatives (as against establishing mutual-veto arrangements). Secondly, in the absence of justiciable rights for minority members, it makes rights a matter of permanent negotiation, 'leading to an ethnification of broad areas of the political process'. Thirdly, it tends to marginalise members of smaller minorities not ascribed political recognition. Finally, it does not represent all members of even larger minorities, as these inevitably contain diverse political perspectives.

In his classic text on constitutional engineering, Sartori (1997: 72) crisply encapsulates the risk: 'If you reward divisions and divisiveness ... you increase and eventually heighten divisions and divisiveness.' Yet an often implicit essentialism in the comprehension of identity politics has tended to drag the international community towards the second approach, based on *Realpolitik*, with very conservative outcomes.

This reification of ethnicity, 'soundly condemned by a number of theorists' as it is, 'silences inherent complexities' while being 'used to create identifiable units, often set in diametrically opposite sides of the political, social or cultural field of analysis' – as 'Albanians' and 'Serbs' in Kosovo, for example (Blumi, 2003: 218). Inevitably, the declaration of independence in Kosovo by ethnic-Albanian leaders in 2008 heralded, after the celebrations, a de facto partition along the Ibar river and division in the European Union, as well as stimulating Serb secessionism in B-H.[2]

This chapter is based on secondary sources on Macedonia and B-H. A key resource is the independent journalistic network in the Balkans responsible for the production of *Balkan Insight*, successor to the *Balkan Crisis Report*, a regular e-mail newsletter.[3] With a reach across former Yugoslavia and beyond, and in contrast to the way much of the media in Yugoslavia, particularly in broadcasting (Thompson, 1994), fragmented into nationalistic centres paralleling political break-up, the newsletter offers a valuable archive of objective analysis. It attracts expert authors and contributors from reputable think tanks, as well as locally recruited journalists, and impartial reportage and comment are clearly demarcated.

Bosnia-Herzegovina

Nearly a decade after Dayton the Bosnian – his description – poet and Sarajevo bookshop owner Damir Uzunovic complained of the fate of his homeland: 'The problem was that religious practice became national identity: the Christians became Serbs and the Catholics Croats, and now people like me, Bosnian Muslims, are called Bosniaks. It does not help, and we need to move on from it.'[4] Such essentialist labelling tends to foster a fatalism about communalist identities, leading to 'solutions' which vary from consociationalist power-sharing to partition, *de jure* or *de facto*. Both have been tried in Ireland at various points in the last century, and the *de facto* partition of B-H was clearly driven by this weary acceptance that 'ancient hatreds' were at play – even though no intellectually serious work on the war endorsed that perspective (Malcolm, 1996).

The policy pursued by the international community, which failed to challenge elite-driven nationalism on the basis of universal norms, was justified by the associated notion of 'Balkan exceptionalism' (Gallagher, 2003: 5), as 'outsiders insisted that the Yugoslavs were not like them' (Woodward, 1995: 19) – we have already seen the similarly pervasive characterisation of Northern Ireland as 'different'. As Klejda Mulaj (2005: 16) describes that policy, 'In the comprehension of Western mediators, the way to deal with the conflict was to reach a compromise between community leaders, which in effect implied taking on board the very perception of the conflict that nationalists wished to propagate.' The assumption that 'peculiarly Balkan hatreds' were to blame led to a parallel underestimation of the relationship between domestic factors and the international environment (Woodward, 1995: 3).

The Badinter committee (Donia and Fine, 1994: 231) established by the European Community recommended that the internal boundaries of Yugoslavia become international ones for successor states recognising minority rights. Yet the EC recognised Croatia, against Badinter's adjudication. And the committee itself ruled that while B-H also fell short of the recognition criteria, this could be reviewed following a supervised referendum – despite its 'far-reaching consequences' and 'inherently destabilising' character (*ibid*: 234), given the predictable reaction of the leaders of the Serb minority there. As we will see with the British State and Northern Ireland, and for the same reasons, 'the assumption of the comfortable attitude of a distant observer' of supposedly historically determined ethnic factionalism in Yugoslavia enabled the international community to represent the war in Bosnia as 'an exocentric conflict', rather than 'a direct result of the failure of the West to grasp the political dynamic of the disintegration of Yugoslavia' (Salecl, 1994: 231).

Tom Gallagher (2003: 76) concludes: 'EC decisions in this crucial period were made not on the basis of general principles but according to the degree of pressure certain countries were prepared to exert. It was a bad omen when what was called for was a clear indication that the EC was not partial to, or antagonistic towards, any ethnic group or republic.' Recall the argument in Chapter 2 about the importance of impartial authority – in this case transnational – in dealing with communal division, and of universal norms.

In B-H an amoral approach was adopted, notably by the UK, based on minimising intervention – particularly by refusing to commit troops to a peace-enforcing role. This not only failed to prevent the horrors of 'ethnic cleansing' but ensured it was ultimately to be rewarded by the communal carve-up of B-H by the ethnic protagonists at Dayton. As overall in former Yugoslavia, victory reflected the argument of force rather than the force of argument, falling 'not to the just, but to the strong' (Silber and Little, 1995: 388).

The B-H constitution, contained in a Dayton annex, recognised the effective wartime division of the country into two entities, the Federation of Bosnia and Herzegovina (in which power was further devolved into ten cantons), populated mainly by Muslims and Croats, and Republika Srpska. The constitution named 'Bosniacs' (implicitly Muslims), Croats and Serbs as 'constituent peoples', along with – but clearly residually – 'others' and 'citizens of Bosnia and Herzegovina'.

Communalism was the guiding institutional principle. A tripartite executive presidency would comprise a Serb elected by the people of Republika Srpska, and a 'Bosniac' and a Croat elected from within the federation. This meant, in contravention of all democratic norms, that, for example, Croats and Muslims in Republika Srpska could only vote for a Serb representative – hardly conducive to the return of displaced persons with minority affiliations. As Bieber (2006: 56) contends, it entailed 'the near total exclusion of "others" or "citizens" from the power-sharing arrangements'. This despite the fact that 43 per cent of respondents to an Oxford Research International (2007: 49) survey said they defined themselves primarily as B-H citizens and three-quarters of those who defined themselves primarily as 'Bosniacs', Croats or Serbs also subscribed to B-H citizenship.

In terms of the State legislature, the Parliamentary Assembly was divided into two houses, the House of Representatives and the House of Peoples. The former was directly elected, whereas the latter comprised 15 representatives – five from each of the three 'constituent peoples' – drawn from the House of Peoples of the Muslim-Croat Federation (ten) and the Republika Srpska Assembly (five). If representatives of any 'community' declared a proposed decision of the Parliamentary Assembly to be 'destructive of a vital interest', the measure could only pass with the support of concurrent majorities of each of the 'constituent peoples' in the House of Peoples, conferring ethnonational vetoes all round (Chandler, 2000: 67–9). James Gow (2008: 50) describes this as 'a recipe for potential constant deliberate frustration of work in the Parliamentary Assembly'.

Powers rested predominantly with the entities – responsible for the armed forces, police, fiscal policy, telecommunications, transport, health, education, agriculture, industry, power and public broadcasting – so that the central government was initially 'threadbare' (Bose, 2002: 24). Being the result of 'ethnic cleansing', the entities were overwhelmingly Muslim/ Croat (the federation) or Serb (Republika Srpska). In the wake of rulings by the Constitutional Court in 2000, declaring substantial parts of the entity constitutions themselves unconstitutional – as not securing equality among the 'constituent peoples' – the High Representative of the international community imposed constitutional amendments in 2002. These entailed arrangements at entity level mirroring those at the level of the State, including strong communal-veto powers which 'accentuated the predominance of group representation over individual rights' (Bieber, 2006: 130).

As Misha Glenny (1999: 651–2) observed, 'Dayton brought the fighting to an end, in itself a considerable achievement. But as a model for reconciliation and for rebuilding a shattered society, it was and remains limited … The three local élites are comfortable with the arrangements as it guarantees their hold on power within their own communities.' With further hindsight, Christopher Solioz and Tobias Vogel (2004: 16–17) similarly conclude: 'Insofar as stopping the war was its key objective, the GFAP [General Framework Agreement for Peace] has succeeded with remarkably little disruption and a rather small deployment of foreign troops … However, insofar as the GFAP aimed to create a cohesive state with effective government, it has abjectly failed.' And Bieber (2006: 4) affirms: 'Significantly, the elaborate mechanisms of power-sharing have increased group inclusion at the price of governability and cross-national identity.'

Gallagher (2003: 172–3) concurs. He recognised that as ethnicity would be 'the basis for political representation and decision-making in post-war Bosnia' – at the expense of those civil-society organisations which had comprised a 'peace constituency' – '[e]thnic rights would take precedence over individual human rights'. Indeed, while Dayton committed B-H to compliance with 15 international human-rights conventions, including the Framework Convention for the Protection of National Minorities, this was vitiated by the system of collective rights for the three 'constituent peoples': members of other communities (such as the Roma), members of the 'constituent peoples' in polities where they constituted a minority and those who did not identify themselves along national lines were all deprived *de facto* of their rights (Bieber, 2006: 33).

A former senior editor with the independent newspaper *Oslobodenje* and director of an NGO coalition finds Dayton particularly wanting in this regard (Dizdarević, 2004: 38):

> In the Constitution, the citizen, the *citoyen*, the individual, goes unmentioned: the terms 'Bosniak', 'Croat' and 'Serb' dominate everything, giving irrationally inflated significance to the national, to the detriment of the more modern and democratic concept contained in a civic approach and in civil-society values. It goes without saying that such provisions, constitutionally enshrined, severely restrict the potential for human rights and freedoms to be respected.

Belloni (2007: 6) similarly concludes that the Bosnian experience demonstrates that the 'group rights' associated with consociationalism do not only favour 'immobility and inflexibility'. They also 'entrench the power of those nationalist elites responsible for war and complicate the emergence of moderate political alternatives', they 'undercut the exercise of individual rights' (such as refugee return) and they 'create considerable hurdles in undermining zero-sum notions of identity and establishing civic notions of citizenship'. In sum (*ibid*: 160–1), 'consociationalism's propensity for inefficiency, bureaucratisation and patronage along ethnic lines has suited the interests of the political/economic elite that emerged from the war, and precluded the emergence and affirmation of civic-minded political and social forces'.

The Social Democrat Bozidar Matic became chair of the Council of Ministers in B-H in 2001 as part of a moderate Alliance for Change, which assumed power in the context of a nationalist boycott of the institutions. Matic promised to 'work for the good of the whole of Bosnia-Herzegovina' but his elevation was denounced as 'historically shameful' by the Croatian Democratic Union (HDZ), since though a Croat himself he was not seen as representing the ethnic interest.[5]

In elections the following year, the Social Democrats were ousted by the nationalists on a low turn-out, with the party's support falling from 26 per cent in 2000 to 16 per cent.[6] The principal nationalist parties – the HDZ, the Serb Democratic Party (SDS) and the ('Bosniac') Party of Democratic Action (SDA) – secured around 45 per cent between them and took the respective seats in the tripartite presidency (OSCE, 2003: 20).

While the nationalist elites pursued a politics which was 'the continuation of war by other means', the 'weak, disunited and dysfunctional state that is post-Dayton Bosnia' (Bose, 2002: 6) could only function under constant international supervision, with key decisions being abrogated to the Office of the High Representative (Zahar, 2005), whose initial one-year mandate was extended to three years and then expanded and extended indefinitely (Jenne, 2009: 278–9). This set in train a cycle of dependence (Chandler, 2000: 3) and oppositionalism – similar to that in post-agreement Northern Ireland which made Mitchell reluctant to return to sort out implementation crises,[7] though eventually he was prevailed upon to do so.[8]

When he took over as High Representative in 2002, Paddy (now Lord) Ashdown realised this was an impossible system. He called for 'a long hard look at how this country is governed' – with B-H enjoying 760 legislators, more than 180 ministers (with 14 prime ministers) and four levels of government, for a population of 4 million. He also complained of the 'corrosive effects' of educational division along ethnic lines, which he had 'detested' in Northern Ireland and said he liked no more in B-H.[9] An education law passed in 2003 should at least have meant that mathematics, science and other less controversial subjects would be taught with the same textbooks across the State, but the Council of Ministers failed to endorse it.[10]

Frustrated with the associated deadlocking and stagnation, the European Stability Initiative (ESI) sent an open letter to Ashdown a year later. It asserted that the High Representative's so-called 'Bonn powers' – assumed in that city in 1997 at a meeting of the Peace Implementation Council, to override ethnic vetoing (Zahar, 2005: 132) – only encouraged the nationalist politicians to leave the 'hard choices' to him.[11]

In 2004, the Council of Europe Parliamentary Assembly (2004) described the Dayton constitution as 'extremely complicated and contradictory' and declared: 'As the outcome of a political compromise reached in order to end the war, it cannot secure the effective functioning of the state in the long term and should be reformed once national reconciliation is irreversible and confidence is fully restored.' The motion pointed *inter alia* to 'the need to ensure that any future constitution brings the concept of "constituent peoples" and their specific rights into line with the principle of the primacy of individual rights'.

In 2005, the Venice Commission reported on the constitutional position of B-H and the powers of the High Representative. Following a fact-finding visit, the commission complained (European Commission for Democracy Through Law, 2005: 12) that 'the state institutions are structured not to represent citizens directly but to ensure representation of the constituent peoples'. This not only risked neglect of the interests of persons who deemed themselves not to belong to the 'constituent peoples' but also engendered the 'strong risk that all issues will be regarded in the light of whether a proposal favours the specific interests of the respective peoples and not of whether it contributes to the common weal'. Further, elections could not 'fully play their role of allowing political alternance between majority and opposition'.

The commission suggested that the constitution was incompatible with the equality provisions of the European Convention on Human Rights (*ibid*: 20) and it attacked the 'dependency culture' associated with the Bonn powers (*ibid*: 22). It concluded (*ibid*: 25): 'Constitutional reform is indispensable since present arrangements are neither efficient nor rational and lack democratic content.' The aim should be one of 'changing the emphasis from a state based on the equality of the three constituent peoples to a state based on the equality of citizens'.

As he was stepping down later that year, Ashdown was frank. He said of Dayton: 'It was a superb agreement to end a war, but a very bad agreement to make a state. From now on, we have to part company with Dayton and try to build a modern democratic state, for which I have tried to lay the foundations.' He was contemptuous of the Bosnian political class.[12]

A week later Ian Traynor, a journalistic expert on the Balkans, revealed that representatives of the eight main parties in B-H had been invited to Brussels to discuss a blueprint for constitutional reform for which the prime mover was a former State Department official who had served as deputy to the High Representative and was now with the United States Institute for Peace (USIP). As Traynor reported it, 'At the blueprint's centre is an emphasis on individual human and civil rights, supplanting the previous accent on the privileges of the rival ethnic collectives.' It would give B-H 'the "normal" trappings of an integrated, non-ethnic parliamentary democracy: a national parliament with full legislative powers, central government and cabinet enjoying full executive power, and a titular head of state'. The entities would be retained but stripped of most of their powers. Critically, the tripartite presidency would be replaced by a largely symbolic single head of state, elected by the Parliament, and its powers would pass to the Prime Minister.[13]

The Bosnian Serb representatives vetoed any move to weaken Republika Srpska, while the Croat politicians demanded a new entity of their own.[14] At least, however, the parties turned up in Brussels, and subsequently in Washington, where they even signed a 'Commitment to Pursue Constitutional Reform'.[15] A month later, one of the members of the US delegation at Dayton put their name to a jointly authored article on the accords. The authors – also affiliated to the USIP – welcomed the peace, but said B-H was 'not yet a functioning state':

> Under a convoluted constitution, all positions of government authority are apportioned under ethnic criteria and each ethnic group can block decision-making. Politicians do not yet seem prepared to change these fundamental aspects of the constitution. The same parties that fought the war remain in power and, although the discourse is now more civil, politics remains almost entirely ethnic-based.
>
> … In this dysfunctional system, progressive citizens who have sought to penetrate political structures or create bottom-up movements are disheartened and disengaged … Ethnic divisions are becoming more entrenched. Neither Bosnian moderates nor international actors have effectively challenged the grip of the nationalists. Schools are ethnically segmented, with three different nationalist versions of history taught and small linguistic differences among the three communities magnified into separate 'languages'. Religious leaders have become increasingly entangled in Bosnia's ethnic politics. Children grow up more divided than ever.[16]

Similarly, a report by the International Crisis Group (2007: 9) was to argue that the Dayton constitution constrained 'individual rights in favour of ethnic group rights' and over time had become 'a straitjacket'. Separate schools and curricula, which had emerged as a way to encourage refugee return, were teaching 'a new generation their parents' nationalist hatreds with government imprimatur' (*ibid*: 17).

In April 2006, most of the parties in B-H agreed a package of constitutional reforms (Sebastián, 2007). But elections in October (OSCE, 2007: 30) favoured critics of it. The vote in the Serb constituency for the collective presidency saw victory for Nebojša Radmonović of the Party of Independent Social Democrats (53 per cent), easily defeating his main rival from the SDS (24 per cent). The 'Bosniac' vote favoured Haris Silajdžić of the Party for Bosnia and Herzegovina (63 per cent) over his principal competitor from the SDA (28 per cent). The Croat poll was however topped by Željko Komšić of the Social Democratic Party (40 per cent), prevailing over the HDZ candidate (26 per cent). The leader of the Party of Independent Social Democrats, Miloran Dodik, repeatedly called for a referendum on secession of Republika Srpska from B-H, whereas Silajdžić demanded the abolition of the two sub-state entities.[17]

The dysfunctional character of B-H is highlighted by the north-eastern district of Brcko, which was left outside the two entities at Dayton due to lack of agreement on where it should go. Brcko has a multi-ethnic education system and is now the most prosperous part of the State. The mayor of Brcko, Mirsad Djapo, explained its success thus: 'Here ... members of all three nationalities are first and foremost citizens. This approach has created a much more friendly environment, and it should be institutionalized by including it in the Constitution.'[18]

It is not true to say that nothing has changed in B-H since Dayton. Support for secessionism has weakened: in predominantly Croat areas, it fell from 22 per cent in a 2000 survey to 4 per cent in 2003; in the same period in Republika Srpska, it declined from 69 per cent to 43 per cent (Bieber, 2008: 15). The entity defence ministries have been substituted by a single State ministry and the armed forces brought under unified command, while the initial arrangements for the Council of Ministers have been rationalised, with a single chair replacing two co-chairs (of different ethnicities) and single deputy ministers (of another ethnicity from the minister) replacing double-deputy arrangements. The State is still weak, but not as weak as it was (Bieber, 2006: 46–8).

Having said that, there have been regressions in human-rights protection. Annex Six of Dayton envisaged that the extensive commitments on human rights, however nominal, would be policed by a Human Rights Commission, comprising an Ombudsman to receive complaints and a Human Rights

Chamber to which they would be referred. Yet in 2003 the chamber, which had received almost 7,000 new cases in its last two years, was abolished, purportedly on budgetary grounds; the following year the Dayton model for the Ombudsman was abandoned when three separate Ombudsmen – one each to represent the three nationalist interests rather than upholding universal norms – were appointed (Nowak, 2004: 55). This was echoed in Northern Ireland when, after a prolonged impasse, in January 2008 the First Minister and Deputy First Minister, the then DUP leader, Revd Ian Paisley, and Martin McGuinness of SF respectively, appointed four 'victims commissioners' to champion the concerns of survivors of the conflict, instead of one as envisaged (Wilford and Wilson, 2008c: 16–17).

In late 2007, hopes rose that the prospect of EU integration could incentivise conciliatory behaviour in B-H, with the parties agreeing a declaration on police reform and a compromise on streamlining government and parliamentary procedures in return for the initialling of a Stabilisation and Association Agreement (SAA). The EU had expected legislation to effect police reform by mid-February 2008 but at an acrimonious meeting that month the parties decided to postpone further constitutional reform until after an SAA had been agreed. EU officials indicated that the SAA would be correspondingly deferred and an exasperated High Representative, Miroslav Lajcak, criticised 'politicians' stupid statements'.[19]

In June, Lajcak told *Balkan Insight*:

> It is clear that some reform of the constitution will be necessary. If nothing else, the current constitution is in conflict with key provisions of the European Convention on Human Rights. Then there will need to be a discussion how to make BiH more functional … But currently there is no agreement amongst the political leadership on how to proceed with this reform. Their visions are completely opposite and there is no common ground.[20]

Moreover, the EU was not itself able to articulate clear guidelines for reform (Sebastián, 2008a: 8). Further inter-party constitutional talks in August came to nothing.[21] The bitter relationships between the parties manifested themselves in the campaign for local elections in October (Sebastián, 2008b). Lajcak, a Slovak diplomat, was reported as saying the atmosphere reminded him of the last years of former Czechoslovakia.[22] The old ethnic parties were duly returned to power.[23]

B-H might seem a more successful power-sharing case than Northern Ireland, in as much as the State institutions, however dysfunctional, have at least been in being ever since the Dayton accords. But the weakness of the State by comparison with the ethnically defined entities is debilitating – indeed in October 2008 Ashdown and Holbrooke warned that the country was 'in real danger of collapse'.[24] In 2009, Lajcak stepped down prematurely and his successor, Valentin Inzko, found himself in a trial of strength with the Republika Srpska Assembly, which sought to claw back powers from the State – a challenge he rebuffed by resort to the Bonn powers but amid declining European appetite for further engagement.[25] Moreover, while it is true that the Belfast agreement is a consociationalist scheme, as noted in Chapter 2 it does contain subordinate integrative elements, tending more towards a civil society rather than one permanently riven by ethnic division – albeit these took a back seat during implementation.

Macedonia

Pace Ashdown, it is central that power-sharing is *not* presented as a necessary concession to end political violence. Apart from the moral hazard this creates – with the risk of countervailing violence from the other 'side' or a recrudescence of violence from disillusioned paramilitaries, as became evident among 'dissident' republicans after the 'honeymoon' following the renewal of devolution in 2007 expired (Wilford and Wilson, 2008b: 15) – it is also impossible to bring a critical mass of the ethnic-majority community behind change if nationalists in *that* community can successfully present this as a 'sell-out to terrorism'. In Macedonia importantly, interethnic dialogue after the outbreak of civil conflict could be presented instead, as Brussels was keen to do, as an integral part of the path to eventual EU membership, via an SAA.[26]

A positive factor in moving a divided society beyond those divisions, as mentioned in Chapter 2 *vis-à-vis* peaceful Indian states, is civic leadership, given the need for impartial authority. The late President of Macedonia Boris Trajkovski, though coming from the more nationalistic VMRO-DPMNE Slav-Macedonian party, played a key role in this regard in the context of the Ohrid agreement (Ilievski and Taleski, 2009: 359–60). Such leadership had also been evident even during the war in B-H in the 'peace enclave' of Tuzla (Katunaric, 2003), thanks to 'the strength of the civic-minded municipal government' there (Gallagher, 2003: 135). In B-H the Dayton architecture ensured this could not become a peacetime trend: with the trio of ethnic presidency partners – as with the system of first and deputy first ministers in Northern Ireland – only ethnic representation was, by definition, conceivable.

Another key factor is a commitment to 'a shared future'. As a European Stability Initiative (ESI) (2001: 22) report on south-eastern Europe put it, 'Democracy is unlikely to be stable where basic state architecture remains a matter of dispute.' A month later, just before the worst of the violence in Macedonia, a US-commissioned poll found that while 69 per cent of ethnic Albanians were sympathetic to the paramilitary National Liberation Army, 87 per cent said it was important to them personally that Macedonia remained united.[27]

This was reinforced externally by a resolution of the European Council, meeting in Gothenburg, which underlined the inviolability of the borders of Macedonia, though as a multi-ethnic state. It indicated that a political solution required dialogue between Slavs and ethnic Albanians, substantial constitutional reform and a consolidated ceasefire. The EU also agreed to establish an office in Macedonia to pursue this agenda, including security co-operation with Nato.[28]

This initiative followed condemnation by the EU of an accord, the 'Prizren platform'. This had been agreed between Arber Xhaferi, leader of the Democratic Party of Albanians – power-sharing partner with the representatives of the Slav-Macedonian majority before the conflict – and (along with the leader of a smaller ethnic-Albanian party) Ali Ahmeti, leader of the National Liberation Army. It would have given the NLA a veto on decisions relating to Albanian rights.[29] The platform, brokered by a US diplomat, was very similar to the Hume-Adams agreement of September 1993 on the principle of 'Irish self-determination'. The latter was widely welcomed by, in particular, its US audience despite its polarising effect at home, as discussed in Chapter 2.

During a breakdown in the talks leading to the Ohrid agreement, the accommodating Trajkovski insisted they could only be premised on 'a civil society' in Macedonia, not one based on ethnic 'communities' that would open the door to secession of Albanian-dominated areas.[30] These fall to the north and west, with Albania and Kosovo over the border.

A European Centre for Minority Issues expert, Farimah Daftery (2001: 8), agreed. She counselled in favour of redefining Macedonia constitutionally as 'a state for all of its citizens, regardless of ethnic, religious or linguistic origin', whereas to recognise ethnic Albanians as a second constituent people would 'further accentuate tensions' and annoy members of other, unrecognised minorities.

Trajovski's adviser revealed that the Slav-Macedonian side would accept removal of all references to the (ethnically coloured) 'nation' in the constitution, to be replaced by 'citizens'. Similarly, all references to the Orthodox Church could go, to be replaced by commitment to a secular state and equality among members of religious communities.[31] This chimed with an academic study of the history of eastern Europe (Bideleux and Jeffries, 1998: 641), which more generally concluded: 'The region must escape from the tyranny of ethnic collectivism.'

Human rights represent a key universal norm for divided societies. The EU made clear its condemnation of state repression in Macedonia in the name of 'security' operations against the NLA. In a toughly-worded communiqué, a meeting of foreign ministers in Luxembourg in June 2001 called for resumption of political dialogue and warned the results would affect 'the possibility of further assistance' for Macedonia.[32]

Writing in the wake of the agreement eventually concluded at Lake Ohrid, Maria-Eleni Koppa (2001: 59) argues that in the choice between recognition of Macedonians and Albanians 'as two equal elements of the Macedonian state' and defining the latter 'as the state of all the people living in Macedonia', the second option prevailed. She continues: 'The only option for the viability of the state is genuinely unlinking nationality and citizenship. This is necessary for an open, tolerant and democratic society.'

Observed by the EU's foreign-affairs envoy, Javier Solana, and the Nato Secretary-General, Lord Robertson, the Ohrid agreement fell broadly within the framework of the evolving international standards on minority rights, notably the Framework Convention for the Protection of National Minorities and the European Charter for Regional or Minority Languages (Council of Europe, 1992). Among proposed amendments in an annex to the constitution of Macedonia (Council of Europe, 2001), it affirmed that the 'fundamental values of the constitutional order' were 'the basic freedoms and rights of the individual and citizen, recognized in international law and set down in the Constitution' and 'equitable representation of persons belonging to all communities in public bodies at all levels and in other areas of public life'. Critically, it proposed to change the constitutional preamble to indicate that sovereignty rested no longer with 'the Macedonian people' but the 'citizens of the Republic of Macedonia'.

Ohrid nowhere referred to 'Albanians' or 'Macedonians', except with regard to a proposed Committee for Inter-Community Relations, where reference was also made to members drawn from other communities, including Turks, Vlachs and Romanies. But there were extensive provisions for minority rights, including in the use of language, self-government and police recruitment, and in the Assembly to ensure the Slav-Macedonian majority could not ride roughshod over others on constitutional or culturally sensitive issues.

The issue of the rule of law was also not fudged. The NLA was not represented at the talks, with the paramilitaries only forming the Democratic Union of Integration as a political vehicle *after* the accord. By contrast, in the talks leading to the Belfast agreement, SF's 'chief negotiator', Martin McGuinness, was chair of the IRA army council (Moloney, 2002: 486). As Jonathan Steele wryly noted, 'The political and military parts of the package are skilfully synchronised so that parliament has to pass the laws needed to enshrine the offers of greater rights to the Albanians in the same period as the guerrillas complete their handover of weapons. No delays on "decommissioning" here.'[33]

Ahmeti insisted: 'All weapons will be handed over.'[34] NLA arms were handed up, in front of TV cameras, to Nato soldiers, following an independent Nato estimate of the size of the NLA's arsenal. Indeed, more than the 3,300 weapons demanded were collected.[35] Not only that, but the process began before the Macedonian Assembly debated the ratification of the accord[36] and was completed within six weeks after it was promulgated. Two days later, the NLA disbanded, with Ahmeti saying: 'Mutual trust has to be created between the two communities.'[37]

Another feature of Ohrid was the way the constitutional status of Macedonia was settled, whereas the Belfast agreement, as discussed in Chapter 2, merely reiterated the 'consent' formula on constitutional change. Ohrid, picking up a phrase from the Prizren Platform, baldly affirmed (Council of Europe, 2001): 'There are no territorial solutions to ethnic issues.' In that sense, it addressed the 'stateness problem' which had bedevilled the consolidation of democracy in the country since independence (Daskalovski, 2004). Unlike in B-H, the aim was to foster inter-ethnic integration in a unitary state (Paintin, 2009: 14).

In the Assembly, Trajkovski defended the document in the face of Slav-Macedonian opposition by stressing its alignment with universal norms: 'The agreement we have in front of us embodies European values of human rights, democracy and compromise. It eliminates the reason for war and inter-ethnic conflict in the republic of Macedonia.'[38] The vote on Ohrid carried with well over the required two-thirds majority, with 91 deputies in favour and 19 against.[39]

There was, however, foot-dragging from the Slav-Macedonian side on implementing the constitutional amendments, particularly the redefinition of the preamble. The EU Commissioner for foreign affairs, Chris Patten, responded that a donors' conference planned for mid-October 2001 would not now go ahead.[40] Solana, Robertson and Mircea Geoana, chair of the Organisation for Security and Co-operation in Europe, descended on Skopje to apply pressure.[41]

Eventually, this issue was fudged in a deal between Trajkovski and Xhaferi. And the civic character of the new constitution was significantly diluted by communalism – though at least on a plurinational rather than binational basis – by inserting after the reference to the 'citizens of the Republic of Macedonia,' the clause 'the Macedonian people, as well as citizens living within its borders who are part of the Albanian people, the Turkish people, the Vlach people, the Serbian people, the Romany people, the Bosniac people and others taking responsibility for the present and future of their fatherland'. Xhaferi secured assistance for an Albanian-language university as part of the deal.[42] The reforms then easily passed through the Assembly, with Trajkovski subsequently announcing an anticipated amnesty for NLA members, barring any that could be indicted by the ex-Yugoslavia war-crimes tribunal.[43]

This important qualification aside, as Bieber (2005: 109) argues, the Ohrid agreement 'largely avoided institutionalising ethnicity' in the manner of Dayton. It did not parcel out government ethnically nor establish major sub-state ethnic entities. The result was 'greater room in Macedonia for non-institutionalised, but nonetheless co-operative, politics'. By contrast, 'power-sharing in Bosnia is laid down by the Dayton constitution and subsequent legislation to the last detail' (Bieber, 2006: 48).

Recall the empirical argument in Chapter 2 that, from a broader European perspective, the counterposition of (majoritarian) Westminsterism and (non-majoritarian) consociationalism, as if these exhausted the alternatives, excludes states which are 'plural' in Lijphartian terms and yet operate with 'majoritarian' systems. Only if 'communities' are conceived as homogeneous political entities is this impossible to imagine. Once it is recognised that different parties compete within, and communicate across, communities, more flexible forms of power-sharing, as in Macedonia, can be envisaged – indeed are more compelling (Ilievski and Taleski, 2009: 359).

This did not however mean all was now sweetness and light. Indeed, it was reported at the time of the Trajovski-Xhaferi deal that the 'polarisation of the two communities is as sharp as ever'.[44] The cultural arena was marked by apartheid, not just in literature, music and art but also in the popular sphere, including football.[45] Attempts to desegregate education were shelved after an integrationist initiative at two schools led to protests.[46]

Elections in September 2002 were to lead to a new government, with the Social Democrats (SDSM) defeating the nationalist VMRO-DPMNE on the Slav-Macedonian side and being thereby able to renew power-sharing, despite DUI – 'the equivalent of Northern Ireland's Sinn Fein'[47] – outflanking the more moderate Democratic Party of Albanians in that community.[48] But the picture of sustained division was picked up in another US-sponsored poll, which showed a clear deterioration in inter-ethnic relations by comparison with a year earlier. By now almost half (48 per cent) of all ethnic Albanians favoured a greater Albania, while nearly two-thirds (63 per cent) of Slav Macedonians were opposed to Ohrid.[49]

It took the carrot of the postponed donors' conference to bring to an end months of haggling about local self-government legislation.[50] And an ESI

(2002: 11) paper warned that the underlying, and differential, socio-economic challenges facing Slav Macedonians and ethnic Albanians had to be faced, to avoid exacerbating 'worrying signs that the ethnic Macedonian population tends to see the Framework Agreement as a capitulation to Albanian interests, under heavy international pressure'.

By the time of the third anniversary of Ohrid in 2004, there was a further crisis as a large majority of Slav Macedonians opposed a new law on municipal boundaries, out of fear it would lead to ethnic partition, which drove Ahmeti – at a press conference where for the first time he appeared under a Macedonian flag – to insist he had no intention of dividing the country.[51] But the law was passed in August that year and an opposition-inspired referendum only secured a 26 per cent turn-out in November, well short of the 50 per cent threshold required for the result to be recognised.[52]

Erwan Fouéré, appointed in 2005 to head the EU mission in Macedonia, said that 'reconciliation' was a prerequisite of 'long-term stability' and he looked forward with concern to the 2006 election.[53] Macedonia was subsequently recommended by the EU for candidate membership status – a big step on the road to integration, a driving force behind implementation of Ohrid.

Yet Fouréré's fears were to an extent realised, when the July 2006 election led to victory on the Slav-Macedonian side for the VMRO-DPMNE, which refused to renew coalition with the DUI, preferring instead the DPA, even though the latter won fewer votes. A DUI leader warned that this could 'lead to uproar and violence among the Albanian voters and the use of force and Kalashnikovs'.

A report, however, in June 2006 by the United Nations Development Programme found that interethnic relations had stabilised, with social distance between members of the different communities not out of kilter with elsewhere in Europe. Nenan Markovic, of the Institute of Democracy in Skopje, said that following the legal outworking of the Ohrid accord, 'the major chapters' of ethnic issues had been 'closed', adding: 'All the polls unambiguously say the greatest problems now for citizens are unemployment, poverty and corruption, not ethnic issues.' Gross domestic product, for example, remained 15 per cent below the level at independence in 1990.[54]

In May 2007, the DUI ended a five-month boycott of Parliament.[55] But Macedonia's interethnic future was in the long run dependent on integration into transnational, particularly European, institutions. Enter Greece, which placed a blockage on this route to civic modernity by vetoing Nato membership at the organisation's summit in Bucharest in April 2008, because of its unresolved dispute with Macedonia over the name of the state.[56] Elections were called following the summit[57] and in this atmosphere the

VMRO-DPMNE correctly anticipated a convincing victory over the Social Democrats when the polls took place in June.[58]

Coalition was renewed with the DUI, thus as in Northern Ireland placing the two most ethnically militant parties in power, with the inevitable associated tensions. Many Albanians, prioritising the European integration agenda, resented the unbending position of VMRO-DPMNE on the name question. Ethnocentric VMRO-DPMNE initiatives to build an Orthodox church in the main square in the centre of Skopje and to erect a statue of Alexander the Great also alienated minority members. Most Albanians boycotted the presidential election in April 2009, won by the VMRO-DPMNE on a low poll.[59]

Before this externally stimulated hiatus, Macedonia's post-Ohrid trajectory had been significantly less bumpy than post-agreement Northern Ireland, with the constitutional unit of society conceived to a greater degree as the citizen rather than the 'community', and with a stronger 'pull' towards a universalist, European normative perspective. With the political-party system now polarised, Macedonia's advantage was receding. At the time of writing, however, a ray of hope was that the landslide victory in the Greek general election of October 2009 for the social-democratic PASOK, led by the cosmopolitan George Papandreou, might temper the row over Macedonia's name.[60] And while intercommunal mistrust and associated stereotyping, associated with increasingly segregated education, were worrisome, the country remained a 'relative success story' (Paintin, 2009: 31).

Conclusion

At their summit on the western Balkans in Thessaloniki in June 2003, EU leaders declared: 'Fragmentation and divisions along ethnic lines are incompatible with the European perspective, which should act as a catalyst for addressing problems within the region.'[61] Yet it was a fragmented and divided western Balkans which the International Commission on the Balkans surveyed in its report of 2005.[62]

The commission's diagnosis (International Commission on the Balkans, 2005: 15–16) was, first, that the constitutions deriving from the negotiations to end the wars of the preceding decade had been 'shaped by elites associated with armed conflicts'; rather than reflecting popular mandates, they represented 'hard-nosed trade-offs to persuade the elites to stop fighting or avoid destabilising acts'. Secondly, each of the frameworks 'allocates power by group affiliation', and since groups are defined in ethnic terms, this 'reinforces claims that the societies themselves are riven by ethnic differences which help to undermine central state institutions'. Thirdly, and consequently, these were now weak states, because 'state actors became cumulatively weaker while powerful private actors, including political parties, oligarchs and criminal syndicates spawned by the wars of the 1990s, have remained influential and largely escaped scrutiny'. The report called on the EU to play a more active role in strengthening state institutions.

The commission argued that the post-Dayton structure in B-H was indeed 'dysfunctional'. It needed to move to 'sustainable self-government guided by the process of EU accession', which would entail removing the High Representative (*ibid*: 24–5). By contrast, Macedonia was described as 'a modest but significant success story', which 'illustrates our thesis that a final and clear constitutional arrangement and the institutionalization of European perspectives are the two instruments that can work apparent miracles in the Balkans'.

As we have seen, building on pre-conflict power-sharing experiences, in Macedonia government is formed by interethnic coalition-building, with post-election alternation. Whereas in B-H power-sharing is 'constitutionally prescribed', in Macedonia it is subject to 'greater flexibility' (Bieber, 2005: 115). This can lead to tensions because of the resentment of those left out, but at least it has led, most of the time, to functioning, shared governance.

As long as inclusion in the political community provides the opportunity to participate in government, as against guarantees that this or that party will be included for all time, it is difficult to legitimise violent opposition – as evidenced by the empty nature of DUI's threats and the failure of its parliamentary boycott after the 2006 Macedonian election. Horowitz (1994: 35) warns: 'Again and again in divided societies, there is a tendency to conflate inclusion in the government with inclusion in the community and exclusion from government with exclusion from the community.'

The supposed comforts of grand coalition, by contrast, import into government – and entrench there – deep communal division, which means that genuine power-sharing (as against international supervision and/or deadlocking internal vetoes) can remain a chimera. Thus in B-H 'it is noteworthy that the particular system of presidency emphasizes the fact that its members primarily represent their respective constituency, rather than the country at large' (Bieber, 2006: 52).

As in B-H, in Northern Ireland power is allocated by 'group affiliation'. Of both, *fin-de-siècle* comments by Martin Woollacott still ring true:[63]

It is now sadly obvious that many of the peace settlements of the 90s did not wholly deserve that name. Carl Bildt, analysing what has gone wrong in Bosnia, says of the local leaders: 'For most of them peace was just the continuation of war by other means.' ... Bosnia was a forced settlement, imposed by outsiders, but a tendency similar to that which Bildt sees there can be found in situations where the parties came to an independent recognition of the need for agreement, as they did in Ireland ... There has been perhaps too much concentration on skilful ways of moving conflict from a violent phase to a non-violent phase and on military intervention to suppress the violence and not enough on tackling fundamental differences.

This chapter has shown that a taken-for-granted communalism has had very negative effects on societies recently riven by ethnic conflict. Constitutional engineers should set their sights on entrenching 'the individualist conception of society', via human and minority rights for the citizen, if they are to allow such societies to begin to leave a divided past behind.

The next chapter will explore how policy-makers in London and Dublin, unenlightened by any such benefit of hindsight, grappled with the unfamiliar crisis that exploded in Northern Ireland in the late 1960s. While it is in many ways critical of their efforts, it does demonstrate that these deserve rather more positive consideration than became the fashion in the retrospective official narrative of the late 1990s – on which Chapter 5 will focus.

Notes

1   'Yes, minister', *The Economist* (4 December 1999).

2   Gordon Katana, 'Kosovo fuels secession talk in Bosnia', *Balkan Insight*, 124 (21 February 2008). Interestingly, after a year of stalemate on the implementation of the Belfast agreement, one minister confided: 'Kosovo is beginning to look easy in comparison with this.' See Patrick Wintour, 'Final bid to save peace process', *Observer* (20 June 1999).

3   See www.birn.eu.com/en.

4   Louisa Waugh, 'Peace movements', *Guardian* (15 January 2005).

5   Amra Kebo, 'Bosnian Croats flex their muscles', *Balkan Crisis Report*, 223 (2 March 2001).

6   Janez Kovac and Gordana Katana, 'Bosnia: nationalists prevail in elections', *Balkan Crisis Report*, 373 (11 October 2002).

7   Joe Carroll, 'The longest years in the life of a peacemaker', *Irish Times* (3 April 1999).

8   Joe Carroll, 'Mitchell returning "with reluctance"', *Irish Times* (4 September 1999).

9   Paddy Ashdown, 'Reform will bring justice and jobs', *Balkan Crisis Report*, 341 (7 June 2002).

10 Predrag Popovic, 'Harmony a long way off in Bosnia's disunited schools', *Balkan Insight*, 54 (13 October 2006).

11 European Stability Initiative, 'Open letter to Lord Ashdown', *Balkan Crisis Report*, 447 (23 July 2003).

12 Ed Vulliamy, 'Farewell, Sarajevo', *Guardian* (2 November 2005).

13 Ian Traynor, 'Revealed: US plans for Bosnian constitution', *Guardian* (10 November 2005).

14 Gordana Katana and Gordana Igric, 'New constitution poses challenge to Serbs and Croats', *Balkan Insight*, 10 (18 November 2005).

15 Steven R Weisman, 'Bosnia's 3 groups reach unity agreement', *New York Times* (23 November 2005).

16 Laurel Miller and Deborah Isser, 'Outsiders can't build a nation for Bosnia', *Balkan Insight*, 15 (23 December 2005).

17 Nerma Jelacic and Saida Mustajbegovic, 'Poll upset for big three in Bosnia', *Balkan Insight*, 53 (5 October 2006).

18 Saida Mustajbegovic, 'Brcko left on sidelines in Bosnia constitution talks', *Balkan Insight*, 91 (4 July 2007).

19 Srecko Latal, 'Bosnia constitutional reform: a new deadlock', *Balkan Insight*, 122 (6 February 2008).

20 Nidzara Ahmetasevic, 'Bosnia must free itself from international tutelage, *Balkan Insight*, 139 (5 June 2008).

21 Srecko Latal, 'Bosnian constitutional talks derailed by election campaign', *Balkan Insight*, 151 (28 August 2008).

22 Srecko Latal, 'Local polls deepen sense of crisis in Bosnia, *Balkan Insight*, 156 (1 October 2008).

23 Srecko Latal, 'Old leaders emerge triumphant in Bosnia election', *Balkan Insight*, 157 (9 October 2008).

24 Paddy Ashdown and Richard Holbrooke, 'A Bosnian powder keg', *Guardian* (22 October 2008).

25 Srecko Latal, 'Bosnian Serbs call international envoy's bluff', *Balkan Insight*, 194 (18 June 2009); Dan Bilevsky, 'Bosnia Serbs and envoy are at odds on powers', *New York Times* (20 June 2009).

26 Ian Black, 'With one eye on the EU, Macedonia prepares for talks with its Albanians', *Guardian* (2 April 2001); Jonathan Steele and Ian Black, 'Macedonian army brutality condemned', *Guardian* (10 April 2001).

27 Tim Judah, 'Albanians back Macedonian unity', *Balkan Crisis Report*, 250 (25 May 2001).

28 Paul Gillespie, 'Agenda reflects growing presence on world scene', *Irish Times* (18 June 2001).

29 Veton Latifi and Agim Fetahaj, 'Albanian deal threatens coalition', *Balkan Crisis Report*, 250 (25 May 2001).

30 'Further fighting is feared as Macedonia peace talks collapse', *Irish Times* (21 June 2001).

31 Borijan Jovanovski, 'Macedonian labour pains', *Balkan Crisis Report*, 258 (22 June 2001).

32 Ian Black, 'Negotiate peace or we cut off aid, says European Union', *Guardian* (26 June 2001).

33 Jonathan Steele, 'The final confrontation', *Guardian* (11 August 2001).

34 Rory Carroll, 'Albanian rebels bask in sun and sense of victory', *Guardian* (20 August 2001).

35 'NATO says arms handover complete', *Irish Times* (26 September 2001).

36 Nicholas Wood and Richard Norton-Taylor, 'Albanian guerrillas queue up to hand over weapons to Nato', *Guardian* (29 August 2001).

37 Nicholas Wood, 'Macedonian rebel chief calls off war', *Guardian* (28 September 2001).

38 'Macedonian President pleads for peace plan', *Irish Times* (1 September 2001).

39 Nicholas Wood and Richard Norton-Taylor, 'Skopje sticks to deal by voting for reforms', *Guardian* (7 September 2001).

40 Vladimir Jovanovski, 'Macedonia: constitutional U-turn', *Balkan Crisis Report*, 287 (10 October 2001).

41 'EU says fulfil peace accord', *Irish Times* (19 October 2001).

42 Veton Latifi, 'Macedonia: Albanian education battle', *Balkan Crisis Report*, 297 (16 November 2001).

43 Nicholas Wood, 'Macedonian MPs finally ratify peace-deal reforms for Albanians', *Guardian* (17 November 2001).

44 'Better and worse', *The Economist* (17 November 2001).

45 Veton Latifi, 'Macedonia: no end to cultural apartheid', *Balkan Crisis Report*, 353 (26 July 2002).

46 Ana Petruseva and Boris Georgievski, 'Macedonia: school desegregation plans shelved', *Balkan Crisis Report*, 462 (3 October 2003).

47 'A hopeful outcome', *The Economist* (21 September 2002).

48 'Rebel leader demands role in Macedonia', *Irish Times* (17 September 2002); Ana Petruseva, 'Elections "huge victory" for Macedonia', *Balkan Crisis Report*, 368 (18 September 2002).

49 Tim Judah, 'Macedonia: "Greater Albania" gathers support', *Balkan Crisis Report*, 341 (7 June 2002).

50 Ana Petruseva, 'Macedonia: new law clears way for aid', *Balkan Crisis Report*, 313 (31 January 2002).

51 Ibrahim Mehmeti, 'Protests may destroy Ohrid deal', *Balkan Crisis Report*, 510 (5 August 2004).

52 Ana Petruseva, 'Macedonians turn away from ethnic divisions', *Balkan Crisis Report*, 525 (12 November 2004).

53 Jamie Smyth, 'A tough challenge ahead at a time of escalating tension in the Balkans', *Irish Times* (7 November 2005).

54 Tamara Causidis, 'Nationalist politicians keep playing with fire', *Balkan Insight*, 46 (3 August 2006).

55 Sinisa-Jakov Marusic, 'Macedonia's tight EU timetable', *Balkan Insight*, 118 (10 January 2008).

56 Sinisa-Jakov Marusic, 'Greek sword hangs over Macedonia's future', *Balkan Insight*, 130 (1 April 2008).

57 Sinisa-Jakov Marusic, 'Macedonia poll may derail EU and NATO bids', *Balkan Insight*, 132 (16 April 2008).

58 Boris Georgievski, 'Macedonia Social Democrats mull lessons of defeat', *Balkan Insight*, 139 (5 June 2008).

59 Sinisa-Jakov Marusic, 'Macedonia stalemate makes ethnic Albanians restive', *Balkan Insight*, 191 (28 May 2009).

60 'An emphatic win', Economist.com (5 October 2009, www.economist.com/daily/news/displaystory.cfm?story_id=14580584 [accessed 5 October 2009]).

61 See Thessaloniki Declaration at www.stabilitypact.org/reg-conf/030621-

thessaloniki/declaration.asp [accessed 12 July 2009].

62 Hugh Griffiths, 'Balkans overhaul urged', *Balkan Crisis Report*, 552 (15 April 2005).

63 Martin Woollacott, 'Why peace processes are breaking down all over', *Guardian* (22 December 2000).

4

Power-sharing, Mark 1

Introduction

As already hinted in Chapter 2, there is an important relationship between intellectually worked-up ideas and 'common sense' understandings. Gramsci (1971: 323) articulated this relationship, in his arresting claim that 'all men are "philosophers"'. What he meant was that every social actor operates with a certain conception of the world, and while only some have the function of intellectuals all embrace a *mélange* of by no means coherent ideas which have sedimented themselves as 'common sense', encompassing 'Stone Age elements and principles of a more advanced science' (*ibid*: 324). One of the reasons why the rich repertoire of political categories developed by Gramsci is deployed here is that they derive from a non-essentialist perspective on the relationship between the economy, civil society and the state, which makes his thought particularly relevant to the treatment of ethnicity (Hall, 1996b).

The officials who worked painstakingly through the protracted talks on constitutional arrangements for Northern Ireland did not read, still less think through and criticise, the major writers on consociationalism – those interviewed for this book made plain almost without exception that neither these, nor any other intellectual sources had guided them. Yet the conception of the world with which they worked, for the most part implicitly, was framed by an essentialist categorisation of 'unionism' and 'nationalism', represented as the unproblematic, antagonistic voices of exclusive 'communities' defined by their 'ancient hatreds' – and, contradictorily, by the belief that these ethnopolitical blocs should nevertheless coalesce in permanent government together, in what became known as 'community government' (Bloomfield, 1994: 163). Indeed, precisely because all this was taken for granted, rather than subject to careful scrutiny, it was all the more pervasive and unquestioned, despite its intellectual incoherence and normative fragility.

When the Northern Ireland crisis erupted in 1968–69, this was to lead to starkly stereotyped perspectives. Richard Crossman (1977: 381), minister in the 1964–70 Labour Government, noted in his diary how his children were enjoying his reading to them of *Gulliver's Travels*, with the Lilliputians' disputes between Big Enders and Little Enders: 'Well, this is just like Ireland.' Oliver Wright was a senior diplomat seconded by the Government to the Northern Ireland Cabinet Office, following the influx of British troops in August 1969. Six months on, Wright was to report that society in Northern Ireland was 'tribal', and that 'the Micks' and 'the Prods' liked each other 'about as well as dog and cat, Arab and Jew, Greek and Turkish Cypriot'.[1]

When the Conservatives took over in June 1970, Reginald Maudling as Home Secretary assumed responsibility for the region. Maudling (1978: 180) reflected: 'Above all, there was the historic hatred, blind, unreasoning, unrelenting ... I realised the virtual hopelessness of any attempt by reason to bring peace and reconciliation.' When direct rule was introduced as Stormont fell, William Whitelaw as first Northern Ireland Secretary took the brief. In his memoirs, Whitelaw (1989: 78) observed: 'Of course, with his clear and logical brain, Reggie Maudling found the Irish mentality almost impossible to understand.' And after the power-sharing initiative had failed, the CPRS report mentioned in Chapter 2 argued that 'the hatred between the communities' was such that there was 'no more chance of their living together in harmony than there is of Turks and Greeks living together in Cyprus, or Jews and Arabs in Palestine'.[2]

Within this stereotyped perspective, of course, the British State saw itself as passive and reactive, rather than its interventions framing concrete outcomes in Northern Ireland. This was to blind its representatives, official and political, to the critical importance of impartial public authority, as explored in Chapter 2, in cauterising ethnic division. In particular, it was to lead to the contradiction that human rights abrogations, which bore down most heavily on members of the Catholic community, were to exacerbate the very 'alienation' which the consociationalist political démarche the State eventually embarked on was meant to assuage.

This chapter and the next explore how official discourse, in London and Dublin, came over time to define the Northern Ireland 'problem' and how, as a result, only certain solutions were conceivable – notably excluding those based on universal norms – even if these were to prove unsustainable or, at best, sub-optimal. These chapters also highlight how essentialist conceptions led to an oscillation between hyperactive interventionism and fatalistic disengagement – both of which could be justified by the view of the population of the region as inherently recondite and irrational.

Consociationalism remained as the 'common sense' answer during activist periods. The Chief Executive Officer of the Community Relations

Council (and political scientist), Duncan Morrow, explained its instrumental attraction bluntly: '[I]t makes sense if you don't have to live under its consequences. So it is common sense from an international perspective. It takes Northern Ireland off the equation. You don't have to think about it.'[3]

The State responds

Notoriously, when the civil-rights movement emerged (Prince, 2007), responsibility for Northern Ireland in the Home Office was confined to the General Department – also dealing with the Channel Islands and the Isle of Man, as well as sundry minor responsibilities such as state-owned pubs in Carlisle (Callaghan, 1973). Decades of political insulation from the region, despite frequent day-to-day official contacts (Mitchell, 2004), had been buttressed by the Speaker's convention at Westminster, preventing discussion of issues germane to the devolved Stormont Government, despite its failure to comply with the universal norm of non-discrimination.

The Home Secretary, James Callaghan, for whom direct rule was 'the last thing' he wanted, recalled (Callaghan, 1973: 22): 'At that stage we knew little enough at first hand about what was going on, and had few reliable means of finding out.' The Defence Secretary, Dennis Healey, concerned that the Prime Minister, Harold Wilson, was strongly interventionist on Northern Ireland, confided to the Health Secretary, Crossman (1977: 478), that 'we shall be as blind men leading the blind if we have to go in there knowing nothing about the place'. Crossman himself confused 12 July and St Patrick's Day in his diary.

The State was forced to reorganise itself to address the challenge: Crossman refers to a Cabinet committee on Northern Ireland, of which he secured membership in April 1969 and which included the Prime Minister, the Foreign Secretary, the Home Secretary and the Defence Secretary (*ibid*). After the June 1970 General Election, a note by the Cabinet Secretary, Burke Trend, marked the renewal of what was formally entitled the Ministerial Committee on Northern Ireland. It similarly comprised the Prime Minister, the Foreign Secretary, the Chancellor, the Home Secretary and the Defence Secretary. Its broad terms of reference were 'To keep under review the Government's policy in relation to Northern Ireland' and it was serviced by the Cabinet Office.[4]

The extent of collective strategic attention paid by the British governing class to Northern Ireland in the early 1970s was to be remarkable: in October 1971 the Conservative Prime Minister, Edward Heath, directed that the ministerial committee should meet once or twice a week.[5] This 'unprecedented concentration of hegemony', to borrow a phrase in another context from Gramsci (1971: 238), was in sharp contrast not only to the inattention which was to come later but also to the narrowly presidential and media-conscious approach eventually adopted by Blair.

A further note by Trend said Heath had ordered that a parallel, cross-departmental official committee be constituted, chaired by Sir Philip Allen, Permanent Secretary of the Home Office.[6] In a striking demonstration of the degree to which Northern Ireland had previously been perceived as *outre-mer*, another note in October indicated that Trend had determined that responsibility for the region within the Cabinet Office would move from the Defence and Overseas Policy Section to the Home Affairs Section.[7]

In Dublin, there were similar if more modest developments. An official Interdepartmental Unit (IDU) was established in June 1970,[8] to act 'as a clearing-house for the activities of Departments generally in relation to the North'.[9] A meeting in January 1971 heard that the Irish embassies in Canada and Belgium had furnished 'a large quantity of documentation about constitutional, legal and other safeguards for minorities in those two countries'.[10]

At Stormont, meanwhile, as the regime was unravelling, the then Unionist Prime Minister, Brian Faulkner, proposed in June 1971 that nationalists be offered positions as chairs of two committees, as part of an expanded committee system, in the Parliament. He argued that 'we must aim to govern with the consent and acceptance of a far wider majority than is constituted by those who elect the governing party', and thus 'provide a means for all responsible elements in our community to play a constructive part in its institutions' (Faulkner, 1978: 104).

This was a modest attempt at what Gramsci (1971: 58) called *transformismo*, 'the formation of an ever more extensive ruling class'. It did not conform to the democratic norm of equal citizenship (International IDEA, 2002: 13) so critical to members of the minority community – Catholics could chair committees but Protestants would still govern – and, while it led to a round of talks with the opposition parties, it fell foul of the withdrawal of the Social Democratic and Labour Party from Stormont in July. This came in the wake of the killing of two Catholic civilians by the army, setting in train a 'path-dependent' process by which the SDLP progressively withdrew from its initial reformist stance to a conventional nationalist perspective, in which it became aligned with, and dependent upon, the Irish State (McGrattan, 2007).

The introduction of internment in August was recognised within the Stormont Ministry of Community Relations as leading to the wholesale alienation of Catholics from the State.[11] This in turn heightened tensions between London and Stormont, as was evident at a meeting that month between Heath and Faulkner at Chequers, attended by the heavy hitters from the ministerial committee – the Home Secretary, the Foreign Secretary and the Defence Secretary.

Heath anticipated rising public pressure for 'some political initiative' but Faulkner said it was hard to see what further initiatives were possible: 'A coalition government would not be practicable.' Maudling however said that, if dissension was to be avoided at Westminster, the UK Government had now to 'be seen to take some initiative towards regaining the confidence of the minority community'; otherwise, he warned, 'the pressure for a tripartite solution involving the Republic would grow'. He said he had recently proposed to Faulkner a meeting between him and members of the Stormont Parliament, at which he (Maudling) would preside, 'to find a means of providing permanent and guaranteed participation by the minority in government and administration' while respecting the constitutional position of Northern Ireland as part of the UK, but Faulkner had rejected the suggestion. Faulkner said he could not 'take part in discussion whose scope might include the supersession of the democratic principle of majority rule'.[12]

At a Stormont Cabinet meeting in September, at which the Prime Minister's idea of 'minority' committee chairs and other suggestions – enlarging the House of Commons, changing the Senate and introducing proportional representation – were discussed, the Minister of Commerce, Robin Bailie, said nothing short of executive power would satisfy the SDLP and sections of the British press would not support anything less than the 'community government' of some European countries.[13] Faulkner's proposals were however expressed in a Green Paper of October 1971 and he was still adhering to them as late as December 1972 in discussions with Whitelaw.[14]

Yet in one paragraph the Green Paper signalled, albeit without commitment, a transition to the fuller project of *transformismo* which was to define the efforts under direct rule to establish power-sharing (Bloomfield, 1994: 152–3):

> Between General Elections the power of a British government is, in some respects, as absolute as democratic power can be, but this exercise of power is accepted by a parliamentary minority who know that sooner or later their turn to exercise it will come. When that expectation does not exist, there is clearly a risk of disenchantment with the democratic, parliamentary process. Because of this, it has been argued in some quarters that means must be found to give 'the minority' in Northern Ireland a share in the effective exercise of power. The Government believes that this important issue should be openly and dispassionately considered by Parliament and public.

Heath (1998: 423) claimed in his autobiography to have 'come to the view years before that there was only one way of achieving any permanent solution for Northern Ireland: some form of power-sharing between the two communities', while also believing 'that the Republic of Ireland had to be brought into the relationship once more'. In September 1971, the CPRS submitted a report outlining the options as internal partition, power-sharing or condominium. Heath made plain his preference for the second, allied to the revival of the Council of Ireland stillborn from the 1920 Government of Ireland Act (*ibid*: 430).

In the Commons that month, Maudling described 'decision making at the political level' in Northern Ireland as 'a very hard problem indeed', and he went on:

> We are all supporters of the system of democratic election, of democratic assembly, based on universal adult suffrage, but, as I have said in the House before, in effect our system in this country works in practice by giving almost unlimited powers for a few years to the party that happens to possess a temporary majority in the House of Commons. This is acceptable because the party in government changes. But one must recognise that there are different circumstances in a country where the majority does not change.

He said that the object of talks with the Northern Ireland parties was 'to find agreed ways whereby there can be assured to the minority and majority communities alike an active, permanent and guaranteed part in the life and public affairs of Northern Ireland'.[15]

Meanwhile, Heath had met the Taoiseach, Jack Lynch, at Chequers. Lynch told reporters afterwards that he had put Heath 'completely in the picture' as to the republic's attitude. This was that to 'impose a parliamentary system' on Northern Ireland 'as operates in Westminster' was 'not possible in the kind of community that existed where by reason of the polarisation only one side will be permanently in Government'. He argued for 'some other structure of government, as has been devised in other countries where there had been racial, religious, linguistic differences, in fact all three in some cases e.g. Switzerland, places like the Lebanon and Belgium'.[16]

Lynch reported to the Dáil that, while in his view the only ultimate solution was a united Ireland, 'new structures were required in the North because the attempt to govern the area with a Parliament based on the Westminster model had been such a total failure'.[17] This implied 'enactment without delay of a form of administration for Northern Ireland in which the minority … will participate by right'.[18]

A meeting of the Whitehall official committee in November 1971 discussed 'Possible courses of action', based on a paper of the same name by Allen, which described current policy as 'to try to reach an agreement in discussion with representatives of the communities in Northern Ireland on ways in which both the majority and the minority can have an active permanent and guaranteed role in the life and public affairs of the Province'. The meeting considered possible proposals beyond Faulkner's Green Paper, 'but based fundamentally on the present constitution'. It recommended that ministers decide on 'the degree of coalition which we should press Mr Faulkner to accept, e.g. would we insist on having members of the elected minority in the Cabinet, and if so in what strength?'[19]

In December, the official committee decided to 'prepare a study of arrangements made in other countries for providing a minority with a role in government'. Allen wrote a note, following reports from British embassies, on Belgium, Cameroon, Canada, Cyprus, Czechoslovakia, Fiji, Finland, Italy, Lebanon, Mauritius, Switzerland and Yugoslavia. This concluded: 'Not surprisingly, there is no one model which seems exactly to fit the Northern Ireland situation.' Given Northern Ireland's size (ruling out a federal solution) and admixture of population (ruling out extra minority seats in parliament), Allen argued that an effective role for 'the minority' depended on specific provision 'for places for the minority in the government'. This could be done by requiring inclusion in the Cabinet of minority party representatives in proportion to seats held, guarantees of specific portfolios or matching of senior and junior ministers on a majority–minority basis, as well as 'blocking devices' at executive or parliamentary level. It was 'doubtful' this could be arrived at by inter-party agreement and Faulkner had made clear it would be 'unacceptable'. But Allen wrote: 'Nevertheless, there are circumstances in which such a scheme might be tolerated as a solution imposed from Westminster.' This implied drafting a bill detailing 'a new constitution'.[20]

Against the backdrop of months of intense violence following the introduction of internment, the Deputy Secretary to the Stormont Cabinet, Ken Bloomfield, meanwhile met the then UK Government observer, Howard Smith, though he was anxious no one at Stormont should know. Bloomfield had 'thought long and hard' before 'reluctantly' coming to 'a deep change in his assessment of the situation here and in his view of what was needed', which entailed 'strong remedies'. He said: 'The Green Paper proposals would certainly not be enough ... Nothing less than a share in governmental power would do: that is to say, community government.' As Smith noted, Bloomfield contended:[21]

A solution would only be found if the British government steeled themselves to intervene directly. They should impose a new constitution under which at the next general election the single transferable vote would be used to elect an enlarged house from which a community government would be appointed[22] on a basis reflecting party strengths in the house, with blocking provisions in the government as well as in parliament to safeguard minority interests in selected fields. Bloomfield emphasised that it would be essential to protect minority interests in executive as well as legislative decisions: hence the need for blocking provisions in government.

Smith concluded: 'Whatever view one takes of Bloomfield's proposals, the fact that a man of such high ability, who has been at the centre of things for so long, and who has served three prime ministers so closely, has come to these conclusions about the situation and the need for radical action by the UK government must, I suggest, be given a good deal of weight.'[23]

On Christmas Eve, Trend sent a note to Heath's Principal Private Secretary, Robert Armstrong, saying the latter would be 'interested to see this surprising – and possibly significant – approach by the Deputy Secretary of the Cabinet at Stormont'. Trend suspected that the proposal 'might prove to be simply a recipe for indefinite stalemate' but described as 'interesting' Bloomfield's conviction that only an 'imposed solution' would do.[24] Armstrong noted that it was also 'interesting – and significant – that someone so near the centre of Stormont' should have unburdened himself to Smith. Despite the Christmas break, Armstrong was able to report back to Trend on 2 January that the Prime Minister had 'read the signal with great interest'.[25]

This found a ready echo in Dublin. Addressing the FF conference in February 1972, Lynch reiterated his commitment to a united Ireland. But, in terms of 'interim policies', he argued that 'the first essential is that the monopoly of power now residing in one community because of the operation of the British system of parliamentary democracy should be replaced by a different kind of representative democracy in which power is deliberately shared between the two communities'.[26]

What was interesting about this emergent discourse on 'community government', however, is that it ultimately relied on representing itself as a necessary departure from the taken-for-granted constitutional hegemon – Westminster. Vernon Bogdanor (1999: 102) presents the mindset clearly:

> Successive governments have insisted ... that any new system of devolution [to Northern Ireland] must, unlike the parliament which existed from 1921 to 1972, be such as to be acceptable to both communities in the province. This has been interpreted to mean both that the government of Northern Ireland should contain representatives of both communities, and that the aspirations of the nationalist minority should be recognized through the Irish Dimension, some form of institutionalized connection with the Irish Republic.
>
> Such an approach involves a striking departure from the Westminster model of government, which is based on the possibility of alternating governments.

Dithering over intervention

The British State had, however, been remarkably reluctant to intervene. Callaghan (1973) as Home Secretary had recognised that British military intervention would have political implications and he commissioned contingency plans for direct rule as early as the winter of 1968. But when Crossman (1977: 463) joined the Cabinet's Northern Ireland committee in April 1969, he was told that while preparations had been 'roughly' made for an army intervention, direct rule was a prospect 'perhaps in the last resort'. A three-clause bill to introduce direct rule was prepared but never pursued and Callaghan opposed resolutions in favour of direct rule at Labour's 1970 conference (Kellner and Hitchens, 1976).

Under the Conservatives, from the first meeting of the ministerial committee on in July 1970, direct rule was a scenario on the agenda. The committee considered a memo from Maudling, who said it was 'prudent to prepare against the worst eventuality', including the collapse of the Northern Ireland Government and the requirement that the UK Government would 'take urgent action to suspend the Stormont Parliament and take over the government of Northern Ireland'. The paper set out a contingency plan, including rushing a bill through in a day and legislating for Northern Ireland by order in council. It was recognised in discussion that this would 'create major political problems' but there was agreement with Maudling's view that if security had to be taken over there would have to be 'a total assumption of responsibility'.[27]

Yet the next meeting of the committee, four days later, recognised also that '[o]nce the Stormont Government and Parliament were suspended it might be difficult to revive them'. And, under the heading of 'Longer term prospects', Heath said: 'Either we must resign ourselves to having to maintain large numbers of troops in Northern Ireland indefinitely with all the strain on our financial and military resources that this entailed, or we must seek to achieve a political situation.' He proposed a small working group 'to consider possible political solutions'.[28]

When Cecil King (1975: 80) met Whitelaw, Lord President of the Council, after a Cabinet meeting in January 1971, he put it to him that the Government's policy was limited to a wish that Ireland and the Irish should go away. Whitelaw responded: 'Exactly.' Direct rule thus remained what the committee felt at a meeting in March 1971 to be 'a last resort'.[29] When Faulkner (1978: 128) met members of the ministerial committee in August, and raised the possibility of direct rule, he recalled: 'Sir Alec [Douglas-Home] threw his hands in the air: "Not direct rule," he exclaimed, "anything but direct rule." It was a point of view clearly assented to by all present.'

As late as 10 January 1972, Trend wrote to Heath, saying: 'I imagine that Ministers will continue to wish to find some means of maintaining the Stormont system if at all possible.'[30]

At Christmas 1968, the Stormont Prime Minister, Terence O'Neill, had confided to Bloomfield (1994: 108): 'The only solution – direct rule from London – will of course never materialise and so we shall drift from crisis to crisis ...' Nor did it, at least not quickly, with Callaghan (1973: 15, 25, 71) so reluctant to be 'sucked into the Irish bog', 'quicksands' and 'quagmire'. This resistance to intervention was disastrous: it inevitably led to shoring up the Unionist regime beyond its political shelf life, at the expense of Catholic alienation. Amid the consequent downward spiral, summing up an official committee meeting in March 1971, Allen said that even though 'it would not help the military position' internment 'had political attractions as a means of placating the Unionist Party'.[31]

This did not reflect a pro-union orientation on the part of the British State. The very same resistance to intervention underlay a strong preference for Irish unification, rehearsed by Allen at the same meeting:

> It was desirable to look at the Irish problem both in the short term, i.e. while an acceptable regime lasted in Northern Ireland, and in the longer term (perhaps the next 30 years) in which we must seek a final answer. Our objectives in the short term must be to find means of improving life in Northern Ireland and of sustaining a moderate Government in power. We would come face to face with the need to define our longer term objectives (which must include the creation of a united Ireland) as soon as a situation arose in which it became necessary to impose direct rule.

Allen's parenthetic comment was not idiosyncratic, for the minute records: 'In discussion of the longer term problem, the committee noted that direct rule on a Scottish or Welsh pattern might not be consistent with our ultimate intention of promoting a united Ireland.'[32] Heath's view was similar. In August 1971, the Irish Ambassador, Donal O'Sullivan, reported to Dublin on a meeting with the Prime Minister, who had shown reluctance to consult the Irish Government on finding a solution yet had 'talked freely about reunification, which he is confident must come about'.[33]

From early February 1972, ministers met regularly, now including Whitelaw, as the clock ticked down on the Stormont regime. Cabinet discussed Northern Ireland on 3 February, before a meeting with Faulkner the next day, noting: 'It had been found possible elsewhere, for example in the Lebanon, to devise an acceptable method of allocating governmental responsibilities between representatives of different religious groupings.'[34] This was a telling formulation: power-sharing would indeed be a project of top-down *transformismo*, of allocation of power rather than reconciliation of a divided society.

At a meeting of the ministerial committee six days later, 'there was general agreement that the moment for a political initiative had arrived'.[35] But a meeting on 15 February, discussing 'Political reform in Northern Ireland', noted:[36]

> As to the concept of community government, while it might be supposed that Faulkner was conscious of the trend of our thinking, he was probably unaware that the form of 'community' government which we had in mind involved the representatives of the Roman Catholic minority being chosen from among the elected members of the Opposition in the Northern Ireland Parliament.

As it happened, the Stormont Cabinet met the same day, with Faulkner (1978: 147) writing to Heath on 16 February, saying that it had agreed that an entrenched role for members of the Catholic community in government would 'strengthen sectarian divisions and eliminate attempts to create non-sectarian political alignments'. That this was manifestly self-serving did not detract from the fact that the counterposition of 'community government' to Westminsterist one-party government, by treating the 'community' rather than the individual citizen as the unit of democracy, weakened power-sharing as a hegemonic project. Conceived as an exercise in *transformismo*, it was less intellectually and morally robust than would have been the case if linked to more flexible, citizen-based power-sharing arrangements, founded on universal norms – as explored in Chapter 3 *vis-à-vis* Macedonia.

Continuing their meeting that day, the UK ministers concluded that an 'interregnum' of direct rule should precede the implementation of reforms, though Heath was still saying that 'direct rule was a very unpalatable measure to take'.[37] A further meeting on 25 February anticipated 'that it would take some 2 years to bring a permanent reformed constitution into force if there was to be effective consultation with all the interests concerned'. Ministers concluded that 'proroguing' rather than 'dissolving' Stormont and including a border poll in the plan might help assuage 'majority' reaction. Summing up, Heath said *inter alia* that contingency plans should be made for the establishment of a Northern Ireland Department.[38]

On 2 March, ministers considered a letter from Faulkner which said, as reported, that 'a provision guaranteeing a permanent place in the Cabinet of Northern Ireland for a minority would be wrong in principle and unworkable in practice' and argued in favour of his Green Paper. It was agreed that this 'fell far short of meeting the needs of the situation'. Heath summed up saying 'that the Meeting was agreed, albeit with reluctance', that the only course was to resort to a temporary period of direct rule.[39] At Cabinet that day, Maudling backed a 'decisive political initiative' as the 'Roman

Catholic minority' was now 'totally alienated'. Such 'political reform' would require London to assume direct responsibility for administration of Northern Ireland for 'an interim period'.[40]

A memo from the Home Secretary the next day fleshed out his thinking. Less than five weeks after 13 civilians had been killed by British soldiers on 'Bloody Sunday' in Derry, he rather insensitively asserted that sometimes 'it seems almost as if the people of Northern Ireland, or at any rate their political leaders … are possessed of a death wish'. Maudling warned: 'Our whole position in the world is being seriously affected by Northern Ireland, and however hard we try we will not get other countries to understand the reality of the situation.' The UK could benefit even from the failure of a policy that was seen as 'just and equitable', he calculated coolly. Maudling argued that Protestants cared most about the border but Catholics cared most about not being 'second-class citizens'. So he recommended a plebiscite on the border, with no successor for 'a period of 15 or 20 years', as otherwise 'stability on the constitutional issue' would be lacking. He described the idea of a bill of rights as 'interesting' but did not betray a close understanding of human rights in his subsequent reference to 'majority rights':

> Providing the minority representatives with their proper share in the life and public affairs of the Province is a far more intransigent problem. The majority has its rights as well as the minority. The normal Westminster system will continue for many years to come to provide automatic Unionist majorities. If we are to ensure minority participation we must therefore depart from our accepted systems.

The Home Secretary claimed that 'the simple fact is there are only three alternatives – a Cabinet with minority representation chosen by the minority; a Cabinet that continues to be totally dominated by Unionists, which I believe is no longer acceptable to the minority; or no Cabinet at all'. Yet, as indicated in Chapter 2, this treatment of Westminster as the model failed to appreciate the European norm (including in Lihphart's consociationalist cases) of coalition governments formed by agreement. Maudling argued for a secretary of state to take over Stormont's functions, as a 'clean break' in the interim, in the context of 'widespread' distrust of Faulkner and the latter's refusal to continue if control over policing was transferred to London.[41]

When his proposals went to Cabinet, concerns emerged about the 'serious risks' involved, echoing Lijphart's (1977) argument that consociational democracies depended on common commitment to the polity:[42]

> 'Community Government', with statutory allocation of Cabinet portfolios according to representation of the Parties in the Northern Ireland House of Commons, could not be reconciled with the democratic concept of responsibility to a Parliamentary majority. In those countries where Ministerial offices had been

distributed by statute or by convention among opposing political Parties there had at least been general agreement upon the broad objective of preserving the integrity of the State. In Northern Ireland this basic prerequisite was lacking. But if for this reason 'Community Government' proved to be unworkable in practice, we might find ourselves committed in perpetuity to the system of direct United Kingdom rule which we had envisaged as only a temporary expedient; and in earlier discussions Ministers had frequently agreed that direct rule represented a policy of last resort.

These divisions were out in the open. The Conservative-aligned *Spectator* editorialised: 'The cabinet is divided. The administration is divided. Tory backbench opinion is divided. The party in the country is divided.'[43] On 8 March, having met this unease in Cabinet, Heath indicated that there would be 'considerable political advantage, both in Northern Ireland and in Great Britain, if the Government were seen to have been compelled towards direct rule by Faulkner's refusal to continue in office following a transfer of the responsibility for law and order'. On 23 March, with Faulkner rejecting a handover, direct rule was duly agreed.[44]

Pace Whitelaw's comment about Irish 'irrationality', official perspectives in Dublin tended to be more nuanced than in London. Lynch presciently warned Heath, in the wake of the establishment of direct rule, against periodic border polls. The Taoiseach anticipated that the 'advent of the pleb-iscitary period would, on each occasion, lead to renewed polarisation of the communities'.[45] The plebiscite was to face a widespread Catholic boycott when run on 8 March 1973 (Bew and Gillespie, 1999: 60).[46]

Indeed, Whitelaw advised fellow ministers in July 1972 to the same effect. But in the wake of the revelation of his ill-judged secret talks with the IRA leadership a fortnight earlier (*ibid.*, 1999: 54) – he later recalled that 'they simply made demands'[47] – he said that 'pressure from the Protestant side for an immediate commitment to a plebiscite had become intolerable' and in its absence 'extreme Protestant feeling might go to the point of armed insurrection'. It was argued in discussion that the proposal was 'untimely, contentious, and irrelevant to the solution of the problem in Northern Ireland' and that it would be an 'anomaly' to go ahead 'without an indication of the proposed constitutional solution'. Yet Heath, summing up, said of Whitelaw, in another odd projection of policy incoherence in London on to a suppos-edly irrational population in Belfast: 'The conditions he faced in Northern Ireland were not always susceptable [sic] to logical argument.'[48] On such a flimsy basis was the idea of a border poll to make its way into official dis-course, re-emerging despite its contradictions in the Belfast agreement, as described in Chapter 2.

Transformismo in action

In August 1972 Whitelaw told colleagues he would invite the parties represented in the old Stormont Parliament to send representatives to a political
conference in late September – this was to be held at Darlington but no nationalists attended, in protest at internment – though the chances of agreement
were 'remote'. He thought that 'it would be necessary for the Government
to impose the solution which it judged most likely to be acceptable and lasting; and to legislate to that end'.[49]

At Darlington (Bew and Gillespie, 1999: 55), Alliance suggested a
structure based on committee chairs taking over the functions exercised
by ministers before direct rule[50] – the position to be adopted by the Ulster
Unionist Party in the 1990s. But as proceedings were conveyed to the Irish
Government, 'Mr Faulkner remained adamant for a two tier system, with
executive ministers and advisory committees, emphasising the "parliamentary democracy" aspect'.[51]

A document prepared in the Department of the Taoiseach in August,
headed 'Possible lines of an imposed settlement', had noted the unionist
proposal but argued that since the committee chairs could 'presumably
delay controversial legislation, but not ultimately veto it' they would 'have
no real effect on the Unionist power monopoly'. The document argued that
power could be shared via the proposal by the northern industrialist Fred
Catherwood (Elliott and Flackes, 1999: 202) for a two-thirds weighted-
majority requirement for certain bills, by 'PR' government or by election of
ministers from the legislature as in Switzerland.[52]

The UK Government Green Paper of October 1972, *The Future of
Northern Ireland* (NIO, 1972), marked the next stage in the evolution of
official thinking. There were, however, continuities: Bloomfield (1994:
177–8) wrote the first draft, having also drafted its Stormont predecessor
(2007: 192), and his contribution was singled out by Whitelaw (1989: 108).
Bloomfield said that his draft – written 'furiously' over a weekend at his
aunt's in London – had been 'mucked about with' afterwards. 'Nevertheless,
the outline of a potential settlement, without being terribly bombastic about
it, was my outline. What was so interesting was that I would have liked to
see the thinking that had already been going on in the Home Office, and
there wasn't really any.'[53]

The Green Paper said that the 'most striking feature' of the government
of Northern Ireland over the previous half century had been the unbroken
dominance of the Unionist Party (NIO, 1972: 4):

> The alternation of governing parties which has for so long been a characteristic of
> the British political system, and which has undoubtedly contributed in a marked

degree to the stability of Parliamentary Government in Great Britain, accordingly did not exist in Northern Ireland ... The special feature of the Northern Ireland situation was that the great divide was not between different viewpoints on such matters as the allocation of resources and the determination of priorities, but between two whole communities. The 'floating vote' for which rival parties would normally compete was almost non-existent ... Such a situation was unlikely to foster either sensitivity on the part of the permanent majority or a sense of responsibility on the part of the permanent minority.

The Green Paper thus concluded (*ibid*: §58):

[I]t can be argued that the British democratic system only works where a regular alternation of parties is possible; that the real test of a democratic system is its ability to provide peaceful and orderly Government, and that by that standard the existing system has failed in Northern Ireland; that other countries with divided communities have made special constitutional provision to ensure participation by all; that a number of these countries have had stable and successful coalition governments over many years; and that there is no hope of binding the minority to the support of new political arrangements in Northern Ireland unless they are admitted to active participation in any new structures.

Note that key phrase, 'binding the minority to the support of new political arrangements', which identifies the project as one of *transformismo*. Expressing sympathy with election of an assembly by single transferable vote (*ibid*: §53), the Green Paper considered four ways in which this could be done via executive formation (*ibid*: §60):

(a) 'entrenched government': government would be constitutionally required to include 'minority elements', which could 'present very difficult problems of definition, and impede the development of non-sectarian party structures';

(b) 'proportional representation government': all 'substantial elements' elected to the legislature would be proportionately represented in the executive, which could 'exclude the possibility of any Opposition as currently understood in the legislature and would not be made easier by the very broad range of political opinion';

(c) 'bloc government': the party(ies) commanding a majority in the legislature would be required to coalesce with the party(ies) commanding a majority of 'the minority', which would ensure some residual opposition and make possible the exclusion of 'small irresponsible groups' but 'would be apt to prove a somewhat complex, inflexible and artificial device'; or

(d) 'weighted majority government': government on establishment and facing votes of confidence (and possibly other business) would require assembly endorsement by a majority 'so weighted as to make necessary a broad range of support', not confined to 'representatives of a single community' – in the 1970s demographic context of a more substantial Protestant majority, the paper suggested a threshold of 75 per cent.

The paper promised a border plebiscite (*ibid*: §82), while also introducing the phraseology of the 'Irish Dimension' in the context of forthcoming common EEC membership – 'to make possible effective consultation and co-operation in Ireland for the benefit of North and South alike; and to provide a firm basis for concerted governmental and community action against those terrorist organisations which represent a threat to free democratic institutions in Ireland as a whole' (*ibid*: §78). 'Exceptional measures' were taken to engage the Northern Ireland public in debate around *The Future of Northern Ireland*: nearly 13,000 copies were sold, 200,000 leaflets were distributed and a tabloid summary was circulated with the newspapers to more than 1.2 million readers (NIO, 1973: §3).

The Green Paper was welcomed by Lynch, in a speech in November in Cork. The Taoiseach said: 'One essential part of the search for peace is the need to find a political structure which can command the consent of the separate communities in the North.'[54] In fact, he had been the only recipient of an advance copy from the UK Government, sent four days before its appearance on 30 October, and was asked to avoid comment suggestive of having had time for its study.[55] It would be 'very embarrassing' if this fact became known, the Irish Ambassador reported.[56]

Lynch had earlier spoken of the need to find a 'centre ground', which he identified with 'community government'.[57] But his Cork comments indicated the difficulty, for he went on: 'We must find ways to live and work with one another which do not intrude on personal values, traditions and loyalties.'[58] The 'centre ground' in that context could only be of the thinnest, and most fragile, character where 'values, traditions and loyalties' were counterposed, rather than being constrained by universal norms and arbitrated by impartial public authority.

At a meeting in January 1973, the ministerial committee, addressing 'New institutions for Northern Ireland', was told by Whitelaw 'that there was no basis of agreement between the political groups representing various elements in the community; and that it would be necessary for the United Kingdom Government to work out a solution and to give a clear lead towards its implementation'.[59] At a February meeting,[60] Whitelaw tweaked the options for executive formation, based on an accompanying memo, 'A new executive'.

The menu comprised:

1 reserved seats for 'statutory Catholics' (which the memo rejected: 'Its

disadvantage is that it institutionalises the sectarian basis of politics in Northern Ireland');

2 the majority party would have posts proportionate to its strength and minority positions would be filled by the Secretary of State (which the memo argued might work but would be dangerous to legislate for);

3 proportionate government (or 'PR government', which had 'few advantages');

4 an executive dependent on weighted-majority support in the Assembly (which risked rejection or the possibility that the 75 per cent figure might not be enough to ensure a cross-community coalition if there was an element of nationalist boycott); and

5 to leave it to the Assembly in consultation with the Secretary of State to decide detailed arrangements.

The memo suggested that the first three options should be ruled out. It is particularly noteworthy that option 3, which was to be deployed in 1998 – after only the most cursory consideration in the talks – via the d'Hondt rule, was rejected in Whitelaw's paper as 'likely to encourage intransigence and face us with a group who have nothing in common and have no intention of working together'. The first, and especially the second, period of devolution after the Belfast agreement bore out this forecast. The memo contended that the fourth option might well prove 'the right answer' but that it was safer not to commit absolutely to it. In contemporary circumstances, the demographic and political strength of members of the Catholic community would render the concern about a boycott nugatory, while the 75 per cent figure would be unduly high as a super-majority requirement.[61]

But Heath, summing up the discussion, said there had been 'substantial support' for the fifth option,[62] which was to lead to the unforeseen problem of a struggle among the parties over the number and balance of executive seats. Pursuit of the super-majority approach would have had – and would continue to have – the contrary advantage of requiring the parties aspiring to join an executive to reach agreement in advance.

A more considered brief had been offered by the IDU in Dublin in December 1972. It provided an exegesis of the options set out in *The Future of Northern Ireland*, and noted that 'weighted majority government' was the only one not specifically criticised. The brief said 'the overriding consideration' was that any administration which 'the majority and minority representatives' were prepared to accept and work 'would probably be acceptable to the Dublin Government'. This implied the republic would have gone along with the weighted-majority option, which Whitelaw had personally favoured (and, as we have seen, Mitchell was subsequently to prefer).

On the Council of Ireland, the document argued that if it were to operate properly it would 'require acquiescence at least from the Unionists'. This suggested a council which would deal 'at the outset with matters which are fairly mundane, pragmatic and unlikely to cause confrontation'. It listed areas of prior cooperation and proposed only seven new areas: physical planning, mineral/oil exploitation, industrial promotion, the Arts Councils, broadcasting, a single civil service commission and some link with semi-state agencies (of these only industrial promotion would have been really controversial). It suggested it should function on the EEC model, with a Council of Ministers, an Assembly and a 'small' secretariat.[63]

Whitelaw took a similarly modest view of the Council of Ireland at this stage. A note in February 1973 to ministerial colleagues said while it should have a capacity to develop by mutual consent into 'something real and influential', it would be 'counter-productive' if one were to 'give the impression that the institutions were deliberately designed to pave the way towards unification', and movement on the republic's territorial claim should be sought.[64]

In a note to Cabinet later that month, Whitelaw offered without preference the single transferable vote (STV) and the additional member system (AMS) as voting systems for an assembly with about 80 members that would be compatible with existing electoral boundaries – the former with Westminster's, the latter with those for the old Stormont. He suggested the forthcoming White Paper should not give hostages to fortune on executive formation and he felt the executive would end up being appointed by him. Notably, he added:

> There is however a good deal to be said for providing that all parties with a specified number of seats should have a right to a place in the executive if they wish to take it up; and even more to be said for a scheme by which a panel of members of the assembly, elected by a weighted vote (say 75%) by all members of the assembly, act as Heads of Department since this would make necessary some form of coalition government.

There should be a committee system, based on the departmental structure, with chairs distributed 'as far as possible' in proportion to assembly party strengths. On a 'Bill of Rights', the constitution bill following the White Paper should enshrine non-discrimination. This of course implied that the only threat of abrogations of human rights came from Protestant-majority rule, not the activities of the British State. Finally, on the 'Irish Dimension' he said: 'We have a tightrope to tread here. On the one hand, we have to avoid arousing the fears of the majority community and this means that the proposal for a Council of Ireland must be part of a wider settlement; on the other, we have got to satisfy the minority community and the Government of Ireland that we really mean business.'[65]

The electoral system was discussed at the ministerial committee two days later. STV was favoured over AMS – though Bloomfield (2007: 40) advocated a version of the latter – because it would not require use of the old Stormont constituencies and because it had already been agreed for elections to the new district councils.[66] In June 1972, Whitelaw had argued in a memo to Cabinet: 'It may be that PR itself will not succeed in breaking the political polarity, but there can be little doubt that it is one of the most potent instruments in attempting to do that.' Interestingly, STV had then been favoured over the list system, because the former had been used in Ireland, north and south, and because the latter 'tends on the whole to the dominance of parties'[67] – precisely the reason, of course, why Lijphart (1977) supported it.

But there was very little appreciation of the pertinent effects of different systems. Bloomfield recalled: 'Well, to be honest of course we were all infants on this. We were dealing with an area that people hadn't thought about very much.'[68] But as Horowitz (1985: 645) observes, while PR as such represents 'a feasible strategy to achieve proportionality where first-past-the-post has distorted the results', it offers 'an unlikely vehicle to create a new fluidity'. The fundamental difficulty with STV in heterogeneous constituencies is that it does not incentivise parties to appeal for, or citizens to offer, tactical preferences to boost the chances of moderate candidates from the 'other side', rather than seeking to secure core communal support – and the larger the number of seats per constituency, the greater the problem. Linked to this, it does not encourage moderate parties to establish embryonic interethnic coalitions in advance of an election (Horowitz, 2003: 124).

Interestingly, there was some distaste in Dublin for the idea of 'community government', at least after the change of government following the election of March 1973, which saw a Fine Gael–Labour coalition replace FF. Civic republicanism, as the official ideology of the State, is after all – however much diluted by nationalism in practice – ill at ease with communitarianism, privileging as it does the individual citizen. And a memo sent to London, a few days before the White Paper appeared, warned that power-sharing should involve 'not just some representation for the *minority community* (a sectarian concept)'. The alternative offered, however, was Whitelaw's option three – 'participation of *political groups* in the executive on a basis broadly proportionate to their strength in the Assembly itself elected by P.R.' (original emphasis). But this was linked to a proposal for a 75 per cent super-majority requirement to pass Assembly motions on issues identified by a bill of rights, rather than communal designation, and the memo did recognise that a mechanism could be needed to resolve deadlocks in this context.[69]

When Garret FitzGerald, the newly elected Minister for Foreign Affairs, met Heath and Douglas-Home in London that evening, he urged judicial protection for human rights. But he faced the obstacle of the British State ideology of 'parliamentary sovereignty'. Heath exclaimed: 'What! Her Majesty's judges overruling Her Majesty's Parliament? Constitutionally impossible!'[70]

In March, the Government's proposals were firmed up in the White Paper, *Northern Ireland Constitutional Proposals* (NIO, 1973). This repeated, verbatim, the objective of 'binding the minority to the support of new political arrangements', stressing (*ibid*: 13): 'There is no future for devolved institutions of government in Northern Ireland unless majority and minority alike can be so bound.' Equally, on the 'Irish Dimension', it said that a Council of Ireland would require 'the consent of both majority and minority opinion in Northern Ireland', to be thrashed out at a tripartite conference involving London and Dublin (*ibid*: 30).

A whole section of the White Paper was devoted to 'A Charter of Human Rights' but this stressed the conservative convention that 'the principal protection is that afforded by our parliamentary democratic tradition and by the common and statute law'. And while it did say that the Northern Ireland Constitution Bill implementing the White Paper would outlaw discriminatory legislation by the Assembly and that a Standing Advisory Commission on Human Rights was to be established, it also promised that in the presence of paramilitary 'intimidation' internment would continue and the Special Powers Act, under which it was introduced, would be replaced by successor legislation (to become the Emergency Provisions Act 1973).

In April, Whitelaw hosted FitzGerald at his office and said acceptance of the White Paper had 'exceeded his wildest dreams'. While he would meet the Northern Ireland party leaders about it, the resultant legislation would 'faithfully carry out the fundamentals' of the document, which he was not going to change.[71] But FitzGerald was unhappy about the detail when Whitelaw published the bill. At a meeting in June at the Irish Embassy, the Minister for Foreign Affairs expressed concern about the adequacy of the reference to the European Convention on Human Rights. He was also unhappy that the power-sharing executive was not defined and so lacked any requirement for collective responsibility. Whitelaw tellingly presented this as a bonus: 'The great catch was that if the members do not want to act collectively then they won't.'[72]

The Assembly election, to a 78-seat chamber, was duly held on 28 June under STV. The moderate Alliance (8 seats) and Northern Ireland Labour Party (one) did less well than expected, and unionists opposed to the White

Paper, albeit fragmented, secured more seats (26) than Official Unionist supporters of it (24); the SDLP (19) however performed solidly, with SF declining to participate in the poll (Elliott and Flackes, 1999: 533).

Heath (1998: 440) did not claim in his memoirs that STV was deployed to encourage cross-sectarian transfers but rather that it was 'to ensure that the Assembly would reflect the state of public opinion in the province as accurately as possible, and that the viewpoints of smaller minorities would also be represented'. He had, indeed, been presciently warned by FitzGerald, at a meeting in March in London, that elections based on the Westminster constituencies would mean too many candidates per constituency, leading to less benefit for 'Moderates' from lower preferences – merely to assert in response that 'the best expert advice' which he had been able to obtain 'suggests that elections by PR and based on the Westminster Constituencies will help the moderates'.[73]

London had previously received official advice from Dublin to that effect. In April 1971, a Mr Pemberton from the Home Office, whose speciality was described as electoral reform, divulged to an official in the Department of the Taoiseach that the Home Office was looking at 'multi-seat proportional representation' and that 'Mr Heath had made Northern Ireland his "own thing" two weeks ago and had fully informed himself on the subject'. He hinted that 'the whole apparatus of Whitehall' was 'now concentrating on imposing a new kind of set up in the North while maintaining a facade of Unionist government there'. The Irish official reassured him that multi-seat PR 'had not resulted in political fragmentation in the South – instead it tended to move politics to the centre and this surely was the primary case for introducing multi-seat PR for Stormont'.[74]

If *transformismo*, with its conservative implications, defined the predominant strand of official discourse on Northern Ireland, there was also a subordinate, more progressive, discourse of reconciliation. In an address to the Blackrock branch of his party in June 1973, the Taoiseach, Liam Cosgrave, accepted the essentialist premiss of defining Northern Ireland as 'a divided community' of 'two apparently incompatible aspirations'. Yet Cosgrave drew from this not a conclusion about elite *Realpolitik* dealing but the urgency of reconciliation.

Consensus should be sought, he said, 'by seeking to promote reconciliation as the essential preliminary basis for a settlement', this calling for 'a growing recognition of common interest transcending past bitterness and division'. The 'great need' was for political institutions which would encourage this process and he concluded: 'Only if we are prepared to approach the whole problem of Northern Ireland in genuine friendship and with a sincere concern for their tragic problems, can we hope to lay a foundation for reconciliation within Northern Ireland itself.'[75]

Cosgrave's approach sidestepped rather than solved the problem of 'apparently incompatible aspirations' but it was the best that could be done with the limited intellectual resources to hand. Cosgrave's predecessor, Lynch, had similarly told the Dáil in July 1972 that if a 'regional form of administration' were to be formed, involving 'the legitimate representatives of both Northern communities and the representatives of the Governments in Dublin and Westminster', then 'a necessary preliminary must be reconciliation'.[76]

Setting out his political agenda for shared power in 1972, FitzGerald (1972: 133) had made the standard consociationalist 'move' in recommending as an alternative to the Westminster model, 'government à l'anglaise', something akin to the grand-coalition arrangements in Switzerland. But he went on (ibid: 140): 'A system that eliminates all political opposition, by incorporating all groups of significance in government, does not seem likely … to provide a satisfactory long-term solution.'

Understandably, FitzGerald set a high bar for the supersession of the consociationalist arrangements, suggesting that this should require 75 per cent agreement in a devolved assembly or Northern Ireland referendum. But he concluded (ibid: 141):

> Hopefully, over time the proposed system of joint government could lead to an end to the sectarian polarisation of Northern Ireland politics and to the emergence of some other division, possibly on the basis of divergent economic ideologies. In this event the people and politicians of Northern Ireland might feel themselves ready to return to a more normal type of parliamentary system, and the possibility should be faced and provided for.

Even as he published the White Paper, Whitelaw (1989: 109) indicated in a broadcast to the people of Northern Ireland, as he described it, that he saw this as 'a chance to free themselves of violence, of sectarian strait-jackets, above all of the sterile politics based solely on the border'. Indeed, this was the basis for the SDLP's critique of the document, which said that 'we have always taken the view that power sharing is not just a matter for those at the top but must clearly be seen to permeate all levels of society in Northern Ireland to be fully effective'. In language quite different from the nationalist stance the party adopted in 1998 – when the arrangements it supported for communal designation and mutual vetoes inadvertently empowered anti-agreement unionism, as the next chapter explains – the SDLP took the civic-republican high ground: 'In addition, as a Party which is completely dedicated to the removal of sectarianism as a force in politics in this part of Ireland, we would be anxious to avoid any suggestion of power sharing that would institutionalise sectarianism in Northern Ireland.'[77]

UK ministers, too, tended to look *in the longer run* to non-sectarian politics, which they interpreted as the replacement of communalism by class. Callaghan (1973: 157–60) saw the NILP as the vehicle for a cross-community alternative to unionism. Maudling (1978: 188) similarly expressed the wish that the political agenda in Northern Ireland move on to a left–right axis. But these were to prove wistful hopes as political polarisation deepened in subsequent years – arguably, a polarisation sustained by the very politics of recognition which, in the immediacy of their interventions, ministers embraced.

Power-sharing in practice

The five-month duration of the power-sharing Executive between January and May 1974 (Bloomfield, 1994: 196–223) was to be taken by London and Dublin at a distance of two decades of hindsight to indicate that its organisation around the 'political centre' of the UUP, the SDLP and Alliance had made it unstable. Yet in the 1980s the fear of the 'republican movement' was that just such an 'internal deal' would be concluded at its expense, until and unless it secured a political veto over developments (Frampton, 2009: 22, 47), which the Hume-Adams agreement of 1993 achieved. And it was not the arrangements for executive formation which were to be the downfall of the experiment: on the contrary, relationships within the Executive were better than was to be the case, fitfully, from December 1999 to October 2002 and after May 2007. The Achilles Heel was the Council of Ireland arising from the Sunningdale conference of December 1973 (Bew and Gillespie, 1999: 72–5).

The principle of power-sharing became widely accepted as a result of the public debate following the introduction of direct rule; in that sense, the transformist project was remarkably successful. Indeed, so accepted did it become that in opinion polls throughout the years following the Executive, despite its collapse, strong and cross-sectarian support for power-sharing was almost invariably demonstrated.[78]

Francis Pym, who replaced Whitelaw as Northern Ireland Secretary in early December 1973, sent a note to the Ministerial Committee on Northern Ireland in February 1974, saying: 'The Executive itself is working encouragingly well. It is getting on with its business, reaching internal understandings, and presenting a solid and united front in public.'[79] Merlyn Rees similarly discovered power-sharing was 'working well', when he inherited the experiment as Labour Northern Ireland Secretary after the general election later that month (Rees, 1985: 45).

Ministers had agreed on collective responsibility at their first meeting after Bloomfield, as Secretary to the Executive, had ensured it was on the agenda.[80] Indeed, inconceivable as it might seem now, a Unionist Party proposal, from the liberal Education Minister, Basil McIvor, to begin integrating education in Northern Ireland was endorsed by the SDLP (*ibid.*: 45–6).

Bloomfield said of Faulkner and his SDLP partner, Gerry Fitt: 'Yes, they got on amazingly well.'[81] While accepting there was a 'personality conflict' between Roy Bradford (UUP) and Paddy Devlin (SDLP), Sir Oliver Napier, the then Alliance leader, recalled: 'We got on unbelievably well.'[82] Devlin himself (1993: 250) was to reflect: 'The collective effort of the ministers, so ably led by Brian Faulkner, is still an unexcelled model and legacy for future attempts to govern our perplexed community.'

When Faulkner met Cosgrave at Baldonnel on 16 January 1974, according to Dermot Nally's account he had said of the Executive: 'It was working well as a team. In fact, he had never, in his experience as [sic] Government, seen any better determination on the part of a group of men[83] to work together.'[84] After the experiment collapsed, Faulkner, responding to a letter from the Taoiseach expressing his regret, sent a warm, handwritten note, which included the following: 'It was tragic that evil men were able to bring down the Executive for I am satisfied that it was the most worthwhile political development up here in 50 years and it was working well.'[85]

While the power-sharing Executive had been the product of extensive public *deliberation* – with the Green Paper, the White Paper and the implementing Northern Ireland Constitution Act – the Council of Ireland was to be the outcome of intensive private *negotiation*. Successful *transformismo* entails a capacity for hegemony rather than mere 'domination' (Gramsci, 1971: 57–8). This the power-sharing project achieved, while the emergence of the Council of Ireland, driven only by *Realpolitik*, did not. Faulkner (1978: 237) dismissed it as 'necessary nonsense', required to secure agreement from the SDLP and Dublin on the status of Northern Ireland, acceptance of the Royal Ulster Constabulary and cooperation on dealing with paramilitarism.

'Sunningdale' has often been incorrectly used as a shorthand for the 1974 arrangements as a whole, as in the widely-cited suggestion by the SDLP Deputy First Minister, Séamus Mallon, following the Belfast agreement, that the latter represented 'Sunningdale for slow learners'. Yet, according to Napier, the SDLP and Dublin negotiators 'did crucify Faulkner' at the Berkshire conference;[86] Devlin (1993: 252), one of the SDLP team, was later to write that he had been 'always uneasy that Faulkner, whose support was haemorrhaging dangerously, had been asked to swallow too much in one gulp at Sunningdale'. And it was precisely because the Council of Ireland could be publicly represented by one SDLP figure at the time as 'a vehicle for trundling unionists into a united Ireland' (Bew and Gillespie, 1999: 77) that it handed to unionists hostile to power-sharing the powerful electoral rallying cry 'Dublin is only a Sunningdale away' (Rees, 1985: 90). This slogan, for all its egregiousness – given the procedural constraints built into the evolution of the Council of Ireland – was given legs by the failure of the republic at the time to countenance withdrawal of the territorial claim in *Bunreacht na hEireann* (FitzGerald, 1992: 222–4).

At his meeting with Faulkner at Baldonnel, the Taoiseach said a referendum on Articles Two and Three of the constitution would be 'extremely risky', but Faulkner said developments such as the *Boland* legal challenge[87] to Sunningdale – defended only on technical terms by the Irish Government – had 'really robbed the Sunningdale supporters of credibility'. This when 'the whole concept of a Council was much more difficult to sell' to unionists than 'the concept of power sharing', as they perceived it 'as a half-way house to a united Ireland'.[88]

A further meeting between the pair, joined by other ministers and officials, took place at Hillsborough on 1 February. Faulkner again emphasised the dangers threatening Sunningdale: even supporters of the Executive opposed the Council of Ireland and though support for the agreement as a whole was increasing, there were still deep suspicions about the council. He argued it should take executive decisions but not engage (as the republic wished) in executive actions, thereby being seen as 'an embryo all-Ireland government'; rather, it should 'concentrate on practical and non-controversial matters'.[89] Faulkner followed up these assertions with a letter: 'There is already encouraging support for our Coalition Executive but the Council of Ireland is proving an obstacle which, if wrongly handled, could bring down the whole affair.'[90]

The February 1974 Westminster election, when anti-Faulkner unionist candidates assisted by first past the post won eleven out of twelve seats, worsened Faulkner's legitimacy crisis (Anderson, 1994: 146–7). In a memo for a ministerial committee meeting at the beginning of April, Rees wrote that the council had proved a 'potent and emotional issue' in the election, and he warned: 'There is no doubt that this issue has brought together moderates and extremists in the Protestant community.'[91]

Whitelaw was later to tell the author:

I think at the time the power-sharing executive of itself when it was formed and when it was working had a great deal of support. What didn't have support, particularly in the Protestant community – much wider than the narrow loyalist world who had the loyalist workers' strike – much wider in the Protestant community was fear of the Council of Ireland. Now I think in retrospect perhaps the project – not the project but the proposition – about the Council of Ireland went too far.[92]

Whitelaw added, however: 'But on the other hand it was something that was necessary for the SDLP to come into the power-sharing executive.' Yet, in turn, the SDLP's heavy investment in the council reflected the unwilling-ness of the British State to countenance the abolition of internment and, more generally, the rendering of 'security' policy consonant with human-rights obligations (Bew and Patterson, 1985: 59–60; Cunningham, 2001: 16). Rights, and social-class, issues were much more resonant with northern Catholics on the ground. A senior Dublin official reported after a visit to Stormont:

> There appears to be no doubt whatsoever among SDLP backbenchers about what they regard as the absolute necessity of the Council of Ireland with executive functions. They seem to look at it, however, not in terms of the Council for its own sake but in terms of 'that's what we negotiated and we're not going to be pushed around by Faulkner'. The Council is not a burning issue among their constituents, who continue to be concerned by internment and by violence, as well as by the conventional problems of jobs, houses and prices. I spent some time with a deputation of about fifteen people who had come from Derry to see Austin Currie about housing repairs, and found their interest in the Council of Ireland minimal.[93]

There was real, and understandable, hostility in the incoming Labour admin-istration to accepting the *bona fides* of the critics of Sunningdale, given their sectarian associations and even paramilitary roles. For example, a note by Sir John Hunt as Cabinet Secretary, approved by Wilson following a meeting with other senior ministers and Faulkner, Fitt and Napier from the Executive as the latter was collapsing, said: 'The argument is not about Sunningdale, the Council of Ireland, etc. It is basically an attempt by extremists to estab-lish an unacceptable form of neo-Fascist government.'[94] Pusillanimity on the part of the British State towards paramilitary intimidation at the onset of the strike (Fisk, 1975; Donoughue, 1987: 130–1) and the involvement of 'democratic' politicians such as Paisley alongside the paramilitaries played, moreover, key roles in its success (FitzGerald, 1992: 243, 238).

A huge irony is that calculations by officials in Dublin indicated that in its maximalist conception the Council of Ireland would have been unwork-able. In January 1974 a working group produced a bulky confidential report, 'Transfer of Functions to the Proposed Council of Ireland'.[95] A letter from Nally, the Assistant Cabinet Secretary, to Cosgrave highlighted that if all those functions which it would be technically feasible to transfer to the council were to be transferred, it would have more than 12,400 employees (including more than 6,000 civil servants), at a cost of IR£62 million per year. 'I think that the transfer of staff and functions of this scale to a Council initially is just not on,' he wrote.[96] Nally was to reflect that the Council of

Ireland had been 'far too ambitious'.[97] To put this in context, the implementation bodies established by the Belfast agreement employed 733 staff by 2006 (Coakley, Caoindealbháin and Wilson, 2007: 39).

The IDU had thus prepared a shorter list of competences, whose transfers had 'apparent and substantial' advantages and so 'could be justified in the way in which the Unionists *must* justify them – in that they will bring economic or other benefits, other than the sort of benefit we see in their tendency to encourage unity'. Ministers still needed, Nally warned, to recognise this would involve 'the transfer of substantial staff numbers and powers from their Departments'.[98] A note to the Taoiseach three days earlier with the report noted that unionists only anticipated a secretariat of 10–20: 'This means that we simply cannot work on vague hopes and aspirations to unity. We must be able to prove the concrete benefits of a transfer both to North and South.'[99]

A subsequent letter from Cosgrave to Faulkner distinguished a relatively short list of functions, which it would be 'technically possible and mutually advantageous' to transfer, from those where this might be feasible but implementation could remain through existing agencies, and those where it was neither feasible nor desirable.[100] Even then, departmental resistance, north and south, meant that Maurice Hayes, the official in the Executive responsible for identifying items for transfer, found he was being offered just 'sacrificial ewe lambs', with matching departmental bids only on the protection of wild birds (Hayes, 1995: 174). This was the single issue in half a century on which legislation proposed from the nationalist side had been passed by the Stormont Parliament.

At the end of March, Faulkner wrote to Cosgrave saying that he could not envisage early ratification of the Council of Ireland, because of the extent of opposition, notably among the bourgeois heart of his party's support: 'The most moderate and well-balanced people in the professional and business community convey the same message to us.' He warned that 'the mood of the majority, against a background of renewed violence, is such that to press ahead with this concept without modification would be to risk the gravest consequences'.[101]

In early May, Cosgrave wrote to Faulkner, stressing the importance of consensus among the Executive parties on the way ahead.[102] Faulkner replied that he was 'heartened to think we are now in general agreement about the way to proceed'.[103] And when, on 22 May, Faulkner persuaded his Executive colleagues to accept his proposals for the phasing of the Council of Ireland, Dublin said that while the Government would have preferred if it had been possible to implement all aspects of the council immediately, it understood the reasons which made this impossible.[104] But by then, with the

UWC strike a week old and the back-to-work trade-union march the previous day having failed, the political die was cast (Bew and Gillespie, 1999: 84–6).

Indeed, it was remarkable how warm the relationship between the two principals became. A letter from Cosgrave to Faulkner in August 1976, when the latter retired from political life, expressed the 'greatest regret' at this development. Cosgrave took the opportunity to 'say once again how much I valued the close and forthright working relationship we developed in the period since 1973'.[105] And when Faulkner died in a riding accident the following March, his widow, Lucy, wrote a handwritten letter to Cosgrave thanking him for his 'warm personal tribute'. She said her husband had held him 'in the highest esteem' and felt that they had 'a lot in common'.[106]

The official mood in Dublin after the collapse was sober. A discussion document entitled 'Policy on Northern Ireland' produced in the Department of the Taoiseach in June 1974 interpreted the 22 May Executive decision as marking 'for the short term at least, the abandonment of an all-Ireland dimension in the solution of the Northern Ireland problem' and acceptance in effect by the SDLP 'that the problem can be tackled in the immediate future exclusively in a Northern Ireland context'. The document contended: 'The more we involve ourselves the more material damage we will do both to this country and to the minority in the North. Any practical gain would be hard to imagine.' It favoured a short-term policy that would encourage power-sharing talks without overt intervention and '[l]eave it to Northern interests to sustain and develop the Irish dimension'.[107]

In February 1976, at a meeting between the Taoiseach and a delegation of British parliamentarians, Cosgrave was asked if there was a future for power-sharing. According to the official note, 'he felt that, perhaps, at Sunningdale, there had been excessive emphasis on the Irish dimension and that this had produced the reaction which had destroyed Sunningdale'.[108]

One Dublin official involved with Northern Ireland in both the 1970s and the 1990s reflected on how, to his surprise, more modest north–south arrangements had come to be accepted by his superiors in 1998. And he said: 'I think it's fair to say in '74 we … weren't as conscious of the fears that this would have for Unionists as we should have been. With the benefit of hindsight guys like Conor Cruise [O'Brien] and so on who raised warning doubts, they had a good bit of right on their side.'[109] Another official observed that in 1998 'the north/south arrangements were a lot tighter and were less potentially contentious and all-embracing than the 1974 ones'.[110]

Constitutional convention

The collapse of the Executive had a searing effect on the British State. During the strike, Wilson agreed with his adviser Bernard Donoughue (2005: 124) that 'a small contingencies committee' should be established, to consider 'the unmentionable' of withdrawal from Northern Ireland. The Prime Minister subsequently wrote a memorandum which represented a counsel of despair, suggesting dominion status and a five-year taper of financial support, with a 'Doomsday Scenario' of withdrawal – an abdication of responsibility which did not survive a horrified SDLP response or US hostility (Patterson, 2006: 248).

Since the only reference point was an archaic Westminsterism, rather than universal norms and a political project of reconciliation, no longer was any hegemonic project to be essayed from London because no other project could be conceived. The implicit approach was increasingly to be to accept anything which the communal politicians in Northern Ireland would be willing to endorse.

A ministerial committee meeting in mid-June 1974 was told by Rees, under the heading 'Future policy':

> There was a widespread feeling in Northern Ireland that the people should be given the opportunity of working out for themselves the future pattern of constitutional government; and it was clear that an imposed solution at this stage had no chance of acceptance. He proposed, therefore that we should make arrangements for elections to a Constitutional Assembly or Convention, charged with the task of making recommendations.

This was approved by Wilson in his summing up.[111] Rees (1985: 91) recalled:

> If in May 1974 the Whitelaw policy road was coming to an end, I would have to find something more long-term to take its place. If Sunningdale had been too orientated to London and Dublin, I would have to bring policy back to Ulster, and try to involve all the politicians there in a search for a better way of sharing power in a devolved government.

This even though he believed at the time the chances were 'not great'. As he put it more pithily in a minute to the Prime Minister two days after the strike was called off (*ibid*: 93), 'Let Ulstermen try to work it out between themselves.'

Also in June, FitzGerald met Frank Cooper, Permanent Secretary of the NIO, in Dublin. Looking ahead, Cooper said that 'the strongest discernible pattern in Northern Ireland at the moment was that "Ulstermen [sic] should be left alone to have a shot at a settlement on their own"'.[112] In September, Wilson hosted Cosgrave in London. He told him that after the UWC strike 'they had formed the view that it was unreal of the British Government to attempt to draw up another Constitution'. The conclusion had been: 'Right, you have taken the law into your own hands. If you will not accept an English [sic] solution, you must sit down and produce a set of proposals of your own.'[113]

Wilson (1979: 78) put it less bluntly in his memoirs:

While it may have seemed negative, almost defeatist, the Government inevitably had no new proposal for the future of the Province. The initiatives taken at Darlington and Sunningdale, the policies of the Heath Government and of our own had reached a dead end. No solution could be imposed from across the water. From now on we had to throw the task clearly to the Northern Ireland people themselves. Let Parliament see what they could come up with, and we would consider it – a Northern Ireland solution.

Indeed, there was no official optimism that this displacement of responsibility – however consonant with the stereotyped view that the 'Irish' should deal with their 'ancient hatreds', which had nothing really to do with the British State – would succeed. A memo by Rees to the ministerial committee in October, 'Northern Ireland: future trends of policy', admitted: 'It is idle to pretend that the Convention has a strong chance of succeeding; there must be a high likelihood of failure.' Reflecting the loss of intellectual confidence in prior policy, he wrote: 'There can be no real doubt that "power sharing" in the constitutional form which it took in the Northern Ireland Constitution Act 1973, is dead; the very use of the term is now a liability.' As to the 'Irish dimension', he asserted: 'Institutional arrangements, particularly of a symbolic nature such as a Council of Ireland, are dead.'[114]

Official desperation was reflected in a paper drafted by officials on 21 November – the day 19 people were to be killed by IRA bombs in Birmingham – for a ministerial committee four days later. 'Northern Ireland: contingency planning and policy options' presented a menu should the convention fail: 'Unilateral withdrawal', 'Unification', 'Negotiated independence', 'integration', 'imposed devolution' and 'Playing it long'. It asserted that no new pattern of 'imposed devolution' was likely to work and, as to the last scenario, it demonstrated that the stereotype of Irish irrationalism could equally favour prolonged direct rule: 'This points to perseverance with some form of direct rule to allow more time for Northern Ireland to come to its senses.'[115]

In a series of pre-convention discussion papers, the NIO published in February 1975 *The Government of Northern Ireland: A Society Divided*, which reiterated the by now familiar analysis – Westminsterism allied to an essentialist characterisation of Northern Ireland's 'difference' (NIO, 1975: 4):

In the United Kingdom, while the government is normally drawn from the elected majority, parties in office change, and power and responsibility are shared over the course of time. Thus a governing party in the United Kingdom has all the power of office for part of the time. In Northern Ireland, a governing party, drawing virtually entirely from only one part of a divided community, had all the power for all the time.

It is the nature of the division in the community which has caused the failure in Northern Ireland of institutions based, without substantial modification, on the British pattern. The population is divided – as it is not elsewhere in the United Kingdom – into two distinctive communities, each with its own heritage, culture, religious affiliations, traditions and aspirations. This division permeates the conflict of parties, and fixes the relationship between majority and minority.

Yet this was no longer associated with a confident assertion of a constitutional *desideratum*: the paper meekly affirmed that 'it is not the purpose of Government to commend any particular pattern or structure' (*ibid*: 17). Interestingly, the report had been preceded by a comparative assessment of arrangements in the Netherlands, Switzerland and Belgium. It concluded that the safeguards for minority rights in these countries could 'never be adequate to provide that genuine sense of participation by both communities which is needed in Northern Ireland' (*ibid*: 12). But this was to view the cases through a communalist lens.

Lijphart's least plausible European consociationalist case was the Netherlands: it did not have grand-coalition government but Lijphart (1977: 32) weakly claimed that a broadly-based Economic and Social Council played the same role. The point about the Netherlands, however, was that it provided a 'genuine sense of participation' for Protestants and Catholics *as individual citizens* via the range of parties which formed non-inclusive coalitions by agreement. Indeed, buried in the final annex to *The Government of Northern Ireland* were these comments (NIO, 1975: 43): in the Netherlands, there had been a 'steady removal of sectarian bitterness from the political field' and coalition governments, reflecting changing public attitudes, had been 'increasingly prepared to make common cause rather than maintain entrenched and divisive positions'. The stereotypical conceptual grid applied to Northern Ireland prevented the logical conclusion – of flexible power-sharing arrangements, based on equal citizens rather than 'communities' as the social unit – from being drawn.

The (STV) election on 1 May 1975 to the convention returned a strong phalanx of unionist MPs opposed to power-sharing, now cohering in the United Ulster Unionist Coalition (UUUC), in the name of 'British parliamentary standards'. The UUUC's 46 seats dwarfed those held by the former Executive parties, the SDLP (17 seats), Alliance (8) and the Faulkneriterump Unionist Party of Northern Ireland (5) (Elliott and Flackes, 1999: 541).

Admitting that prospects were 'gloomy', Rees (1985: 107) concluded: 'My only hope for the future was that the "Ulster nationalism" of the loyalists would grow into something capable of uniting a divided community.' However perverse this conclusion, given the limits of such schematic, 'divided community' thinking it was a tempting straw to clutch at. Even more extraordinary was the claim in the White Paper (NIO, 1974: 19) leading to the convention that there was 'a new awareness in the Protestant and Catholic working class of their real interests' – an *ouvrierist* notion which had some flawed currency at the time (Gibbon, 1977).

In March Wilson had visited Northern Ireland to announce the election date. Once again, he said the reason for the failure of past initiatives could have been 'that they had in some way been imposed on Northern Ireland from outside'. Now he was looking for 'an Ulster solution'.[116] But in private he was pessimistic: he wrote to Cosgrave in May, saying that 'we are well aware that, despite the efforts of all those who wish it well, it may not succeed'.[117] A note by the NIO to the official committee that month, on 'Possible scenarios for the next stages in Northern Ireland', wearily concluded that 'if integration or withdrawal cannot be contemplated, the only course open to us in the circumstances is a further prolonged period of direct rule'.[118] In September a 'mood of near-desperation in Stormont Castle' was reported.[119]

The convention represented a transitional methodology between the 1972–73 démarche and the 1997–98 negotiations. It preserved the idea of parliamentary norms, with an elected membership and public debates, while critically moving the venue of deliberation from Westminster to Stormont. It was supported by papers generated by the NIO, but success or failure hinged not on legislation passed at Westminster but on agreement between the parties, as at Sunningdale. It was, unsurprisingly, to end in failure, despite being given a second chance in early 1976.

There was a flurry of interest around the pragmatic solution of an 'emergency coalition', advocated by the former Unionist minister of home affairs William Craig (Patterson and Kaufmann, 2007: 176–81). But it was bound to fail because it had no articulate intellectual expression, with the mainstream unionist position to resist Cabinet power-sharing with the SDLP by calling in aid the very Westminsterist standards the UK Government insisted did not apply. The convention report, written by the unionist majority, was to stand by the Westminster model and to repeat the same complaint against power-sharing that the Stormont Cabinet had made as direct rule loomed in 1972 (Northern Ireland Constitutional Convention, 1975: 20): 'Such a constitution would provide no impetus or incentive for change with regard to political allegiances. It could freeze and fossilize the existing party structures and, in a phrase, institutionalise sectarianism in government.'

Even while the convention was in operation, a meeting of the ministerial committee in November, discussing 'Northern Ireland: future policy options', received a paper from the official committee which said: 'Our aim must be ultimately to achieve a system of government acceptable to the majority community but which the minority community will also regard as fair and as a sufficient safeguard of their interests, and which will enable us to disengage from the situation with honour.' It favoured, *faute de mieux*, direct rule associated with 'distancing' from Northern Ireland[120] – a policy Donoughue (2005: 506) had pithily defined as 'washing our hands of the consequences'. But the lack of a hegemonic strategy was reflected in dissensus around the Cabinet table. Acording to Donoughue (*ibid*: 562), while Wilson and the Home Secretary, Roy Jenkins, wanted 'separation from Britain' in the longer term, the Northern Ireland Secretary, Rees, the Chancellor, Healey, and the Foreign Secretary, Callaghan, all said 'do nothing'.

In expectation of the winding up of the convention, in February 1976 Hunt as chair of the official committee circulated a paper, 'Northern Ireland after the Convention'. He wrote: 'The choices are getting starker. They seem likely to fall into two broad categories: either the Government administers Northern Ireland directly for an indefinite period waiting for the situation there to change, or we aim deliberately to disengage.'[121]

The latter was simply not a realistic option. The Republic of Ireland department of the Foreign Office commented on Hunt's paper:

> As for the longer term, the Northern Ireland Office continue to hanker after a policy of deliberate disengagement from Northern Ireland, while recognising … that it is not an option which could be taken without a lengthy period of preparation. Probably the less said about this option, the better. Certainly, it is important for our relations with the Irish Government that no word of it should be breathed in public. The last thing that Mr Cosgrave and his Coalition Government would wish to hear at the present tricky juncture is that the British Government was contemplating a final disengagement from Northern Ireland.[122]

This had indeed become a great fear in the mind of FitzGerald (2006) – and he robustly rehearsed it, more than three decades on.[123]

The ministerial committee met again in late February and discussed the ending of the convention. Donoughue (2005: 677–8) cynically reported: 'They all agreed it had been a successful ploy in "playing for time". Now they had to find another one.' The convention was shut down on 5 March and that day Wilson met Cosgrave in London. As the Irish side recorded, Wilson's blunt position was:

> They had decided 'to hell with this – we will not keep going on with it.' Their position now was that they intended to keep their heads down for a while. They

would keep quiet and not trot out with new solutions immediately. Direct rule would continue. There would be no new initiative. If the people of Northern Ireland came together and agreed on something then the British Government would look at it.[124]

In the Commons, Rees announced the winding up of the convention at midnight and said government would concentrate on security and the economy. Devolution remained its aim, 'but it does not contemplate any new initiative for some time to come, though we will always be ready to entertain constructive and responsible ideas from those in Northern Ireland who are prepared to work together for Northern Ireland'; direct rule, he promised, would be 'positive'.[125]

In an adjournment debate later in March, the Secretary of State pointed to polling data showing 'a very large number of people in Northern Ireland accept with equanimity and even approval the idea of continued direct rule'. He promised 'good, fair and firm government' and concluded: 'There are no easy solutions to the problem of Northern Ireland. The beginning of wisdom in Northern Ireland affairs is to accept that.'[126]

A note in May to the official committee by the NIO contained an annexe on 'The future of direct rule'. In stark language, this said: 'We must seek to concentrate more attention on policies and practical issues, and less on constitutional aspirations and hobgoblins.'[127]

At a meeting of the ministerial committee that month on the same theme, Rees's position was reported thus: 'He was firmly opposed to any early new constitutional initiative in Northern Ireland ... A period of constitutional inactivity was what he advocated and what most people in Northern Ireland thought right at present. In his view this could be sustained for some time provided direct rule continued to be exercised in a positive fashion.' In discussion it was argued that devolution would await 'a new generation of politicians' and it was felt: 'The correct policy was a continuation of constructive and purposive direct rule with full emphasis on the maintenance of law and order.'[128]

In contradistinction to the premiss on which he had established the convention, Rees (1985: 282) had concluded: 'The world at large had at last been shown the falseness of the argument that Ulstermen could succeed where the English [sic] had failed.' He anticipated that there would be 'no more political talks and no initiatives' for some time (ibid: 280), and under his successor, Roy Mason, there were not. Cooper of the NIO was subsequently to reflect (Hennessy, 1989: 469) on the exhaustion of the transformist project: 'Certainly, in the early part of ... "the troubles", successive Cabinets paid a great deal of attention to Northern Ireland. But I think it then got into the "too difficult" category ... So they put it, to use an Irish phrase, "on the long finger ..."' Ironically, Mason used that very phrase in conveying his 'first thoughts' in a memo distributed to the official committee in October: 'We need not feel obliged to seek an early constitutional solution but we must remove any impression that we are deliberately putting constitutional proposals "on a long finger".'[129]

In Dublin the mood was similarly despondent: Nally, chairing a meeting of the IDU in April 1977, presented as his first conclusion 'that the policies presently being followed by the Irish and British Governments seemed unlikely to lead to any significant progress in the near future towards a political settlement in Northern Ireland'.[130] This loss of capacity for intellectual and moral leadership was associated with an unstable dalliance in London with contradictory alternatives which would have wished the problem away: withdrawal and integration (Dixon, 2001: 189). The former was advocated by Donoughue (1987: 132–3) and the Downing Street press secretary, Joe Haines (1977: 112). Haines wrote despairingly of UK ministers: 'Since the Ulster Workers' Council strike of May 1974, they have lacked the power to enforce a policy, even if they acquired one.'

Mason was uninterested in further devolution moves, merely presenting a five-point plan in 1977 which did not get off the drawing board. Humphrey Atkins, who took over after the May 1979 Election which returned the Conservatives to power, reiterated the by now conventional discourse, telling the Commons in July: 'I have to recognise, as my predecessors did, that there are two political traditions, two cultures and two sets of aspirations in Northern Ireland.'[131]

The NIO (1979: 3) published a White Paper, which yet again rehearsed the official diagnosis:

> The political divisions of the people of Northern Ireland are such that the alternation of the parties in government which is so important a feature of the Westminster system is unlikely to take place. In the Government's view it is essential for a transfer of powers to be made in a way which will take account of the interests of both parts of the community.

The paper went on to argue (*ibid.*: 8–9) that any new arrangements had to give 'appropriate recognition to the rights of both the majority and minority communities', because 'the representatives of the minority community cannot so broaden their appeal as to expect to win office by way of any future election'. Yet, apart from repeating the canard of 'majority rights', this was merely to demonstrate the constraints of the Westminsterist blinkers. For if the constitutional engineering required potential governing parties to coalesce by agreement – as with a weighted-majority requirement for executive formation – there would *always* be Catholic political figures in government, on a basis of equal citizenship with their Protestant counterparts.

The paper presented a range of options for executive formation but, in a further demonstration of the loss of hegemonic confidence, asserted (*ibid*: 10): 'None of the schemes is Her Majesty's Government's preferred.' It was willing to accept any arrangements emerging from an inter-party conference, provided these appeared likely to be 'broadly acceptable' (*ibid*: 3). These could include a progressive transfer of powers.

The conference went ahead, despite prime-ministerial pessimism (Thatcher, 1995: 387), meeting little enthusiasm.[132] It was boycotted by the Ulster Unionist Party, by now under the leadership of James Molyneaux, who hankered after the complete integration of Northern Ireland into the UK (Walker, 2004: 228–9). And the lack of commitment of the SDLP led to the replacement of its devolutionist leader, Fitt, by John Hume, who favoured moving politics on to a London–Dublin axis.

Prior Assembly

Atkins's successor, James Prior, essayed a modest echo of Rees's convention. In his memoirs, Prior (1986: 179) characterised the problem as 'a legacy of hundreds of years of the same old enmities and distrust' and offered a stereotyped, communalist account – to the extent of describing '[t]he Protestant unionists' as 'a hardworking, stubborn people, of great quality'. Within 'a few weeks of arriving', he judged that a fresh political initiative was 'urgently needed' but he conceived this in exactly the same way as his predecessors (*ibid*: 189):

> I set about talking with the democratic parties, and made it plain from the outset that there was no way in which a British Government would hand back to the people of Northern Ireland responsibility for their own affairs unless and until it could be shown that both communities were involved. In other words, we were not going to give the Unionist majority the right once more, as they had for nearly fifty years under the old Stormont legislation, to govern the Province entirely as they wished, free from any checks or conditions.

Within these terms, he admitted (*ibid*: 190): 'Predictably, therefore, we had a virtual stalemate.' At best, he felt 'rolling devolution' was 'worth a try' (*ibid*: 195). But the Cabinet committee to which he presented it 'was not enthusiastic' (*ibid*: 196) and the Prime Minister, Margaret Thatcher, his factional opponent in the Conservative Party (and sympathetic to the integrationist stance of her ally Airey Neave), was 'very much against the whole idea' (*ibid*: 196).

Again the approach was markedly *laisser faire*. An Assembly was elected in 1982, with powers to accrue devolved competences incrementally, depending on securing 70 per cent agreement – an idea originating with Brian Mawhinney, a Belfast-born Conservative MP and subsequent NIO junior minister (Bloomfield, 2007: 55).

Assisting Prior in the NIO was Lord Gowrie, who in an interview with the *Belfast Telegraph* set out the thinking behind 'rolling devolution'. He did so in mutually contradictory terms which provide another indication of the transition between the early 1970s approach and that adopted in the late 1990s. First, Gowrie reflected the view that Northern Ireland should move towards being a more normal, civic society. In this context the focus of politics becomes the 'communal contenders' (Eide, 1993) open to accommodation, led by those advocating a non-sectarian alternative:

> Elsewhere in the western world, politicians argue about the creation and distribution of wealth, and the maintenance of liberties. The moment you start talking about allegiances, you get away from that. But one of the things Prior and I have noticed is that there are small groups of politicians – some could be called radical and extreme[133] – who realise that you can't run modern economic politics along these traditional tribal or community lines. That doesn't mean that cultural identities and allegiances are not important, or that you downgrade them. They are enormously important, like the people you choose to love and marry. But they must not dominate your politics, or political life will not flourish.

Later, however, the minister anticipated the contrary thinking behind the Belfast agreement – that the role of government was to recognise the 'two communities' and their opposed 'identities'. In this perspective, the focus of attention moves to the determinedly 'ethno-nationalist' parties (Eide, 1993), even to the extent of placing paramilitaries in the vanguard:

> We are working on providing a grammar for the province by which government should be returned, step by step. But that grammar will fail – and the right sentences won't be produced – unless people face the reality that there are two permanent allegiances ... It may sound odd, but some extremists – even paramilitaries or terrorists – seem to have a clearer recognition that Ireland will have these different identities than some legitimate politicians.[134]

The Assembly following the election of October 1982 (O'Leary, Elliott and Wilford, 1988: 81–5) was boycotted by the SDLP and never really got off the ground. His project having failed, Prior drew conclusions identical to those of Rees, with another long gap ensuing before any further devolution initiative was seriously attempted (Prior, 1986: 245): 'Having grappled with the problems for three years I remain convinced that Northern Ireland is different from other parts of the Kingdom. Englishmen [sic], while they can know the situation, can very rarely understand it.'

Anglo-Irish Agreement

The Assembly was dissolved amid chaos in 1986 as unionist members pro-
tested against the Anglo-Irish Agreement concluded between London and
Dublin in November the previous year (O'Leary *et al.*, 1988: 193–4). The
agreement (Department of Foreign Affairs, 1985) was to institutionalise
the 'two communities' paradigm, with its commitment in Article Five to
'measures to recognise and accommodate the rights and identities of the two
traditions in Northern Ireland'.

Its origins lay in the nationalist boycott of the Assembly and the SDLP's
support for an alternative New Ireland Forum in Dublin. The forum, boycotted in turn by unionists, was established by the FitzGerald Government
following pressure from Hume,[135] and ran from May 1983 to May 1984. It
offered a conventional, communalist reading of the Northern Ireland problem, arguing that 'the identity of the nationalist section of the community'
had been 'effectively disregarded' since 1922 (New Ireland Forum, 1984:
§3.9). Its key conclusion (*ibid*: §4.15) was:

> So long as the legitimate rights of both unionists and nationalists are not accom-
> modated together in new political structures acceptable to both, that situation will
> continue to give rise to conflict and instability. The starting point of genuine rec-
> onciliation and dialogue is mutual recognition and acceptance of the legitimate
> rights of both.

The forum translated this conclusion into the constitutional options of a unitary Irish state, a federal Ireland or joint, British-Irish authority over Northern
Ireland. These were infamously rejected by Thatcher after a summit with
FitzGerald at Chequers in November 1984. But while this caught media
and political attention, the summit communiqué accepted the underlying
paradigm, affirming that 'the identities of both the majority and the minority communities in Northern Ireland should be recognised and respected and
reflected in the structure and processes of Northern Ireland in ways acceptable to both communities'.[136] FitzGerald claimed later that the communiqué
had accepted 'the essence of the Forum report approach' and that this was
'the common view' of Thatcher and himself, on which they were 'attempting to build'.[137]

The then Northern Ireland Secretary, Douglas Hurd, said FitzGerald had
been correct in claiming that the forum's analysis marked a 'step forward'
(Dixon, 2001: 194). His successor, present at the signing of the Anglo-Irish
Agreement, Tom King, referred back to this clause in the communiqué in his
account of its emergence.[138]

The notion was fleshed out in a text by the respected Northern Ireland
human-rights lawyers Kevin Boyle and Tom Hadden (1985: 78). This

advocated a 'new Anglo-Irish treaty' within which 'the identities and interests of both communities must be granted full and equal recognition' (*ibid*: 110). It was based on the bleak and stereotyped analysis that 'both communities have shown themselves to be remarkably resilient in maintaining their separate identities and allegiances' (*ibid*: 42) – though in a footnote the authors made the contradictory point that 'giving any single label to either community gives a false impression of unity and common purpose' (*ibid*: 53). In a later volume they came to shift paradigm towards reconciliation, contending that the 'choice' for Northern Ireland was between 'separation or sharing' (Boyle and Hadden, 1994).

The agreement disappointed its advocates. As Hadden and Boyle (1989: 73) concluded over three years later, not only had there been no real progress towards devolution but also 'it cannot seriously be argued that the Agreement has resulted in any marked improvement in the general security situation or in better intercommunal relations'. Buffeted as it was by a series of enervating disputes between London and Dublin, including over reform of the no-jury, 'Diplock' courts in Northern Ireland and extradition of paramilitary suspects from the republic, in 1988 the need for a new departure was widely perceived.

An *Economist* report in February rhetorically asked: 'Is the agreement on its last legs? There are those in both capitals who have begun to think so. But both governments know they have nothing better to put in its place.'[139] In May, the Irish Minister for Foreign Affairs, Peter Barry, said the agreement was not written in stone and could be replaced.[140] By the time of its third anniversary in November, King suggested that talks were needed with unionists to see what could be done to 'accommodate their grievances without losing the benefits of the agreement'.[141]

Conclusion

Most comparative consideration of the 1974 arrangements and those associated with the Belfast agreement has focused on the *agents* involved, or not involved. This chapter has highlighted, however, a neglected but critical *procedural* issue. The former arrangements were the product of a prolonged public debate, organised around successive iterations of official discourse, and were thus the product, at least to an extent, of a transparent and reasoned process.

There were still flaws in the constitutional design. The polarising border poll was introduced to respond to 'loyalist' pressure when the arguments in favour were poor. The human-rights underpinning was not put in place, because of peculiarly British constitutional 'traditions' and a lack of recognition of universal norms. The option of executive formation by agreement, buttressed by a secular weighted-majority safeguard – which would have allowed alternation and evolution of the political agenda beyond constitutional themes – was not developed. And STV was chosen as an electoral system on weak foundations, including illusions about its 'moderating' potential.

But the Achilles heel, as demonstrated by the archives, was the Council of Ireland. The outcome of a process of negotiation, rather than deliberation, this was recognised – unfortunately too late – to be impractical in the form envisaged. Yet the collapse of the Executive was to lead to a loss of hegemonic confidence in London and Dublin. A critical result was the progressive sidelining of structured public deliberation in favour of a passive hope that something would turn up from negotiations among the Northern Ireland parties.

The flaws, though real, were not however so substantial as those accompanying the Belfast agreement. What stands out is just how positive the experience, for all its brevity, proved to be for Executive members. But it would be wrong to look back through rose-tinted glasses. The power-sharing project was one not, primarily, of reconciliation but of *transformismo*. That was to be even more true of what became known as the 'peace process', in which ever more exigent transformist moves were to be made in a protracted roller-coaster ride of negotiations and political crises.

Notes

1 Rachel Donnelly, 'Devious "Micks" no better than "Prods"', *Irish Times* (3 January 2002).
2 Kew, CAB 134/3921, report by Central Policy Review Staff, 'Northern Ireland policy', November 1975.
3 Author's interview, 23 May 2008.
4 Kew, CAB 165/949, note by Sir Burke Trend, 'Ministerial Committee on Northern Ireland: composition and terms of reference', 8 July 1970.
5 Kew, CAB 134/3012, report of sixth meeting of Official Committee on Northern Ireland, 29 October 1971.
6 Kew, CAB 165/949, note by Sir Burke Trend, 9 July 1970.
7 Kew, CAB 165/949, Cabinet Office note, 23 October 1970.
8 Bishop St, DFA 2001/43/1278, report of first meeting of IDU, 18 June 1970.
9 Statement by the Taoiseach, 'Inter-Party Committee on the Implications of Irish Unity' (in which IDU terms of reference are mentioned *en passant*), *Dáil Debates*, vol. 260, col. 1603, 4 May 1972.
10 Bishop St, TAOIS 2002/8/415, report of IDU meeting, 14 January 1971.
11 Eamon Phoenix, 'Memo highlights alienation of Catholics', *Irish Times* (4 January 2003).

12 Kew, CAB 165/950, report of meeting at Chequers, 19 August 1971.

13 Eamonn Phoenix, 'Minority role was discussed', *Irish News* (1 January 2002).

14 Eamonn Phoenix, 'Faulkner rejected power sharing in earlier talks', *Irish Times* (3 January 2004).

15 *Hansard*, vol. 823, cols. 14–15, 22 September 1971.

16 Bishop St, TAOIS 2002/8/487, transcript of press conference by Lynch after meeting at Chequers, 6–7 September 1971.

17 *Dáil Debates*, vol. 256, col. 6, 20 October 1971.

18 *Ibid.*, col. 13.

19 Kew, CAB 134/3012, report of eighth meeting of the Official Committee on Northern Ireland, 30 November 1971.

20 Kew, CJ 4/132, note by Sir Philip Allen, 23 December 1971.

21 Kew, PREM 15/993, report by Howard Smith following meeting with Ken Bloomfield, 17 December 1971.

22 A marginal note by Trend underlines 'appointed' and significantly raises the query: '? By whom'.

23 Kew, PREM 15/993, report by Smith following meeting with Bloomfield, 17 December 1971.

24 Kew, PREM 15/993, note from Burke Trend to Robert Armstrong accompanying report by Smith, 24 December 1971.

25 Kew, PREM 15/993, note from Armstrong to Trend, 2 January 1972.

26 Bishop St, TAOIS 2003/16/472, text of Lynch's speech as party leader to FF ard fheis, 19 February 1972.

27 Kew, CAB 134/3011, report of first meeting of Ministerial Committee on Northern Ireland, 'Assessment of the situation in Northern Ireland', with memo from the Home Secretary, 9 July 1970.

28 Kew, CAB 134/3011, report of second meeting of Ministerial Committee on Northern Ireland, 13 July 1970.

29 Kew, CAB 134/3011, report of first meeting of Ministerial Committee on Northern Ireland, 'The situation in Northern Ireland', 10 March 1971.

30 Kew, CAB 165/951, note from Trend to Heath, 'Political issues: inter-party talks', 10 January 1972.

31 Kew, CAB 134/3012, report of first meeting of Official Committee on Northern Ireland, 15 March 1971.

32 Kew, CAB 134/3012, report of third meeting of Official Committee on Northern Ireland, 'The Irish problem', with a supporting Home Office memo of that title, 19 May 1971.

33 Bishop St, TAOIS 2003/16/466, report from O'Sullivan to H J McCann, secretary of the Department of Foreign Affairs, 2 August 1972.

34 Kew, CAB 128/48/3, Cabinet fifth conclusions, minute 3, 3 February 1972.

35 Kew, CAB 130/560, report of first meeting of GEN 79 committee, 9 February 1972. (GEN 79, as it is referred to in the archives, has a similar cast to the previously, and subsequently, entitled Ministerial Committee on Northern Ireland.)

36 Kew, CAB 130/560, report of second meeting of GEN 79 committee, 15 February 1972.

37 Kew, CAB 130/560, report of third meeting of GEN 79 committee, 16 February

1972.

38 Kew, CAB 130/560, report of fourth meeting of GEN 79 committee, 25 February 1972.

39 Kew, CAB 130/560, report of sixth meeting of GEN 79 committee, 2 March 1972.

40 Kew, CAB 128/48/3, Cabinet 11th conclusions, minute 4, 2 March 1972.

41 Kew, CAB 129/162/1, 'Cabinet: Northern Ireland – memo by the secretary of state for the Home Department', 3 March 1972.

42 Kew, CAB 128/48/3, Cabinet 13th conclusions, 7 March 1972.

43 'The imperative duty', *Spectator* (25 March 1972).

44 Kew, CAB 130/560, report of 12th meeting of GEN 79 committee, 23 March 1972.

45 Bishop St, TAOIS 2003/16/463, message from Lynch to Heath, 29 March 1972.

46 This included this (atheist) author; it was his first opportunity to vote and remains his only electoral abstention.

47 Robin Wilson, 'A proconsul remembers', *Fortnight*, 271 (March 1989).

48 Kew, CAB 130/560, report of 27th meeting of GEN 79 committee, 21 July 1972.

49 Kew, CAB 130/560, report of 32nd meeting of GEN 79 committee, 10 August 1972.

50 Bishop St, TAOIS 2003/16/466, record of first day of Darlington conference, conveyed to Department of the Taoiseach by British Embassy, 26 September 1972.

51 Bishop St, TAOIS 2003/16/466, record of second day of Darlington conference, 28 September 1972.

52 Bishop St, TAOIS 2003/16/466, 'Draft' document, 'Possible lines of an imposed settlement', 30 August 1972.

53 Author interview, 30 January 2008.

54 Bishop St, TAOIS 2003/16/430, text of speech by Lynch in his Cork North-West constituency, 3 November 1972.

55 Bishop St, TAOIS 2003/16/467, letter from John Peck to Lynch with proof copy, 26 October 1972.

56 Bishop St, TAOIS 2003/16/467, report by Donal O'Sullivan on discussion with Whitelaw, 27 October 1972.

57 Michael McInerney, 'Lynch envisages formula to get S.D.L.P. in talks', *Irish Times* (26 January 1972).

58 Bishop St, TAOIS 2003/16/430, text of speech by Lynch in Cork North-West, 3 November 1972.

59 Kew, CAB 130/633, report of first meeting of GEN 79 committee, 'New institutions for Northern Ireland', 15 January 1973.

60 Kew, CAB 130/633, report of third meeting of GEN 79 committee, 19 February 1973.

61 Kew, CAB 130/633, memo by Whitelaw, 'A new executive', 15 February 1973.

62 Kew, CAB 130/633, report of third meeting of GEN 79 committee, 19 February 1973.

63 Bishop St, TAOIS 2003/16/469, IDU brief on Green Paper, 19 December 1972.

64 Kew, CAB 130/633, note by Whitelaw on Council of Ireland, 15 February 1973.

65 Kew, CAB 129/168/7, note by Whitelaw to Cabinet, 26 February 1973.

66 Kew, CAB 130/633, report of fourth meeting of GEN 79, 28 February 1973.
67 Kew, CAB 129/163/10, 'Cabinet: Northern Ireland – reform and proportional representation: memorandum by the Secretary of State for Northern Ireland', 14 June 1972.
68 Author interview, 30 January 2008.
69 Bishop St, TAOIS 2004/21/466, memo to UK Government, 15 March 1973.
70 Garret FitzGerald, 'Ted Heath – one of Britain's strangest PMs', *Irish Times* (23 July 2005).
71 Bishop St, TAOIS 2004/21/466, report of meeting between FitzGerald and Whitelaw, 4 April 1973.
72 Bishop St, TAOIS 2004/21/466, report of meeting between FitzGerald and Whitelaw, 9 June 1973.
73 Bishop St, TAOIS 2004/21/466, report of meeting between FitzGerald and Heath, 15 March 1973.
74 Bishop St, TAOIS 2003/16/465, note on a range of official contacts on Northern Ireland, 6 April 1971.
75 Bishop St, TAOIS 2004/21/441, text of speech by Cosgrave to Blackrock branch of FG, 21 June 1973.
76 *Dáil Debates*, vol. 262, col. 1998, 14 July 1972.
77 Bishop St, TAOIS 2004/21/466, SDLP response to White Paper, 'Northern Ireland Constitutional Proposals: A Critique by the Social Democratic and Labour Party'.
78 See, for example, 'What the people of Ulster think', *New Society*, 6 September 1979; 'Is there another way?', *Sunday Times*, 28 June 1981; 'Poll finds majority backing for devolution', *Belfast Telegraph* (13 February 1982).
79 Kew, CAB 134/3796, note by Rees with minute of conference at Hillsborough of Executive and Irish Government ministers, 5 February 1974.
80 Author interview, 30 January 2008.
81 *Ibid.*
82 '"Hume and Garret crucified Faulkner at Sunningdale"', *Sunday Tribune* (7 October 1984).
83 For all the fraught discussion about how it should be 'balanced' in the negotiations Whitelaw conducted with the parties in late 1973, there was not a single woman in the Executive.
84 Bishop St, TAOIS 2005/7/625, note by Nally of meeting between Faulkner and Cosgrave at Baldonnel, 17 January 1974.
85 Bishop St, TAOIS 2005/7/653, letter from Faulkner's home address to Cosgrave, 26 June 1974.
86 '"Hume and Garret crucified Faulkner at Sunningdale"', *Sunday Tribune* (7 October 1984).
87 Kevin Boland, a former FF minister, contested the Sunningdale arrangements in terms of their compatibility with the constitutional claim. The High Court in Dublin ruled in January 1974 that the Government's affirmation at Sunningdale that the constitutional status of Northern Ireland would not change without majority consent in the north was a mere 'statement of policy' (Bew and Gillespie, 1999: 77).
88 Bishop St, TAOIS 2005/7/653, note of meeting on 16 January 1974 of Faulkner

and Cosgrave at Baldonnel.

89 Bishop St, TAOIS 2005/7/626, note of meeting on 1 February 1974 of Faulkner and Cosgrave at Hillsborough.

90 Bishop St, TAOIS 2005/7/626, letter from Faulkner to Cosgrave, 6 February 1974.

91 Kew, FCO 87/350, memo by Rees, 'The political situation in Northern Ireland', incorporated in brief by Republic of Ireland department of Foreign and Commonwealth Office for 1 April 1974 meeting of Ministerial Committee on Northern Ireland.

92 Robin Wilson, 'A proconsul remembers', *Fortnight*, 271 (March 1989).

93 Bishop St, TAOIS 2005/7/628, report by Sean Donlon of a meeting with the SDLP at Stormont, March 1974.

94 Kew, CAB 129/177/6, 'Northern Ireland: note by the Secretary of the Cabinet', 24 May 1974.

95 A copy is in Bishop St, TAOIS 2005/7/625.

96 Bishop St, TAOIS 2005/7/625, letter from Nally to Cosgrave, 25 January 1974.

97 Author interview, 8 January 2008.

98 Bishop St, TAOIS 2005/7/625, letter from Nally to Cosgrave (underscore in original), 25 January 1974.

99 Note from Nally to Cosgrave, enclosing 'Transfer of Functions to the Proposed Council of Ireland', 22 January 1974.

100 Bishop St, TAOIS 2005/7/625, letter from Cosgrave to Faulkner, 29 January 1974.

101 Bishop St, TAOIS 2007/7/607, letter from Faulkner to Cosgrave, 31 March 1974.

102 Bishop St, TAOIS 2005/7/630, letter from Cosgrave to Faulkner, 3 May 1974.

103 Bishop St, TAOIS 2005/7/630, letter from Faulkner to Cosgrave, 7 May 1974.

104 Bishop St, TAOIS 2005/7/630, Government Information Service statement, 22 May 1974.

105 Bishop St, TAOIS 2006/133/692, letter from Cosgrave to Faulkner, 23 August 1976.

106 Bishop St, TAOIS 2007/116/759, letter from Lucy Faulkner to Cosgrave, 30 March 1977.

107 Bishop St, TAOIS 2005/707/606, discussion paper, 'Policy on Northern Ireland', June 1974.

108 Bishop St, TAOIS 2006/133/691, note of a meeting between Cosgrave and backbench MPs with an interest in Northern Ireland, 23 February 1976.

109 Author interview, 25 January 2008.

110 Author interview, 8 January 2008.

111 Kew, CAB 134/3778, report of the Ministerial Committee on Northern Ireland, 'Future policy', 12 June 1974.

112 Bishop St, TAOIS 2005/7/631, report of a meeting between FitzGerald and Frank Cooper at Iveagh House in Dublin, 5 June 1974.

113 Bishop St, TAOIS 2007/7/607, report of a meeting between Cosgrave and Wilson in Downing Street, 11 September 1974.

114 Kew, CAB 134/3779, memo by Rees to Ministerial Committee on Northern Ireland, 22 October 1974.

115 Kew, CAB 134/3779, paper circulated by Sir John Hunt to Ministerial Committee on Northern Ireland, 'Northern Ireland: contingency planning and policy options', 21 November 1974.

116 Bishop St, TAOIS 2005/151/704, visit on 25 March 1975 by Wilson to Northern Ireland concerning Constitutional Convention.

117 Bishop St, TAOIS 2005/151/697, letter from Wilson to Cosgrave, May 1975.

118 Kew, CAB 134/3922, note by the Northern Ireland Office, 'Possible scenarios for the next stages in Northern Ireland', 8 May 1975.

119 'Rees risks truce to cut Ulster killings', *Guardian* (3 September 1975).

120 Kew, CAB 134/3921, report of eighth meeting of the Ministerial Committee on Northern Ireland, 'Northern Ireland: future policy options', 11 November 1975.

121 Kew, CAB 134/3921, paper by Hunt, 'Northern Ireland after the Convention', 20 February 1976.

122 Kew, FCO 87/542, brief from Republic of Ireland Department of Foreign and Commonwealth Office for meeting of Ministerial Committee on Northern Ireland on 26 February 1976.

123 Author interview, 27 November 2007.

124 Bishop St, TAOIS 2006/133/691, note of meeting between Cosgrave and Wilson in London, 5 March 1976.

125 *Hansard*, vol. 906, cols. 1716–17, 5 March 1976.

126 *Ibid.*, vol. 908, col. 651–2, 25 March 1976.

127 Kew, CJ 4/1421, NIO note to the Official Committee on Northern Ireland, 'Current prospects in Northern Ireland', 7 May 1976.

128 Kew, CAB 134/4039, report of the Ministerial Committee on Northern Ireland, 'The future of direct rule', 27 May 1976.

129 Kew, FCO 87/544, letter from J. D. W. Janes to Hunt and other members of Official Committee on Northern Ireland, attaching 'valedictory' note by Rees and 'first thoughts' of Mason (latter) 1 October 1976.

130 Bishop St, TAOIS 2007/116/749, draft note of IDU meeting, 20 April 1977.

131 *Hansard*, vol. 969, col. 927, 2 July 1979.

132 Colin Brown, 'Little enthusiasm for Ulster initiative', *Guardian* (26 October 1979).

133 This would appear to be a reference to the Workers' Party, a product of the 'Official' republican movement's turn towards non-sectarianism (while retaining an authoritarian conception of socialism).

134 Barry White, 'Direct rule … is very un-British. It is an absurdity that one has almost absolute power', *Belfast Telegraph* (13 January 1982). Chris Gilligan (2007) presents this 'identity talk' as it emerged in the 1980s as if it were a conscious governmental stratagem to dish republican claims to territorial 'self-determination', yet much more evident has been its unreflexive taken-for-grantedness – and, as Gowrie implied, republicans (and Protestant fundamentalists) were ultimately to prove its beneficiaries.

135 Olivia O'Leary, 'Hume to put New Ireland proposal to FitzGerald', *Irish Times* (17 February 1983).

136 'Text of Chequers communique', *Irish Times* (20 November 1984).

137 'Full text of Taoiseach's speech issued', *Irish Times* (17 May 1985).

138 NIO news release, 'Speech by Secretary of State for Northern Ireland, Rt Hon Tom King MP, to the British Irish Association: Oxford, 10 January 1986'.

139 'Gloom', *The Economist* (27 February 1988).

140 William Graham, 'Accord could be replaced says Barry', *Irish News* (18 May 1988).

141 Fergus Pyle, 'Room to meet some Unionist demands on accord – King', *Irish Times* (16 November 1988).

5

Power-sharing, Mark II

Introduction

In 1974 power-sharing governance had a consociationalist inflection, though the coalition was not 'grand' and the mutual vetoes were implicit. Yet its failure was paradoxically to lead to the ultimate adoption in 1998 of a more robustly consociationalist scheme, with the Executive Committee 'inclusive' and communal designation undergirding the 'parallel consent' test of 'cross-community support'. In Horowitz's (2002b) analysis of long-running conflicts, like Northern Ireland and Cyprus – where consociationalist arrangements have also been consistently, though entirely unsuccessfully, essayed – he notes how political inertia arises from the tendency of the international community to define a settlement in terms of the 'crumbs' left on the 'negotiating table' after this or that element, deemed unacceptable by one or other party, has been removed. This inevitably leads to a lowest-common-denominator package, rather than one which, more challengingly, seeks to promote the highest common factor.

One Dublin official with longstanding experience of Northern Ireland said that 'we were proceeding in a practical way I suppose, playing out a certain number of principles which had been laid down from early on in the process like power-sharing, like the Irish dimension and so on'.[1] Similarly, a veteran London official said:

> The strategy put negatively was to bring direct rule to an end. Put positively, it was to hand power back to local politicians, and it's operated always on the assumption you couldn't hand power back again to a one-party state, so therefore there had to be some form of sharing of power. That was the strategy and it was the strategy soon after I came in '72. It was the strategy in 1990; it was the strategy in 1997–98.[2]

Another London official said that, while the aim in the negotiation of the Belfast agreement was to achieve a 'practical' outcome, nevertheless: 'If they could agree on anything, if they'd agreed that the moon was made of blue cheese was the sort of ludicrous example I used to give, we would have been happy – sure, fine, okay.'[3] Yet the specifics of constitutional design matter: the fact that some or all of the contending parties endorse a draft accord is not a sufficient condition of success and 'some political institutions are more likely than others to successfully facilitate conflict management in divided societies' (Belmont, Mainwaring and Reynolds, *et al.*, 2002: 3).

The lowest common denominator of the Northern Ireland parties is, of course, the communalist paradigm – the 'common sense' essentialism which translates religious background automatically into political affiliation. There are other elements in the parties' make-up, such as the subordinate social democracy of the (officially) Social Democratic and Labour Party, the very mild Christian democracy of the Ulster Unionist Party and the more robust liberalism of Alliance. But particularly as the ethnonationalist parties came to dominate the political stage during the 'peace process', London and Dublin came to favour greater and greater institutionalisation of ethnicity.

It was not, of course, how this was officially articulated. On the contrary, the case was put that the two governments had recognised that the focus in 1973–74 on the 'moderates' had been misplaced and it was better to prioritise the 'extremes'. While the lesson drawn could have been to foreground the task of reconciliation, to address the polarisation of the society, the predominant conclusion was instead to pursue an ever more ambitious project of *transformismo*, engaging the 'republican movement' (in both its guises) to arrive at the Belfast agreement – and, when the post-agreement institutions collapsed, further to embrace the DUP.

A senior London official said:

> I've always believed that the end of these very polarised political issues is likely to come when the extremes do get involved. You are more likely to reach agreement when you've got the extremes moving towards each other than by expanding the centre ground because the centre ground is always worried about being outflanked by the extremes.[4]

A Dublin official concurred:

> The previous experiment, and it was a very fragile version, left obviously large amounts of grievance on either side and really just addressed the concerns of moderates within both communities. Now I think the power-sharing element has far more promise and has far more potential in terms of delivering the services needed for governance in Northern Ireland, because it is representing the full gamut of opinion in the North and doing so in a way which offers each sufficient protection.[5]

In a 2000 lecture, the then Northern Ireland secretary, Peter Mandelson (2000), said that 'Sunningdale' had been 'constructed on the supposition that the "moderate majority" in both unionist and nationalist communities would assert itself against the "extremes"'. But, he said, 'we learnt, very painfully in 1974, the centre ground did not hold'. He went on: 'The Good Friday Agreement only works because it offers every significant section of the community in Northern Ireland an opportunity to take part and the guarantee that they can never be excluded from the government of Northern Ireland.'

Unfortunately, as Mandelson's theme was proportional representation, to which in a British context he was opposed, this led him to a contradictory assertion at the outset of the same lecture: 'I do not believe that perpetual coalitions make for efficient or effective governments.' And whatever claims have been made for the fitful experience of devolved government since 1998, 'efficient' or even 'effective' have not been prominent amongst them (Wilford and Wilson, 2004, 2008a).

A senior London official defined the 1990s approach, by comparison with that of the 1970s, by its 'comprehensive' character, in two senses:

> [I]f I look at that phase of the process, '90–'98, the two key features of what we were trying to do was to have a process eventually with a comprehensive cast list, that's to say everyone who was prepared to sign up to constitutional/democratic means and renounce violence – hence the arguments about how far people really did that, what qualifications there were, but, anyway, that was the rules of the game – and the other thing was a comprehensive agenda.[6]

Yet it is a misreading to claim that 1974 failed and 1998 succeeded because the former did not embrace extremism. As Horowitz (2001) points out, constitutional engineers are vulnerable to model bias – as indicated in Chapter 3 with regard to South Africa – and historical bias, in terms of an incorrect but taken-for-granted historical narrative. What went wrong in *both* periods was that *moderate* Protestants became increasingly disaffected with the arrangements, respectively over the Council of Ireland – as demonstrated in Chapter 4 – and delay in paramilitary arms decommissioning.[7]

In autumn 2000, as the *Observer* declared that a 'majority of the unionist community no longer supports the Good Friday Agreement',[8] the *Irish Times* quoted 'an authoritative British government source' thus: 'Let's not repeat the mistakes of Sunningdale. We cannot afford to lose moderate unionism and any who think we can are fooling themselves.'[9] Yet, less than three months before the institutions collapsed in 2002, the same paper editorialised: 'Mr Trimble's natural support base has dwindled as moderate unionists have become disillusioned with the Agreement.'[10]

Equally unacknowledged in the aftermath of the renewal of devolution in 2007 was growing frustration within the *Catholic* community over the additional veto powers conceded to the DUP at St Andrews.[11] At the extreme margins, that frustration was to spill over into a murderous challenge from the 'dissident republicans' in 2009. As in 1993, if on a smaller scale, this once more led the trade union movement, with its commitment to non-sectarian solidarity, to organise peace demonstrations in March symbolising support for universal norms of non-violence (Wilford and Wilson, 2009b: 9–13). And, as before, lethal violence dropped subsequently.

This chapter looks at the Belfast agreement, with its long pre-history and long shadow. The last noted how the emphasis in the 'peace process' was on private negotiation. This was paralleled by another feature: the directly political role of ministers in articulating the case for policy in public was largely displaced by the role of officials in drafting private papers for (re)negotiation. Wolff (2005: 51) notes that successive drafts of what was to become the Belfast agreement were 'almost exclusively produced' by officials in the NIO, in co-operation with their counterparts in the republic's Department of Foreign Affairs. (As a rider, one official heavily involved with the 'strand one' negotiations said that while this section began with a draft supplied by the British side to Dublin a fortnight or so before the agreement, 'although the governments did most of the negotiations face to face, on the structures inside Northern Ireland it was the one area where there was probably a fair amount of negotiations between the SDLP and the Ulster Unionists'.)[12] Given officials will be very wary of straying from a political mandate, such a process was particularly prone to the inertia Horowitz (2002b) describes, rather than innovative policy departures – even where the evidence might have pointed in such a direction.

Yet the continuing difficulties the governments found in establishing a power-sharing system that was workable and stable came despite a powerfully favourable backdrop in public attitudes. Continuing the stream of positive polls referred to in the previous chapter, similar results were found in this period.[13] This was true even after the collapse of the institutions established by the Belfast agreement. In the two subsequent iterations of the NILT Survey, in 2002[14] and 2003,[15] respondents overwhelmingly agreed – 88 and 85 per cent respectively – with the statement 'Any Northern Ireland government should have to ensure that Protestants and Catholics share power.'

Brooke

The first serious attempt to re-establish power-sharing after the 'rolling devolution' initiative was essayed by Peter Brooke, as soon as he became Northern Ireland Secretary in July 1989. He met the unionist leaders, Molyneaux and Paisley, the following month. Next day he misquoted a paragraph in the report of the review of the Anglo-Irish Agreement by London and Dublin published that May – which referred vaguely to possible 'changes in the scope and working of the [intergovernmental] conference, consistent with the basic provisions and spirit of the agreement'[16] – to suggest that the two governments might be prepared to consider replacing the agreement with 'alternative arrangements' acceptable to the Northern Ireland parties.[17] This did not meet a hostile reaction in Dublin.[18]

In a speech in Co. Down in January 1990, Brooke claimed to detect 'common ground' among the parties. He described his 'general approach' in familiar terms: 'There can be no denying the existence of the two main traditions in Northern Ireland and the need for each to respect the other and to be given its proper place.' Despite the inherently antagonistic character of unionist and nationalist 'traditions', like his predecessors he asserted: 'Let us remember too, and I say this not only to unionists, that the different traditions can be a source of strength and vitality, rather than division and weakness.'

Brooke repeated that the British State now had no substantive project, as against the promotion of inter-party agreement. He recalled that devolution had been government policy since direct rule was introduced in 1972 but he insisted: 'The government has not prejudged the detailed form that any such political arrangements should take. Those arrangements which local politicians are expected to work they must help create.'[19]

This renewed stress on regional political ownership was superficially attractive, yet in allowing parties who could themselves be party to new governance arrangements to negotiate them it was vulnerable to the charge that they would approach the issue with a purely *cui bono?* disposition. This contradicted the key principle elucidated in Chapter 2 of the impartiality of public institutions in normal, civic societies. The only institutions likely to be negotiated were those that institutionalised the very ethnicity which underpinned the parties' political power.

The approach Brooke adopted gave individual parties implicit vetoes on any new arrangements. And later in January 1990 he was already anticipating failure: 'The matter is really for the parties. I am there to be of assistance and they may occasionally want to assign a particular role to me in order to get things moving a bit further. But unless the parties genuinely want to talk and genuinely want to seek agreement, then we are not going to get anywhere.'[20]

The absence of any fresh thinking on the part of the British State was underscored by the fact that the two key procedural innovations came from one of the protagonists – Hume, the SDLP leader. The talks were to be 'three-stranded', with the 'strands' comprising arrangements within Northern

Ireland, the north–south dimension in Ireland and relations between the two islands of Britain and Ireland. Hume was clear that this last was not between the two states called the United Kingdom and Ireland,[21] which would have legitimised partition, though that was how Brooke characterised it.[22] An associated formula, 'nothing is agreed until everything is agreed', governed relations between the discussions. Nationalists were understandably anxious that unionists would 'bank' any nationalist concessions in 'strand one' and then stonewall in 'strand two' but the risk was protracted stasis, with no incentive for the setting in train of virtuous circles of confidence-building.

Elaborating in the Commons in July 1990, Brooke affirmed a conventional stance on 'strand one' which for unionists remained the alpha and omega: 'Northern Ireland is part of the United Kingdom in national and international law. It is part of the United Kingdom because that is the clear wish of the majority of the people of Northern Ireland.' Yet he simultaneously asserted the 'two traditions' definition of the problem more congenial to nationalists: 'It is the existence in Northern Ireland of the two traditions and the two identities, one of them looking, as it is free to do, to another jurisdiction to the South with which it feels cultural and other affinities, which above all distinguishes its situation from that of other parts of this country.'[23]

Conflict over the relationship between 'strand one' and 'strand two' constitutional concerns was thus to be anticipated when the talks eventually started but was prefigured by a prolonged procedural row. Brooke's plan was for the talks to take place during a pre-arranged gap in meetings of the Intergovernmental Conference arising from the Anglo-Irish Agreement. He had hoped to announce a timetable in his July statement to Parliament, with the substantive talks getting under way in the autumn,[24] but had failed to get the agreement of Dublin. At the latter's behest, a section was deleted indicating that 'substantial progress' in the talks would be required before the Irish Government would become involved;[25] up to six drafts of the statement were rejected,[26] with the Taoiseach, Charles Haughey, insisting on a firm line.[27]

Protracted 'talks about talks' followed, focusing principally on when Dublin would enter the discussions – though a further salient was opened by the unionist leaders insisting they be designated at the talks as part of a 'United Kingdom delegation'.[28] The solution to this pettifogging sequencing dispute was to be the simple formula of 'within weeks' of the start of the talks, and in March 1991 Brooke was finally able to outline the arrangements.[29]

When they began in April, however, the talks were confined for several weeks to bilaterals with the Northern Ireland Secretary and procedural matters – notably the venue[30] and the chair[31] for the talks involving Dublin – amid increasing public exasperation, expressed by trade union and employers' organisations and the churches.[32] With the gap between conference meetings having been pre-set at ten weeks,[33] this left only a fortnight for substantive, multilateral discussions, beginning in mid-June.[34]

Brooke indicated the rationale for the whole initiative when he told the opening 'strand one' plenary that he had 'no blueprint or hidden agenda' but was there as a 'facilitator' – he admitted he had also been described as a 'sheepdog' (Bloomfield, 1998: 103). During the 'Beckettian inactivity' (*ibid.*: 91) of the talks, however, Brooke mused: 'It may have been that I misread the situation as involving slightly more flexibility than there was.'[35] The delegations quickly locked horns on the conventionally presented sovereignty issue, with the SDLP insisting on 'the right of the Irish Government to involvement in the affairs of Northern Ireland' and the unionists seeking to get rid of the Anglo-Irish Agreement which had given expression to it,[36] while unionists were also at odds with London and Dublin in seeking a postponement of the next Intergovernmental Conference.[37]

On 28 June, with the end of the talks a week away, the government presented a paper, drafted by the junior NIO minister Mawhinney, which affirmed what it called 'fundamental political realities'. These included the now familiar formulation of 'the two differing political and cultural aspirations of the protestant and catholic communities'. The paper also listed areas of purported common ground, again conventionally encompassing 'the existence of two communal identities, both needing full political recognition' (*ibid.*, 1998: 129–30). But with the 'aspirations' and 'identities' so stereotypically counterposed, Josias Cunningham of the UUP unsurprisingly described the discussions as 'talking past each other' (*ibid.*: 140). The final plenary took place on 3 July without agreement, and without the second and third 'strands' opening, though Brooke made a 'doggedly upbeat' statement to the Commons (*ibid.*: 145).[38]

Yet, despite the predictable outcome of the two-year effort, given the intellectual limits of the raw material deployed, Horowitz's (2002b) dictum was to be vindicated. Brooke insisted in Co. Tyrone that his approach represented the 'only framework'[39] and the republic's Foreign Minister, Gerry Collins, said before an Intergovernmental Conference in September that it would be 'extremely unwise to discard that particular basis' for talks.[40] As David Bloomfield (1998: 165) put it, 'the key elements of the negotiating framework which Brooke so painstakingly developed over 16 months of bilateral prenegotiation – the three-stranded structure, and the banking principle [i.e. "nothing is agreed until everything is agreed"] among them – proved their longevity and their durability through the subsequent rounds of negotiations'.

Brooke tried to revive the talks in early 1992, but was unable to secure agreement among the parties, with the SDLP failing to secure from the UUP a commitment that talks would continue after the then looming Westminster election.[41] The *Independent* editorialised: 'The Northern Ireland scene is at the moment characterised by a complete bankruptcy of ideas.'[42]

Mayhew

Following the April election, and with a new Conservative Northern Ireland Secretary, Sir Patrick Mayhew, talks were initiated once more. But immediately the difficulties were apparent. Announcing after a meeting in London a further three-month gap in the Intergovernmental Conference, in which the talks would take place, Mayhew and his Dublin counterpart disagreed over the anticipated constitutional outcome. The Northern Ireland Secretary said he believed the talks would end with Northern Ireland still an integral part of the UK, whereas the Minister for Foreign Affairs insisted that the 1920 Government of Ireland Act partitioning Ireland was on the table.[43] Mayhew hardly inspired confidence when he said that it would not be 'the end of the world' if the talks failed and direct rule continued.[44]

In this context, a leaked[45] SDLP proposal[46] for quasi-joint authority raised tensions. It was studiously even-handed, with a new Northern Ireland executive to have three directly elected members plus three appointees – the appointments by the administrations in London, Dublin and Brussels. But it was an elitist project: the envisaged assembly would be only consultative and the executive would not be accountable to it. It thus flew in the face of the tendency among Protestants to identify democracy, as discussed in Chapter 6, with the dimension of 'popular control' (International IDEA, 2002: 13). The UUP said it was 'undemocratic, far worse than the present arrangements for direct rule'.[47]

The UUP, meanwhile, in its submission of the same day,[48] envisaged devolution operating via a committee system, with chairs proportionately distributed by d'Hondt – the position it was to retain until the eleventh hour in 1998. The SDLP found this 'a severe disappointment' – recognising its failure to address the 'political equality' element of democracy (*ibid.*) – but was bluntly told by the UUP: 'It was a fact of life that if a majority reached a view that would be decisive.'[49] The SDLP also could not see – and in this it foreshadowed the failure of the Executive appointed after the Belfast agreement to operate in a 'joined-up' way (Wilford, 2006) – how the UUP proposal would provide for coordination across government: 'Effective strategic planning would be impossible.'[50]

A compromise proposal did however emerge from a sub-committee of the strand one 'business committee', which took from the SDLP proposal the idea of a directly-elected, three-member supervisory 'panel' without the appointees. This also envisaged weighted-majority protections on sensitive issues – a 70 per cent threshold was suggested – against ethnic Protestant dominance in a legislative assembly.[51] The compromise was 'commended' by the UK government representatives in a subsequent plenary but 'reservations' were now expressed by the SDLP – Hume had not been a member of the sub-committee – 'because the question of identities had not been adequately addressed'.[52]

In line with the New Ireland Forum analysis, Dublin stuck to the position of recognising the 'two traditions' while failing to address their irreconcilability. Thus, when the talks eventually moved, after much unionist foot-dragging, to 'strand two', the Tánaiste, John Wilson, read a leaked,[53] 27-page submission which asserted that the outcome could not be 'a result where one tradition has the substance of its aspiration and the other merely a theoretical acknowledgment of legitimacy',[54] and Dublin rejected the idea that articles two and three of *Bunreacht na hEireann* constituted a 'territorial claim'.[55]

Nor, as in 1974, were matters helped by London's hostility to entrenching human-rights norms. The SDLP had sought a bill of rights which would protect those detained or harassed by the police or army, but the UK Government again resisted the idea that a bill could go beyond non-discrimination in transferred matters.[56]

The talks ended without the 'heads of agreement' the UK Government had been hoping to secure.[57] Mayhew reiterated the mantra affirming the loss of any hegemonic project. The Government did not have 'a blueprint of its own', he said. 'The people of Northern Ireland have to take that decision for themselves.'[58] During a visit to Co. Tyrone in April 1993, Major, the prime minister, anticipated an 'early start to further talks'[59] but it was to take four more years. The *Guardian* commented: 'It is hard not to feel a renewed sense of desperation in British policy over Northern Ireland at present.'[60]

Major's predecessor Heath argued for a more proactive approach, reminiscent of the hegemonic thrust of the early 1970s. He wrote in *The Times*: 'It is now up to the British government to take the lead, and to drive through a constitutional reform programme which provides a power-sharing system acceptable to moderates in both communities, and to London and Dublin.'[61] But the political will was no longer there.

'Peace process'

Even though the talks process had his procedural stamp upon it, Hume was unenthusiastic throughout. He repeatedly questioned the willingness of unionists, for example in his address to the twentieth annual conference of the SDLP, to 'make political progress'.[62] He said devolution had failed and pointed to sectarian abuse by unionists of district councils they controlled as an indication it would fail again.[63]

Hume's uninterest in the talks was cast in a fresh light with the revelation of the 'Hume-Adams' initiative[64] with the SF President, which caused considerable tensions within the SDLP, notably between Hume and his deputy, Séamus Mallon.[65] In turn, this lifted a veil on a subterranean political initiative launched around 1986 when Charles Haughey was Taoiseach, with his amanuensis, Martin Mansergh,[66] acting as intermediary with the 'republican movement' (Moloney, 2002).

This initiative developed under Haughey's successor, Reynolds,[67] and was to be given the somewhat vainglorious title of the 'peace process'. It involved no effort to boost reconciliation in Ireland across the unionist–nationalist divide but instead sought to trade an end to republican violence for a powerful political 'nationalist consensus'. Its defining feature was an attempt to shift the emphasis in the constitutional argument from the unionist focus on the majority 'consent' principle to the nationalist ideal of 'self-determination' for the island as a whole, thereby tilting the ethnic balance in the direction of the latter (O'Donnell, 2007).

Yet, in the context of the incoherence of the concept of self-determination highlighted in Chapter 2, Hannum (1992: 31) took the very example of these islands to show its arbitrary implications:

> Within the two islands of Ireland and the United Kingdom, for example, the relevant 'self' might be both islands taken together, despite their ethnic mix of English, Scots, Welsh and Irish; each island separately, despite the mix of the first three in Great Britain and of Irish and Scots in Ireland; the existing states; or each ethnic/geographic group, which would include at least the four separate entities of England, Scotland, Wales, and Ireland, with from zero to two additional groups (Irish Catholics and 'British' Protestants) in Northern Ireland. Citing a multitude of equally irreducible situations will not advance our thinking very far, but their existence does underscore the fact that the assertion by the 'self' of political auto-determination almost necessarily entails the denial of auto-determination to another 'self' which may be either greater or smaller; as is the case with minorities, selves can never be wholly eliminated.

One long-serving Dublin official recalled the Taoiseach's stance, and its implications, in this way:

> Albert Reynolds' approach in the early '90s was very much 'you start with peace and then you try to build structures', where I suppose in 1974 it was 'you build structures which will help to bring peace'. Albert Reynolds' approach was 'who

is afraid of peace?' and I must say at the time I was quite worried because I thought you couldn't get peace without structures which would maintain it, and in a way that proved correct for a long time: it took a long, long time. Having got the ceasefires or whatever they were, it took a long time to put structures in place to get the agreement and to get the decommissioning of arms and all the things. And even now it's only just this year [2007] that really we have the thing.[68]

This inevitably put the two governments at loggerheads. London remained committed to the position that a political accommodation in Northern Ireland should be sought to render politically-motivated violence unsustainable – encapsulated in the comment by the junior NIO minister Michael Ancram that there was no point in 'having peace without a political settlement'[69] – yet it had lost any clear compass as to what that entailed. Meanwhile, Dublin had effectively defined the conflict (tautologically) as the product of paramilitarism, which implied that the political problem would be relatively simply solved via the constitutionalisation of the 'republican movement' once IRA violence was ended. As Reynolds put it, 'If you don't get the people who are carrying out the violence to cease the violence then I don't think that political talks are going to bring an end to violence.'[70] From then on the 'talks' (London) and 'peace' (Dublin) 'processes' diverged and only reconverged during the conclusion of the Belfast agreement.

That inexorably shifted the focus from seeking to build the political centre to establishing the terms on which the IRA would be prepared to countenance a ceasefire. The FG leader, Bruton, warned this meant paramilitaries had a veto on political agreement.[71] More fundamentally, Morrow of the Community Relations Council contended, this was to store up long-term difficulties by privileging short-term considerations:

[T]he fundamental issue is reconciliation, it's to unwind antagonism, it is not to end violence on the surface because actually the obsession with violence on the surface, while an important, clearly a critical, issue, can lead to a whole set of short-termist responses which ultimately get you into blackmail and bribery constructions, as opposed to transformation of situations which turn it into something which might have had a chance of being stable on the basis of viable social relations.[72]

Reconciliation would thus, even more than in the 1970s, take a back seat to *Realpolitik*. One Dublin official, who was involved with the Forum for Peace and Reconciliation of 1995–96, said that the agreement 'will have failed if it doesn't bring about some form of reconciliation', and he stressed that Dublin had endorsed the successful pressure by the Women's Coalition for commitments in the Belfast agreement on victims and reconciliation, integrated education and mixed housing. He said, however:

> We did a lot of stuff, but I think it's fair to say that it didn't permeate around those of our colleagues who were involved more in what you might call the hard core of reaching an agreement ... They didn't share those experiences with us and I don't think the whole thing around victims, reconciliation, all that complex of stuff did loom as large for them and they probably regarded it as a footnote, without being too hard on them ... But the reality is the thing was dominated, there was a heavy focus on getting Sinn Féin on board.[73]

Polarisation was thus, as an unintended consequence, to be the corollary of the 'peace' that eventually ensued. Brubaker's (1996) triadic account of similar ethnonational conflicts in east and central Europe helps explain this apparent paradox. Such conflicts, as in ex-Yugoslavia, tend to be pursued by political protagonists deeming to represent:

- a 'nationalising majority' within the jurisdiction, seeking to ensure the state reflects 'their' ethos;
- a 'national minority' within the same jurisdiction, seeking to secure minority rights;
- a 'homeland nationalism' in the neighbouring jurisdiction, supporting the secession of the 'national minority'.

Conversely, de-escalating such a conflict entails:

- ensuring the state acts impartially towards all citizens, seeking only to elicit a 'constitutional patriotism';
- guaranteeing the rights of members of minority communities, in such a way as to blur the majority/minority divide over time;
- supporting from the neighbouring state both of the above, while eschewing territorial claims or secessionist impulses.

The problem with the position of Dublin in this context was that by asserting rather than consigning to history a homeland-nationalism stance it was fuelling division in Northern Ireland and perversely encouraging members of the majority community there to remain in the 'nationalising' (i.e. unionist) camp.

Catherine O'Donnell (2007) has convincingly demonstrated the invalidity of the view that London and Dublin were on all fours as neutral brokers of a settlement from the time of the Anglo-Irish Agreement. It was only, she shows, in the run-up to the Belfast agreement that this became so. This is confirmed in the account by the then Northern Ireland Secretary, Mo Mowlam (2002: 208), who reflected as the two governments struggled to prepare the draft agreement – on, as it happens, 1 April 1998 – that it was 'back to the old problem' that the Irish Government 'were basically nationalists, closer now to Sinn Féin than the SDLP', whereas the UK Government was 'still working effectively as neutrals'. It also chimes with the argument by Catherine Frost (2006) that the republic still has some way to go to arrive at a 'post-nationalist' political destiny.

Meantime, joint statements between the two governments were awkward compromises. In the aftermath of the failure of the Mayhew talks, London and Dublin had begun working privately on 'Elements of a Shared Understanding'. During the spring and summer of 1993, a Liaison Group of officials pursued this project.[74] Following 'Hume-Adams', this meant seeking to square the circle of 'self-determination' and 'consent' and establishing the conditions for the involvement of the 'republican movement' in talks.

Addressing the UN General Assembly, the Tánaiste, Dick Spring, called for 'radical and innovative compromise as part of a new accommodation'. Yet he immediately reaffirmed the longstanding position: 'Compromise does not mean asking either of the two traditions in Northern Ireland to modify its fundamental beliefs or to suppress its objectives. It does mean asking each tradition to recognise that the other deserves equal respect and must be accommodated on equal terms.'[75]

A painful process of negotiation, still deadlocked at a late stage,[76] led to the Joint Declaration (Department of Foreign Affairs, 1993) concluded between the two governments in mid-December 1993 after last-minute prime-ministerial phone calls.[77] The product of more than twenty drafts, one official reportedly described it as 'the most badly-written declaration in Anglo-Irish history ... and that's saying something'.[78] Two hours were spent discussing the relative merits of a full stop or colon in one paragraph, and even then it was only resolved through the premiers' conversations.[79]

The two key sentences in the declaration, representing the positions of each government, placed 'self-determination' and 'consent' side by side but did not – could not – resolve the contradictions between them. First, with regard to London: 'The British Government agree that it is for the people of the island of Ireland alone, by agreement between the two parts respectively, to exercise their right of self-determination on the basis of consent, freely and concurrently given, North and South, to bring about a united Ireland, if that is their wish.' Secondly, the Taoiseach affirmed 'on behalf of the Irish Government, that the democratic right of self-determination by the people of Ireland as a whole must be achieved and exercised with and subject to the agreement and consent of a majority of the people of Northern Ireland and must, consistent with justice and equity, respect the democratic dignity and the civil rights and religious liberties of both communities'.

The authors of the Joint Declaration had agonised over the phraseology available within the paradigm of 'methodological nationalism' (Beck, 2006: 2) but had failed to transcend it. In a long trajectory from the Anglo-

Irish Agreement, the idea that identity could be a question of affinity rather than ascription, with the associated possibility of overlapping rather than inherently antagonistic identities and the possibility of cross-communal solidarities, had been rendered officially inconceivable.

Mayhew hoped talks could be renewed on just such a basis. Addressing a dining club in Trinity College Dublin, he said the declaration 'complements and underpins the talks process'. The latter entailed as 'a democratic imperative' that Northern Ireland should have 'local political institutions'. But there could be 'no going back to a system which has the allegiance of, and is supported by, only one part of the community' and a comprehensive agreement would have to take account of 'the aspirations and concerns of both traditions'.[80]

After months of ostensibly demanding 'clarification' of its contents, the 'republican movement' formally rejected the declaration, as it had done privately from the outset.[81] But to sustain the 'nationalist consensus' in the face of public pressure (see Chapter 2) it nevertheless established the IRA ceasefire of August 1994, while work was going on between officials on a new intergovernmental statement, fleshing out the Joint Declaration with proposed constitutional changes.

It had emerged in April that this 'roadmap' document was envisaged, with the suggestion that it would be published after the European elections the following June.[82] But again there were intergovernmental tensions as 'sources confirmed that officials were involved in a slow, painstaking process where everything was being teased out word by word'.[83] Inevitably, the issues fell on the 'self-determination' versus 'consent' axis, notably the extent of the north–south bodies linking the two jurisdictions and the linked fates of the territorial claim in the republic's constitution and the Government of Ireland Act.[84]

The document finally emerged in February 1995 as *A New Framework for Agreement* (Department of Foreign Affairs, 1995). Constrained by the essentialist lexicon of the 'two traditions', it set out four 'guiding principles':

- 'the principle of self-determination', as set out in the Joint Declaration;
- resort only to 'exclusively democratic, peaceful means' to achieve agreement;
- 'the consent of the governed', as essential to the stability of any political arrangement;
- promotion of 'the rights and identities of both traditions' and 'parity of esteem' as the basis of any such arrangement.

These 'principles' were, however, by no means self-evident. While non-

144

violence is a universal norm, the reflections in Chapter 2 on nationalism showed that 'self-determination' and the 'consent' principle were derived from a dated understanding of the world, organised around 'nation-states' conceived as if homogeneous, in complete possession of 'sovereignty' and interacting in a relationship of pure exteriority. It also showed that 'parity of esteem' was based on the fading multiculturalist approach to managing cultural diversity – which assumed that 'communities' themselves also had a homogeneous character, and that these could coexist side by side, as mutually exclusive ethnic pillars, under a state which gave them official recognition – represented as if this were the only alternative to assimilation.

It now further becomes clear that the two ideas of 'self-determination' and 'parity of esteem' were also *themselves in contradiction*. For 'self-determination' presumes – as Lansing, if not Wilson, immediately recognised – a territory occupied by a unified 'people' entitled democratically to control it, rather than a space whose territorial boundaries are contested by its communally defined denizens vying for 'parity of esteem'. And there cannot be equality, by definition, between unionism and nationalism as constitutional goals, since they are defined by their mutual antagonism in a zero-sum, 'sovereignty' game.

Thus was set up an unending argument in which unionists would privilege *their* version of 'self-determination' – the 'consent' claim – while nationalists foregrounded self-determination by *their* lights and, meantime, the case for 'parity of esteem'. It was to continue up to the Belfast agreement – and beyond.

Belfast agreement

In the aftermath of the IRA ceasefire, a British government source indicated that substantive inter-party talks were two years off.[85] And so it was to prove, with the prolonged impasse over the decommissioning of IRA weapons issuing in the end of the ceasefire with the bomb in the City of London in February 1996, in the wake of the report on decommissioning by an international commission chaired by Mitchell (The International Body, 1996).

A decision by London and Dublin to set a starting date for talks of 10 June that year quickly followed. As Mitchell (1999: 42) commented drily, 'After a year and a half of seeming inaction, the governments had acted decisively within three weeks of an IRA bomb in London.' The former US Senate majority leader was approached by London and Dublin in May, to ask him if he would chair the talks now envisaged. He asked how long they would take and was told (*ibid.*: 45): 'You should easily be home by Christmas.'

Unionists however objected to Mitchell being given an overall chairing role when the talks were convened the following month.[86] Months of unproductive discussion followed, and Mitchell (1999: 45) was eventually to ask himself, in a manner akin to Brooke's earlier reflection: 'Had I been deluding myself, over these many months, when I thought that progress was possible?'

'New' Labour came to power in May 1997, but how novel it was to be was a matter of contention, with Stuart Hall (2003) suggesting its 'double shuffle' entailed only a partial break with its Conservative predecessor. And while much attention focused on the willingness of the Labour Government to engage with SF, were the IRA ceasefire to be renewed, the party manifesto was entirely conventional on Northern Ireland, in its usage of 'the two traditions' and reference to 'a new political settlement which can command the support of both' (Cunningham, 2001: 117).

Blair quickly set a deadline of May 1998 for an outcome to the talks – a measure 'of crucial significance' in persuading Mitchell (1999: 103) to remain.[87] Despite the entry of SF in September, following the renewal of the IRA ceasefire in July, the UUP remained engaged while other unionist parties walked away. Yet when a meeting in December descended into acrimony over the always neuralgic issue of when 'strand two' discussions could move to Dublin and London, Mitchell reflected despairingly (*ibid.*: 126):

> We had been meeting for a year and a half. For hundreds and hundreds of hours I had listened to the same arguments, over and over again. Very little had been accomplished. It had taken two months to get an understanding on the rules to be followed once the negotiations began. Then it took another two months to get agreement on a preliminary agenda. Then we had tried for fourteen more months to get an accord on a detailed final agenda. We couldn't even get that, and we were about to adjourn for the Christmas break.

Mowlam appreciated that the conventional impasse once again loomed. In January 1998, three days before the publication of the document on 'heads of agreement' advanced by the two capitals, she said north–south institutions comprised 'one of the hardest issues'. It had been envisaged that the draft would be ready by mid-December but Dublin was understood to have resisted the London version, arguing that the emphasis on devolution and a possible council of the islands was not sufficiently 'balanced' by north–south relationships.[88] Meanwhile, in a reprise of the fateful 1974 debates, in phone conversations between Trimble, the UUP leader, and Blair the former resisted use of the word 'executive' in reference to any north–south bodies emerging.[89]

When the 'Propositions on Heads of Agreement' document was published,[90] a 'North–South ministerial council' was presented as independent of a new 'intergovernmental council' embracing the jurisdictions of the islands, but the E-word was eschewed in favour of reference to north–south 'implementation bodies'. In by now routinised language, the document envisaged provision 'to safeguard the rights of both communities in Northern Ireland' through a bill of rights which would *inter alia* respect 'the cultural identity and ethos of both communities'.

The brief formulation on the north–south and 'east–west' aspects of any agreement did not resolve the conundrum. The impasse moved on to whether the north–south council would be accountable to the devolved assembly, also envisaged as part of the settlement, or would derive its authority from legislation by Westminster and the Oireachtas – unionists favouring the first, nationalists the second.[91] Trimble envisaged the council being a 'voluntary' mechanism for discussion of mutual interests, while Hume saw it as a vehicle for dynamic cooperation between heads of departments in the assembly and ministers in Dublin.[92]

Working back from the need to achieve progress before the 'marching season', Mitchell concluded that agreement was required by the symbolically important target of Easter, rather than May, so that referendums could take place that month, with an election to a new assembly in June. He agreed a schedule with the parties so that he could hit a deadline of midnight on Thursday 9 April, with the proviso that discussions could go into the next day or weekend (Mitchell, 1999: 143–5).

Mitchell had hoped to have the first draft for the parties on the previous Friday evening. His staff worked from a version submitted by Dublin and London, but the schedule was disrupted by what Ahern publicly admitted were 'large disagreements' over the north–south institutions (*ibid.*: 153).[93] Mitchell secured the agreement of the two premiers that they would supply him with a 'strand two' draft by the Sunday evening (*ibid.*: 156), though they were unable first to resolve their divergence on the relationship between the north–south bodies and the assembly.[94] And, when it arrived, Mitchell recognised 'instantly' that it would be unacceptable to unionists because of the independence envisaged for the bodies – only to discover that the governments, particularly Dublin, were insisting that not a word be changed (*ibid.*: 159–60).

It was after midnight on the Tuesday morning before Mitchell was able to present the complete draft to the parties, as London and Dublin had spent all Monday haggling over what would be listed in three strand-two annexes as areas to fall under the consultative, harmonising and executive remit of the north–south council (*ibid.*: 163–4) – language identical to that surrounding the Council of Ireland in 1974. Trimble threatened to bring the talks to an end unless Blair was willing to entertain 'fundamental change' and Mitchell told Mowlam that the two premiers would have to renegotiate strand two (*ibid.*: 166): 'Otherwise these talks are over.'

The problem was that Dublin's position had been to get SF into talks and then negotiate an agreement which all nationalists would support, recognising SF would not back anything that represented 'backsliding' from the framework document (*ibid.*: 167). Ahern however agreed to a scaling back, as had Blair, with movement on the release of paramilitary prisoners providing a trade-off for SF (*ibid.*: 171). This breach of rule-of-law norms was, though, to represent by far the largest factor behind 'no' votes in the referendum on the agreement, according to a poll taken in the run-up.[95]

As a result of the focus on strand two, strand one – the key section on governance arrangements for Northern Ireland – was dealt with in just one long night of haggling between the UUP and SDLP on the eve of the agreement. Mitchell covers this in a mere paragraph (*ibid.*: 176), without even mentioning the agreed method of formation of the power-sharing executive – never mind discussing its merits or demerits in tackling sectarian antagonism or even as a system of governance.

The British and Irish talks sherpas could only look on in frustration. A senior London official complained: 'We spent months on rules and procedures, we spent months dancing around decommissioning, but the amount of time they actually spent in a room on the details of the devolved institutions was pitiful, and that was very important stuff and very difficult stuff.'[96] A Dublin counterpart said:

> We didn't get beyond the principles for a long, long time … And then the negotiating process thereafter was extremely pressurised, chaotic and febrile. And so, despite the fact that we'd had, on and off, the guts of two years of a talks process, despite all of that, the level of real open engagement across the major issues was quite small, so perhaps it isn't surprising that there are still so many issues.[97]

The UUP had maintained, as in 1992, that there would be no executive requiring power-sharing, but rather proportionately distributed committee chairs who would also act as heads of the associated departments.[98] The SDLP, meanwhile, sought a veto by insisting, as Mallon put it, that 'no decision would ever be taken again on substantive matters without the consent of the nationalist community', while also endorsing cabinet government with collective responsibility[99] – though the first implied indefinite entrenchment of the 'two communities' division, translated into the communal designation and 'parallel consent' provisions of the agreement, while the second implied mutuality in government and an associated expectation that the executive parties would carry a cross-sectarian majority in the assembly.

It was collective responsibility, so quickly agreed in 1974, which was to be the victim of this contradiction. Its moving spirit then (Bloomfield, 2007: 255) was to write: 'This system was patently unstable and incoherent. It staggered into repeated brief or more prolonged suspensions. Any sense of common purpose was lacking.'

Indeed, 'common purpose' was not much in evidence to those privy to the Castle Buildings talks, chaotic in their final days (Powell, 2008: 92–106). One Dublin official said: 'To be quite honest with you ... I thought during most of the negotiations they were going to fail.'[100] Another was even more sober:

> I think we felt that we had one shot in terms of getting it right and that if this shot failed – and I remember myself, on the Good Friday itself, I and one or two others were seriously looking at a possible failure. On the morning of Good Friday, it looked as if the unionists were in internal disarray and so it was quite reasonable to imagine that this shot had failed. In fact I think our sense was that it would be several years before we could try again.[101]

Only a rushed side letter from Blair to Trimble (Powell, 2008: 105), which promised to review, six months after the establishment of the assembly, the arrangements on the exclusion of SF from office if the IRA did not decommission – a promise Blair proved unable or unwilling to fulfil – secured the support of most of the UUP delegation for the agreement on 10 April (Mitchell, 1999: 179–80). According to Trimble's successor, Sir Reg Empey, the party had been within five minutes of walking out.[102] Trimble's concern had been that the mutual-veto arrangements agreed under strand one required him to secure the support of the SDLP for the exclusion of SF – a veto he sought, unsuccessfully, to bypass.

The predominantly consociationalist character of the agreement did not come about by deliberate design. One Dublin official said it had not been the product of a 'political treatise' but what he, significantly, described as 'pretty much common sense'.[103] Another said: 'I don't recall that we had any particular, as it were, academic inspiration for what we were doing apart from the more technical stuff in relation to the d'Hondt formula.'[104] And one who in retirement gives political science lectures said that, outside of the New Ireland Forum and Forum for Peace and Reconciliation, 'it's fair to say that we did proceed very much without the benefit of academic input or intellectual input or study of models or anything like that. Anything that we did around those things over the years was always very pragmatic and very focused on the practicalities of it and didn't really come from a kind of deep theoretical perspective or anything like that.'[105]

More light-heartedly, a London official said: 'Do you want me to say

the word I can never pronounce, consociative? I think we were fairly pragmatic actually.'[106] And yet another Dublin figure commented, laughing as
he spoke:

> To be quite frank with you, I probably first heard the phrase – this is how far
> apart negotiators live from political scientists – I probably first heard the phrase
> 'consociationalism' long after the Good Friday agreement was signed. I would
> be reasonably certain that would apply to the vast majority, if not all, of my
> colleagues. And I'm somebody here actually who tries to stay in touch with
> academia, conferences, etc, etc … If you ask anyone 'did you have the consocia-
> tionalist model in mind?' most of them would probably ask you 'what?'[107]

But would this be a viable structure of governance? The outcome of the
strand-one negotiations – reminiscent of the horse designed by committee
that became a camel – was that the respective UUP and SDLP propositions
were spatchcocked into a power-sharing executive with the positions distributed by d'Hondt. Treated in a remarkably cavalier way by the responsible
UK minister, Mowlam (2002: 219) – again devoting just one paragraph to it
in her memoirs – this was, and remains, unique in the world.

Executive seats are allocated to the parties to fill in successive iterations
of the d'Hondt rule, and ministers are entitled to run their departments
independently. A year on from the agreement, FitzGerald warned that 'the
structure of the executive will differ from that of normal cabinet government in ways that are likely to test seriously the mutual trust and confidence
of its members', since it did not 'seem that collective cabinet responsibility
will apply to this executive in the manner to which we are accustomed in
this and many other democratic states'.[108] Asked on the day of devolution
in December 1999 whether the system of government would work, Mallon,
the Deputy First Minister, 'shook his head, coughed and sighed: "We just
don't know."'[109]

Several months later, Michael Laver (2000) argued that far from the
method of executive formation encouraging parties to appreciate the need
to transcend partisanship, it instilled the belief that departments were party
'fiefdoms'. Indeed, by the final months of the first devolved Executive in
2002, one former minister confided that relations around the Executive table
at Stormont were 'poisonous' (Wilford, Wilson and Claussen, 2007: 123).

In Scotland the devolved Government has only one permanent secretary,
who chairs a civil service Strategic Board[110] and whose department provides the Cabinet Secretariat,[111] but in Northern Ireland each of the ten (plus
Office of the First Minister and Deputy First Minister (OFMDFM)) departments has its own PS, on a par with the OFMDFM Permanent Secretary
who is also head of the civil service. This means any departmental head can

countermand the head of OFMDFM if he or she secures ministerial cover, militating against concerted action and compounding the risks of unilateralism by ministers whose autonomy was enshrined in the agreement (NIO, 1998: 7). A Belfast official said of the 1999–2002 Executive:

> Permanent secretaries didn't want to lose their autonomy. I mean head of the Civil Service is probably the least powerful position in the Civil Service, a sort of plenipotentiary-type role, and he can huff and puff and do all he wants but even when direct rule happened, where you got more authority, it didn't work ... And here to some extent in '98, and I suspect now, the Executive is seen mostly as a discussion forum as opposed to a decision-making forum.[112]

In the aftermath of the failed attempt to establish an executive in July 1999, Blair said: 'Only one thing remains outstanding: it is a matter of trust.' He warned that if politicians did not 'learn to build trust' then 'normal politics in Northern Ireland' would 'never take root'.[113] Yet the premiss of the architecture of the agreement, the perpetual absence of trust, prevented just this scenario emerging.

The comments of two very experienced officials were instructive. On Dublin's side, one said:

> I don't think it can work with a background of mistrust. I think that the only way an executive can work is with collective responsibility or consensus. You cannot have a minister going off on his own and making policy with which his friends in the Executive don't agree. That would destroy the Executive if they don't look after it properly, and developments must move in that direction. Every successful government must work on the basis of collegiality – of collective responsibility – and that implies a lot of trust.[114]

This concern about the absence of collegiality, compounded by the inability of voters to 'turf the scoundrels out', was echoed by a London official:

> There are a number of anxieties associated with the structure that was adopted in 1998. One of them is how successful any government will be, constructed in effect as a forced coalition, at taking clear decisions, giving a clear direction, giving a lead, if you like, to the community. Secondly, where different government departments are in the hands of different political parties, but operating across those departments rather than within the silos of the departments is important in order to achieve good government, there's an anxiety about whether people will be able to work together, because that's not so much the day-to-day business of ministers themselves [but] whether their civil servants will feel that they've got permission from their own political leadership to do business with each other in a really constructive fashion. And, thirdly, one wonders quite how it will feel as a democracy for the voters when you come to a general election where four of the five political parties that have got, as it were, measurable existence, the Alliance being the fifth, are in government, and if you are feeling a bit disenchanted with government

– and one knows that a lot of democracies experience voting against the government rather than for another alternative positively – I mean what options have you got in that situation in this particular form of democracy?[115]

This was a strong concern among the reconciliation practitioners interviewed for this book. David Stevens of the Corrymeela Community noted the contradictions to which the agreement led:

Well, there's a deep paradox in this: you have a deeply distrustful society and for government to work people have to trust each other. So, we have partly institutionalised distrust and yet we're expecting these people to work together ... D'Hondt is a classic way round distrust and, looking back on it, we shouldn't have gone for this designation thing. We should have gone for certain weighted majorities for certain things and this designation thing will return to haunt us.[116]

Morrow expressed the associated concern about setting constitutional arrangements in stone. He said of power-sharing that 'it's a bit like the withering away of a [socialist] state [in Lenin's theory]: at what point does it wither, do you not need it?'[117]

Because the agreement emerged from what one London official described as 'textual barter',[118] as Katie Hanlon of Ballynafeigh Community Development Association put it, 'there was nothing aspirational in the Belfast agreement about the society that we could become'.[119] Cunningham (2001: 163) concludes his three-decades-long survey of UK Government policy on Northern Ireland by denying that the agreement would herald a 'post-national' politics in which ideas of 'nation, state and identity' were critically interrogated. An adviser to Trimble, Steven King, concurred that the agreement made no attempt to transform Northern Ireland.[120] But if neither unionists nor nationalists were being asked to question their political faith, 'progress' would be something that still took them in opposite directions (Duffy and Dingley, 1999: 50).

The difficulty with the received wisdom about the 'politics of recognition' and the agreement was identified, presciently, by the former Taoiseach Bruton when it was first debated in the Dáil. He pointed out while the parties to the agreement had said their objective was 'reconciliation and rapprochement', the aspirations by which their representatives were to designate themselves in the Assembly were 'opposite and not reconcilable terms'.[121] And in an echo of Habermas's concept of constitutional patriotism, discussed in Chapter 2, he warned: 'The Agreement itself, and the institutions it creates, must become the focus of a new loyalty. The Agreement is not the means to some other end. It must be seen as an end itself. Unless that happens, every ordinary proposal from one side will be seen by the other through a prism of suspicion.'[122]

The interviews for this book betrayed significant unease, particular among serving or former Dublin officials, about the consequences for Northern Ireland as a society. These were, after all, individuals who knew the north well and were closer to the experience of what it was like to live under the dispensations the two governments had sought to establish. One senior official, notably invoking the discourse of citizenship, said:

> Like a lot of people, I think I would like as a citizen to see changes to the current model. I doubt if the current model is in the long term democratically desirable or a particularly good idea from an administrative point of view either. In other words, I would like to see the possibility in due course of evolution towards some form of voluntary coalition arrangement, with some sort of cross-community threshold of support. That would seem to me to make more sense in terms of accountability, the possibility of change, avoidance of entrenchment of interests and corruption years down the road. I've no idea as to when that might be.[123]

In 1993, the Opsahl Commission recommended a consociationalist scheme for Northern Ireland, based on mutual communal vetoes (Pollak, 1993: 112). The report was unexpectedly sharply criticised by the Irish political scientist Peter Mair, whose academic interest ranges over western European politics. Mair highlighted the strong thrust of the submissions to Opsahl, which had been called 'a citizens' inquiry',[124] focusing for once not on the supposed needs of the two governments but on the 'democratic deficit' facing those who lived in Northern Ireland.

This popular aspiration for democracy could however be denied, he argued, by the commissioners' proposal. The permanent scheme envisaged 'would effectively institutionalise the core divide between the two communities, and constitute a built-in barrier against any realignment of politics along other lines, however unlikely this might seem'. It would represent 'government by cartel, in which political actors would enjoy a guarantee of office, and in which there would exist no possibility for alternation in power'. He forecast 'a largely unaccountable government, which could neither be rewarded nor punished by the voters, and hence might well be unresponsive to them'. It might thus, he concluded, 'simply replace one form of democratic deficit with another'.[125]

Implementation

Destabilisingly, the agreement was subjected not just to different readings by Trimble and Adams but mutually exclusive interpretations, as they faced special conferences of their party members the weekend after Easter 1998. The UUP leader told the Ulster Unionist Council in Belfast: 'We are not on a road to a United Ireland.'[126] The SF President meanwhile told a special ard fheis in Dublin that the process was transitional to a united Ireland, the union having been 'severely weakened' (Mowlam, 2002: 230). Bríd Rodgers of the SDLP was to affirm that the agreement was not a settlement: 'It is an agreement to disagree.'[127]

Securing legitimacy for the agreement was thus not straightforward. Ironically, the abandonment of secular democratic majoritarianism in official discourse meant that the anticipated big majority in favour in the May 1998 referendum was not enough: battle was joined for the support of Protestants specifically, with the implication that if only a minority supported the agreement its legitimacy was in doubt.

A joint appearance by Trimble and Hume on stage at a U2 concert, organised as part of the 'yes' campaign – a civil-society effort which substituted for any effective cross-party push – countermanded the image of Adams and McGuinness with their fists in the air at another SF ard fheis which greeted the Balcombe Street IRA gang, released by the Northern Ireland Secretary for the occasion. But it was still nip and tuck, with concerns about the fudge on decommissioning, the release of prisoners and police restructuring leading to only a narrow majority of Protestants voting yes – even after three prime-ministerial visits to drum up support.

The STV election to the 108-seat Assembly the following month showed a similar pattern. The political news was good for the SDLP, with twenty-four seats, and SF, with eighteen. But the UUP secured only twenty-eight, leaving Trimble vulnerable on a 'cross-community' vote in the Assembly, as the DUP, the United Kingdom Unionist Party and three anti-agreement independents also totalled twenty-eight seats. Alliance won six, the Women's Coalition two and the Progressive Unionist Party two, but there was extremely little transfer activity across the sectarian divide, in what was possibly the most communal voting pattern since the reintroduction of PR in 1973 (Elliott, 2001).

The opposing communal claims about the agreement could only lead to recurrent impasses over ethnic-barometer issues. Policing and decommissioning had been left (along with a review of criminal justice) to independent commissions. Both touched on the key question associated with the state in a Weberian discourse of sovereignty: who would hold a monopoly of legitimate force in Northern Ireland – representatives of the British state with Protestant inflection, as unionists wished, or an alternative Irish (though to all intents northern Catholic) counter-state, the IRA? It proved impossible in the aftermath of the agreement to resolve these issues within that conventional discourse.

When the report on policing by the commission led by the former Hong Kong governor Chris Patten (Independent Commission on Policing, 1999) was published in September 1999, Trimble was apoplectic. His hostility to the Patten recommendations focused on the loss of the word 'Royal' from the title of the new service and the dropping of the crown from the cap badge. Disputing the claim that this reflected the nationalist belief that the agreement delivered 'parity of esteem', he said of the commission chair: 'The entirely false argument he bought is the argument that, somehow, Northern Ireland is to be a neutral state, with neutrality between Britishness and Irishness ... It is one sovereignty, and the symbols of British sovereignty flow from that.'[128]

The failure of the IRA, like its loyalist counterparts, to begin decommissioning following the agreement had not held up the election of Trimble and Mallon as respectively First Minister and Deputy First Minister at the first meeting of the Assembly in July 1998, with SF abstaining.[129] But Trimble made it plain he would not countenance the establishment of the Executive Committee by the running of d'Hondt at the second session in September.[130] This meant the implicit deadline of 31 October in the Belfast agreement for the transfer of power was not met, at the cost of a growing rift between Trimble and Mallon.[131] This was an important contrast with 1974, when the personal relationship between Faulkner and Fitt had so impressed Bloomfield – ensuring that the political centre could not hold in the face of the centrifugal pressures upon it.

An intergovernmental joint declaration[132] at Hillsborough in April 1999, following discussions with the parties, failed to attract the support of the 'republican movement', obliging the latter as it did to begin decommissioning within one month of the nomination of ministers by d'Hondt and with the confirmation of those nominations by the Assembly effectively conditional on this 'obligation' being met. Correspondingly, another declaration in July, again following days of negotiations, was rejected by Trimble, as it envisaged government being formed and power devolved in advance of the beginning of decommissioning.[133] A charade followed as d'Hondt was run at Stormont, in the absence of unionists, leading to a notional nationalist administration[134] and the resignation of Mallon as Deputy First Minister.[135] Mowlam issued a standing order that morning requiring that the executive include at least three unionists and three nationalists.

The prolonged impasse was to mean devolution was not established until December 1999,[136] following a review which Mitchell was reluctantly brought back to chair.[137] When decommissioning still did not eventuate, devolution was suspended by Mandelson, by then Northern Ireland Secretary, following the introduction of a suspensory act. This provoked a clash with Dublin, in effect between a political culture emphasising 'parliamentary sovereignty' and one based on a written constitution (into which the agreement had been incorporated).[138]

Initiating a further review, Mandelson described the agreement's advantage thus: 'Northern Ireland finally had a truly representative executive, with members drawn from all the major pro-agreement parties and including two of its opponents. It underlines that there are no second-class citizens in Northern Ireland any more ...'[139] Yet, as discussed in Chapter 2, equality of citizenship regardless of identity is secured by a project of constitutional tolerance. It does not imply that government be by grand coalition, including members – as with the DUP – unwilling to manifest 'constitutional patriotism'. The two premiers, Blair and Ahern, were unable to agree terms for such a review.[140]

After yet more negotiations at Hillsborough, the IRA announced in May that it would 'initiate a process that will completely and verifiably put IRA arms beyond use', in the context of the 'full implementation' of commitments by London and Dublin,[141] and the UUP agreed to renew power-sharing with SF later that month. Against the backdrop of unionist divisions over the re-establishment of devolution, Mandelson said in Fermanagh:

> Some of those who attack the Belfast Agreement play on the fears that it will diminish their particular identity or undermine their tradition. It does no such thing. The agreement does not promote neutrality – it cherishes diversity. It secures British identity while recognising and respecting nationalists and republicans who do not share that identity.[142]

Yet the Executive could thus not resolve the issue of the flying of the Union flag over departmental buildings – the SF ministers were refusing to do so on twenty-one designated days – at its first meeting following the second transfer of power. The UUP Minister for Culture, Arts and Leisure, Michael McGimpsey – the party having chosen the small department in the d'Hondt selection to stop republicans taking it later – said refusal to allow the flag to fly denied the consent principle.[143] The SF Minister of Education, McGuinness, said his party wanted to promote mutual respect for the flags and emblems of both traditions: if the British flag was to fly from government buildings, so should the Tricolour.[144] Mandelson pleased neither side by reducing the designated days to seventeen – including by the exclusion of 12 July.[145]

As Chapter 2 also demonstrated, the only way cultural diversity can be democratically managed is *if the state is indeed neutral*. The widespread legitimacy secured by the Police Service of Northern Ireland, with even SF feeling obliged to support it in January 2007, was to testify to the validity of the neutrality approach: the party could not dismiss the universal norm of the rule of law as long as policing was consistent with human rights.

Only thus can denizens who are not legally citizens, or not only citizens, of the state in which they find themselves enjoy equality with those who are. As also indicated earlier, the Belfast agreement was contradictory in its consociationalist versus integrative aspects. And an integrative element, in contrast to the communalist premises of the consent principle and 'parity of esteem' in the section on 'constitutional issues', was the provision there that individuals could freely choose to be 'Irish or British, or both' (NIO, 1998: 2). In the subsequent decade, 400,000 Irish passports were issued to Northern Ireland residents.[146] Interestingly, when the 2007 NILT survey asked the Moreno (1998) question on identity, used to elucidate overlapping national affiliations in Spain, 58 per cent volunteered some combination of 'Britishness' and 'Irishness' rather than exclusive identities.[147]

In a context where every constitutional element was always up for negotiation – and so renegotiation – the official pursuit of *Realpolitik*, rather than compliance with universal norms, meant that what could have been a framework providing security and the potential, over time, for the reconciliation of a divided society became the subject of a never-ending *process* of ethnonationalist attrition. Nowhere was this more evident than on the decommissioning of paramilitary weapons, which – unlike in Macedonia, as we have seen – precipitated the serial suspensions of the institutions arising from the agreement, including the prolonged hiatus after the resignation by the First Minister, Trimble, in July 2001. Unionists insisted, including in abortive talks sponsored by the two governments at Weston Park that month,[148] that the republican leadership bring about decommissioning, but the latter claimed this was a 'collective responsibility'.[149]

Following an undefined act of IRA decommissioning, devolution was only restored the following November by some Alliance and Women's Coalition assembly members temporarily redesignating from 'other', so that Trimble had sufficient 'unionist' support to secure his re-election via the 'parallel consent' procedure – an event soured by a televised brawl in the foyer of Parliament Buildings, behind Trimble and his new Deputy First Minister partner, Mark Durkan (Wilford and Wilson, 2001).

In disowning 'doctrine, whether of Left or Right', 'New' Labour's 1997 manifesto had also stressed (Driver and Martell, 1998: 180): 'What matters is what works.' Toynbee and Walker (2001: 210) succinctly summarise the implications of this instrumentalism for the region: 'Labour's policy became maximizing concessions to the IRA/Sinn Féin for the sake of minimum levels of violence while hoping the Unionists would stay on board.'

Thus in 2000, as Trimble had faced one of a series of knife-edge votes within the Ulster Unionist Council on the agreement, Blair said that while the situation was 'by no means perfect', nevertheless 'we have paramilitary organisations being brought gradually into the proper democratic process', which it would be 'a big mistake' to give up.[150] This assertion implied the suborning of the rule of law for political objectives, with considerable potential to pollute the 'democratic process' itself.

For historical reasons related to the contested legitimacy of the Northern Ireland State and its opponents, the rule of law has a strong resonance in the Protestant community, in the same manner as the discourse of human rights has a powerful appeal among Catholics (Dawson, 2007). It was fundamentally a sense that the Belfast agreement was undermining the rule of law – as against the concern about north–south arrangements that had proved fatal in 1974 – that progressively alienated moderate Protestants from it, in a manner Blair failed to comprehend. It was thus the arrest of three republicans involved in cooperation with FARC guerrillas in Colombia, a break-in by the IRA at Castlereagh police station, and, finally, revelations of an IRA spy ring at Stormont that were to precipitate the collapse of the Executive in October 2002 (Wilford and Wilson, 2003).

And it was for this reason that successive agreements between London and Dublin on the way forward, articulated in their joint declaration of May 2003[151] and putative 'comprehensive agreement' of December 2004,[152] failed to entice the unionist parties back into government. Meantime, the DUP had overtaken the UUP at the November 2003 Assembly election, when it was clear no Executive would subsequently be formed following the breakdown of pre-election, inter-party 'choreography' over IRA decommissioning.[153] It was only when Blair and Ahern changed tack and made a raft of concessions to the DUP in the St Andrews Agreement in 2006 that devolution was, after a fashion, restored.

Asked in March 2007 if he thought Blair had made any mistakes in Northern Ireland, Mandelson said:

> One problem with Tony's fundamental view of Northern Ireland is that the process is the policy ... So even if you don't have any other policy and don't know what the process is going to achieve – the fact that the process is still happening is the bare minimum policy that you need.[154]

Mandelson contended that 'to keep the process on track' Blair had entertained a series of concessions to republicans which had undermined Protestant support for the agreement. This was echoed by a senior London official, who said of the 1998 side letter to Trimble on decommissioning:

> I do find it quite remarkable that leaders of the Ulster Unionist Party, by which I do mean Jim Molyneaux as well as David Trimble, kept buying three-legged horses from doubtful horse dealers, namely British prime ministers. Why did they do that? They did. There we are. It's commonly said of Tony Blair, and I'm

thinking here of the Iraq inquiry, he does mean what he says when he says it to you, he really is sincere in that sense, but he is an existentialist, he lives in the moment.[155]

According to Mallon, this also stimulated the political polarisation which has marked the post-agreement years. In his swansong Westminster speech in March 2005, he referred to the Prime Minister – following Mark Antony's acid description of Brutus – as 'an honourable man', accusing Blair of 'acting in bad faith' and making 'under-the-table deals' with SF.[156] In excoriating remarks two years later, he reflected:

> In reality his whole strategy in terms of resolution of the Northern Ireland problem – I don't use the term peace process – was 'who do I buy and who do I sell'? … It was strategy. You had [Blair's chief of staff Jonathan] Powell and others in Dublin who had decided that to make this work you had to dispense with middle unionism and middle nationalism.[157]

Powell professed not to understand Mallon's concern. Speaking to the same newspaper a year later, as it serialised his reflections, he said: 'Seamus Mallon's complaint is that we talked to Sinn Féin because they had the guns. My answer to that is: yes and your point is?'[158] Yet in the book he admits (Powell, 2008: 210), as the executive collapsed in 2002, that the Belfast agreement had been implemented 'by giving a few concessions to one side and then a few to the other' and that the 'peace process' had been 'morally undermined' and 'no longer seemed to be based on principle'. Reviewing the book, the former US envoy to Northern Ireland Mitchell Reiss (2008) expressed his unease:

> The peace process devolved into an exercise in serial concessions and indulgences, first to Sinn Fein and later the DUP. Moderate political voices from both traditions, such as John Hume and David Trimble, were shouted down and marginalized by more polarizing figures. The British government never seemed to ask why any of the Northern Ireland political parties would ever agree on closure when they could always expect to extract more concessions at the next meeting or after the next crisis.[159]

A Belfast official agreed that 'the middle ground was treated appallingly by both governments in the aftermath of '98'.[160] Dixon (2001: 306–7) also concurs with Mallon. Criticising the 'secrecy, manipulation and choreography by the political elites in Britain and Ireland of party and public opinion' on Northern Ireland, he warns: 'Manipulation and deceit eats into the culture of democracy, producing cynicism and resentment.'

This elite-dominated politics, recurrently distracted by constitutional debates or proxies for them, had limited purchase on quotidian experiences. With 'bread-and-butter' issues subordinated, the devolved institutions were markedly less successful than their Scottish and Welsh counterparts in generating innovative policies, tailored to regional requirements or preferences (Hazell, 2003: 290–1). In February 2002, the Alliance leader, David Ford, claimed that of twenty-three bills passed by the Assembly only two had shown 'substantial original input' from Northern Ireland ministers, as against legislating for 'parity' with Westminster or 'minor housekeeping'[161] – an analysis endorsed after the institutions collapsed by the former principal adviser to the First Minister.[162] The NILT survey had identified health as the public's priority for action by the Assembly at the onset of devolution,[163] but analysing performance in this domain Scott Greer (2004: 160) reflected: 'The institutional design of devolution lures parties into government by granting them great executive powers in their departments and little formal accountability to the Assembly or the public, and then makes collective decisions nearly impossible.'

The legacy

Four years on from the Belfast agreement, the then Northern Ireland Secretary, John Reid, spoke of 'looking beyond the agreement' and of 'building a society free from the burden of history and liberated from the curse of sectarianism'.[164] It was wishful thinking. As the UK Government admitted in its policy framework on 'community relations', *A Shared Future* (OFMDFM, 2005: 15), 'Continued sectarianism, racism, inter[-] and intra[-]community conflict act as a cancer that eats at the body of Northern Ireland.' By early 2006, in the wake of the ignominious withdrawal by Reid's successor, Peter Hain, of legislation planned to meet a longstanding republican demand for the return of 'on the runs' – itself testimony to the moral hazard engendered by the 'peace process' – the *Guardian* was complaining of 'deepening collective failure in Northern Ireland'.[165]

In October that year, a yet further intergovernmental agreement was essayed, the St Andrews Agreement,[166] associated with talks at the famous golf course. But not only did none of the Northern Ireland parties give it their *imprimatur*, laying political timebombs when commitments, including on the devolution of policing and justice by May 2008 and legislation on the Irish language, were not kept – matters critical to the confidence of SF in the arrangements. In addition, the Prime Minister – his place in history beckoning – was willing to concede to the DUP a *de facto* power of veto in renewed devolved arrangements in the small print of the agreement (Wilford and Wilson, 2007a: 21–7).

The key provision, which the DUP had described as 'mutually assured obstruction' (Powell, 2008: 252), allowed any three ministers opposed to a ministerial initiative to insist the issue be put to a test of 'cross-community' support within the Executive. Any party with 3 ministers out of 12 (including the First Minister and the Deputy First Minister) would almost certainly be in a strong enough position to ensure a blocking power in a 'parallel consent' vote, by being the stronger party in its own communal bloc, even if its ethnic partner took a different view.

Ken Bloomfield (2007: 257) warned presciently: 'If controversial action can be blocked by an absence of cross-community support, may there not be a real and ever-present risk of deadlock as between factions hitherto deeply suspicious of each other?' And, indeed, the DUP sought this power to avoid a repeat of the unilateral decision by the SF Education Minister, Martin McGuinness, just before the 2002 collapse of the Executive, to abolish the '11-plus' transfer test.

Devolution was finally restored, after more than one deadline set by London had been abandoned (Wilford and Wilson, 2007a), in May 2007, the requisite Assembly election having taken place in March. This was not because the DUP had become persuaded of the merits of *A Shared Future*, but was in part because of the accommodation to the rule of law by the republican movement represented by the formal ending of the IRA campaign in July 2005 (Wilford and Wilson, 2006) and the acceptance of the legitimacy of the PSNI (and Garda Síochána) by SF in January 2007 (Wilford and Wilson, 2007b).

What had made the difference, after the republican movement had held so firmly to the legitimacy of its counter-state for so long? In addition to police reform, a new factor was the courageous campaign by the sisters of Robert McCartney, slayed by IRA members outside a central Belfast bar in January 2005, which threatened the substantial support republicans had garnered from the 'international community', particularly the US administration.

This turnaround was symbolised by a meeting between the dead man's sisters and the President, George W. Bush, on St Patrick's Day in March 2005, while Adams was no longer facing an open door on Pennsylvania Avenue (Wilford and Wilson, 2005). The door had been closed by Reiss, who had decided to 'put down some red lines' in the wake of the IRA's robbery of the Northern Bank headquarters in Belfast in December 2004 and the McCartney murder.[167] According to Powell (2008: 267), whose memoir recounts endless prior prevarications by the republican leadership, these events meant they 'had no choice but to dissolve the IRA unilaterally if they wanted to pursue a political future'.

Another factor affecting the DUP, as the party leader, Paisley, made clear, was fear that London and Dublin would move to joint authority over Northern Ireland by default (Wilford and Wilson, 2007c). In April 2006 in

Armagh, Blair and Ahern had warned that if devolution was not restored then they would begin 'detailed work on British-Irish partnership arrangements'.[168] Yet, in a manner typical of the instability of the commitment to such a *dirigiste* position over the preceding decades, in the aftermath of the collapse of devolution Blair had ruled out just such a suggestion: 'If there is an impasse as a result of confusion over paramilitary and political ends, there is no way I can cook up some solution with the Irish Government and slam it down.'[169]

St Andrews provided Blair with a Stormont swansong on 8 May 2007, before he announced his resignation two days later – too late, inevitably, to save his party from a mauling in the Scottish and Welsh elections. Hain, his Northern Ireland Secretary, meanwhile told MPs colourfully that they had 'witnessed the final resolution of what has been, for centuries, the most intractable source of political conflict in Europe' and shown 'the world how a "shared future" can emerge from even the most bitterly divided and blood-stricken past', with its 'age-old enmities' (Wilford and Wilson, 2007c: 12). But, as indicated in Chapter 2, *A Shared Future* was quickly shelved by the new administration. St Andrews had merely changed the balance of ethnic forces rather than establishing a new rapprochement – as became evident in the parties' dispositions towards their Programme for Government (Northern Ireland Executive, 2008).

The second programme of the first devolved Executive had been rejected in the Assembly in March 2001 by the DUP, despite having two ministers in government.[170] By contrast, while the DUP was very keen to claim authorship over the first programme of the second devolved term, SF produced a response to the draft version as if the party did not have three ministers, and the SDLP voted against the programme in the Assembly with its minister tactfully absent (Wilford and Wilson, 2008c: 18). The programme was also a much flimsier document than its two predecessors in the 1999–2002 devolved term (Northern Ireland Executive, 2000; 2001), reflecting the uninterest of the 'ethnonationalist' parties in policy issues as against ethnic protagonism.

SF retained its commitment to a united Ireland, preferably in advance of the centenary of the 1916 rising, yet the declining credibility of this project in the face of DUP obstruction, and mounting southern indifference, led to a stream of defections by party councillors.[171] Arguably the administration's central figure, Robinson, initially Finance Minister and then First Minister (and DUP leader), repeatedly made clear his preference for a 'voluntary' coalition.[172] This and serial vetoes by the DUP, most importantly on the prompt devolution of policing and justice, led to SF blocking the holding of Executive meetings from mid-June 2008, shortly after Robinson took over the first-ministerial reins. As the principal parties met in early September to address their wide agenda of differences, Adams accurately captured the wider Catholic mood (Wilford and Wilson, 2008d: 18): 'There's a real concern out there and it isn't just among republicans that elements within the DUP are not reconciled to the concept of partnership government.'

Little more than a year on from the renewal of devolution relationships among ministers were already being described, respectively by a republican and a unionist columnist, as 'dour and dire' and characterised by 'personal loathing' (*ibid.*: 27). Tony McCusker was an assistant secretary in OFMDFM during the previous period of devolution and, while accepting that the former Executive was 'not without controversy', he argued that the principal parties, the UUP and SDLP, had 'a better appreciation of the fundamental rules'. Against a backdrop of a new government dominated by political advisers and with professional civil servants marginalised, McCusker complained: 'What stands out above all is the virtual absence of any perception of collective Executive responsibility.'[173] As another Belfast official complained in exasperation, 'I don't care what the Executive do; I wish they would just do something!'[174]

Government gradually ground to a halt just as the global crisis of financial capitalism struck the region, reflected in spiralling fuel prices and the credit squeeze – and with the future of transfer to post-primary schools still unresolved, as the abolition of the '11-plus' loomed in 2009 (Wilford and Wilson, 2008d). Already in May, 72 per cent of respondents to a *Belfast Telegraph* poll said a year of renewed devolution had made no difference to their lives (Wilford and Wilson, 2008c: 30). In October, the paper accused the politicians of 'living in some parallel province … unaware of the rising anger'.[175]

With business activity falling and unemployment mounting, particularly in construction, the business community lobbied hard for ministers to return to the Executive table, concerned that public contracts were being held up. The regional director of the Confederation of British Industry complained (Wilford and Wilson, 2009a: 17): 'We are in the midst of the world's worst financial crisis and our politicians cannot agree to sit down and talk to each other.'

In November, with fully 60 papers having accumulated in the Executive Committee's in-tray for signing-off, a deal was cobbled together – though no date for the devolution of policing and justice was secured by SF – which allowed the Executive to reconvene (*ibid.*: 18). But its most distinguishing feature was inertness. Though the Belfast agreement stipulated that the Programme for Government be iterated annually, the 2008 programme was not revised in 2009 despite the dramatic economic deterioration, leading to working-class protests at mounting job losses (Wilford and Wilson, 2009b: 49–50). The middle class voted with its feet too, as most grammar schools defied the SF education minister's opposition to academic selection by signing up for unregulated transfer tests (*ibid.*: 61). The 2008 NILT survey indicated falling trust in the DUP and SF as ministers and declining public belief in the achievements of devolution (Dowds, 2009: 30).

The UUP and SDLP ministers increasingly behaved as an opposition within the Government, casting doubt alongside Alliance on the viability of the DUP-SF relationship. The UUP leader, Sir Reg Empey, described it as 'a coalition of the "ourselves alone" parties, based on the principle of sustaining the divisions and building newer and higher walls' (Wilford and Wilson, 2009a: 12).

The nature of relationships between the two dominant Executive parties was indicated by the campaign for the European Parliament election in June 2009 by the DUP candidate, Diane Dodds, who said it would be a 'disaster' if SF topped the STV poll.[176] She faced an awkward challenge from a party defector, the incumbent MEP Jim Allister – who accused his former colleagues of sharing power with republicans at Stormont by day while attacking them on the doorsteps by night. Bairbre de Brún of SF duly secured most first-preference votes, sending shock waves through the DUP.[177]

Under the arrangements arising from the Belfast agreement, the First Minister and Deputy First Minister were elected together by the Assembly. This was inspired by the joint appearance of the then UUP leader, Trimble, and Mallon of the SDLP in Poyntzpass, Co Armagh, to console the families of two victims – one Catholic, one Protestant – of a loyalist shooting a month earlier. The St Andrews Agreement in entrenching communalism removed this element of partnership, with the First Minister to be nominated by the largest party in the largest Assembly 'designation' and the Deputy First Minister by the largest party in the next largest designation, without a legitimising election. But this was subsequently tweaked in the legislation implementing St Andrews – ironically at the behest of the DUP – to ensure the First Minister would be nominated by the largest Assembly party regardless.[178] The 2009 European Parliament election thus presented a polarising scenario for future Assembly polls, with a political 'arms race' to secure the First Minister position for republicans or to stop just such an outcome. While this scenario would be highly beneficial electorally for the DUP and SF in suppressing intracommunal pluralism, it would provide the worst possible context for genuine post-election power-sharing involving those two parties.

Relationships between them, and in particular the two principals, Robinson and McGuinness, meanwhile continued to deteriorate. In September 2009, the latter accused the former of living in 'Disneyland' for offering unilateral proposals to replace communal designation in the Assembly by a weighted-majority safeguard. While a recurrent theme of this book, this was yet again a case of a non-sectarian proposition nullified by its partisan unionist source.[179] Foot-dragging by the DUP on devolution of policing and justice added to the friction, drawing the Prime Minister, Gordon Brown, reluctantly back into repeated meetings to broker a deal. And SF unilaterally published its proposed version of the successor to *A Shared Future*, indicating it saw no role for further dialogue with the DUP on the matter.

Greatest unease was expressed by interviewees for this book about the, to them unanticipated, endurance – even exacerbation – of deep sectarian division in Northern Ireland. Sir Patrick Mayhew reflected: 'I think it's very disappointing that there are today far more solid blocks on one side or another than when I began.'[180] And a senior London official said: 'One of the depressing things, I think, about Northern Ireland in the last ten or fifteen years is that it's become, if anything, more segregated. During this period of great political progress the population has differentiated itself more even than before.' He was very reluctant to link this causally to aspects of the agreement which institutionalised ethnicity, but he did express moral queasiness about the way communalism had been privileged over citizenship: 'Something you could criticise the agreement for is entrenching the nationalist/unionist [divide]. The plaintive cry in the middle, "I'm a citizen of Northern Ireland, I'm not a nationalist or a unionist, so where do I fit in?", is quite a powerful point.'[181]

The 'peace walls' represent the most visible manifestation of this absence of reconciliation. A Dublin official contended:

> I don't think that anybody who was involved in constructing the Good Friday agreement ever expected that frankly we would still have these fences in place ten years after the agreement, and indeed even in some cases more going up. The idea was not to reinforce sectarianism but was to give people the confidence to move away from it, that they would not have to set up high fences because the political institutions would guarantee that protection.[182]

Another Dublin official, with a strong personal commitment to reconciliation, was particularly vexed:

> I find it very disturbing that there are fences needed. I hear this kind of thing about the growth of sectarianism in Northern Ireland, the growth of separation and I react with a degree of startling realisation sometimes when I hear things about 47 peace fences or whatever number, I find it hard to believe that ... I find that whole thing very depressing and I don't fully understand the phenomenon ... I don't think we would have thought that that would happen when we were talking about reconciliation and all that kind of thing.[183]

If the officials found such developments puzzling, FitzGerald, as former participant and latterly observer, was clear – and clear as to the difference with 1974. He said: 'Oh yeah, they have institutionalised the divisions ... We were aiming to soften them and now they're institutionalised, which poses a problem which nobody has addressed.'[184]

The most charitable interpretation of the arrangements established by the agreement was a neutral one, in the sense that they did not model a process of reconciliation. As a key Belfast official put it, 'power-sharing was essentially just a group of people of different persuasions sitting in the one room together but not sharing power in the sense that you and I would think about actually sharing power: they were actually just sharing the administration on what effectively was a divided basis'.[185]

And the difficulty is that, like the physical law of the maximisation of entropy, the institutionalisation of ethnicity tends to become self-reinforcing. A Dublin official conceded:

> [O]ne has to admit it's far from an ideal system and I do share the worries to a degree that it will continue to inhibit interaction between the two communities, and I do share that too. So that I suppose you would in the longer term, like communists used to look forward to the withering away of the state, in a sufficiently long-term perspective you would look forward to the withering away of that system, you would hope that that would happen. But so far one would say there's not much evidence that it is going in that direction and if anything the system is tending to crystallise or calcify a little bit in those terms.[186]

Officials from Northern Ireland, given they had sought by their lights to provide impartial advice to ministers, were perhaps particularly sensitive to the communal-designation provisions. One said: 'I mean it was very unwholesome really. It's almost like going around with a Star of David on a uniform, all of this.'[187] In a more detached way, another said that while it was essential to have 'a form of government in which all parts of the community can participate at some time', nevertheless 'you get into difficulties once you try reifying that, because you can actually solidify a situation that should be fluid'.[188]

The reconciliation practitioners were more inclined than the officials to link the symptoms of polarisation to the nature of the constitutional arrangements, in line with the theoretical critiques rehearsed in Chapter 2 and the assessments of B-H in Chapter 3. Morrow affirmed: 'The problem with constitutions which embed ethnicity is that it freezes political phenomena as legal entities, creating greater obstacles to transformation over time, particularly in societies that would need to be interethnic, the maintenance of fluidity around that boundary.' He warned that 'what you end up with then is a nasty, narrow-minded, resentful, very communally competitive scenario'.[189]

In materials science, rigid substances are always more fragile in the face of physical shocks. We have already seen how the Macedonian system of power-sharing, with its changes of governmental coalition after elections, has been more flexible and so hitherto more absorbent of political shocks than that in Northern Ireland. Conversely, a Dublin official closely involved with the Belfast agreement identified the Bosnian pitfall. He said:

> [O]bviously Bosnia shows the difficulty of needing the concurrent support of all elements, principally the Serbs, the Bosniaks and the Croats as well. But it's not in the long run I think a particularly flexible or particularly robust form of government. As I say, you end up with either dreadful paralysis internally or, alternatively, the long-term entrenchment of individuals and parties and interests which can't be very helpful.[190]

A London counterpart who occupied a similarly key position during the talks admitted to private qualms about the system. But working within the intellectual framework of Westminster-style alternation versus consociationalist power-sharing, he could see no alternative at the time:

> It's quite difficult to reconcile alternation of power with power-sharing, and that was a worry for me. And I had a private thought that if you could get the thing going at all on a power-sharing basis, get it long enough to become routinised and everybody settled down, become sort of quasi-normal, then it may be at some point people would want to consider ways of redesigning a system to provide for alternation of power. But right then that was a luxury you couldn't have …[191]

It emerges that not only was the agreement on Good Friday by no means inevitable but nor was the 'inclusive' governance it enshrined. One Dublin talks official, while unsure of the representativeness of his views, said he did not believe the republic's position at the talks had been to press for a grand coalition. He said: '[I]nitially, certainly, the governments were thinking in terms of a cross-community government, strong representation on either side. It wasn't mandatory. The SDLP introduced the mandatory frame.' Indeed he went so far as to say: '[T]he two governments never really envisaged that Sinn Féin and the DUP would be in government. I mean if they tell you they did they're telling you lies, basically.'[192]

A London participant at the Stormont negotiations, again with qualification, said the same: 'I think if left to my own devices – none of us were obviously – my instinct would naturally have taken me towards forced coalition between the two strongest parties, or the two parties that were capable of making a coalition, with the others in opposition, which is more like where Sunningdale was, wasn't it?'[193]

The agreement was however represented as if this was its major innovation. Mandelson told a Liverpool audience after devolution was first effected that whereas the 1974 executive had included neither republicans nor unionist 'dissenters', the post-agreement administration was 'truly representative'. And he said: 'It recognises that everyone who has been a party to the conflict must be a party to its resolution.'[194] Two months, and the first suspension of the institutions, later, however, he was telling the Alliance conference: 'Today we need to hear the voice of the centre ground – your voice – more clearly than ever.'[195] And in October 2002, after the collapse, a rueful Prime Minister, recalling 'four and a half years of hassle, frustration and messy compromise', said in Belfast:

> [T]here were those who held the middle ground during the dark days of the Troubles, who provided much of the vision underpinning the Agreement, only to see the attention apparently given to the others as we tried to address the problems holding up the implementation of the Agreement. I know especially how frustrating this has been for the SDLP whose leadership has often felt its very reasonableness meant they counted for less.[196]

One Belfast official was robust on the democratic failings of the post-agreement system for executive formation. He said:

> I think the almost total inclusion now enjoined upon us by law is inherently undemocratic and unstable … I feel very strongly about it and here we are with virtually no opposition, with no recourse to the basic democratic device [where] … after a few years you throw the rascals out. Now, we have a situation where in theory you throw the rascals out and you get the same rascals back again.[197]

A Dublin official with a *longue-durée* perspective said that 'as a general proposition I would be personally quite open to the thought that power-sharing in its present form can't really be permanent'.[198] A Belfast official concurred, saying he did not think the arrangements could be for the long term: 'I think it's something to get you from where you are back to what people regard as in a sense more normal politics.'[199]

Reflecting on his four model cases, Lijphart (1977: 2) did then believe that communal divisions were 'declining', because consociationalism had been successful, representing thereby 'a passing phase'. Unfortunately, this proved with hindsight to be least true of the case which best embodied his four consociationalist elements, Belgium.

FitzGerald urged the parties subordinated by the current arrangements to present themselves as 'an alternative government'. He continued: 'Once you have alternative cross-party groupings then the situation could evolve away from sectarianism over time. It may not happen but it's the only way out.'[200]

The reconciliation practitioners were, understandably, the most concerned that change should not be blocked by constitutional rigidity. Michael Wardlow of the Northern Ireland Council of Integrated Education said that his 'biggest concern with the current power-sharing is there isn't an opposition'.[201] And Stevens affirmed: 'What we want in Northern Ireland is the possibility of evolution into more normal and creative politics and we don't want things that institutionally inhibit that.'[202]

Morrow concurred:

> I think the thing that is most difficult is the straitjacket of the designation system. If you moved to a weighted-majority system you would at least force coalition-building and see coalition-building as an art and as a goal, as opposed to something imposed for which no responsibility was taken ... There is no incentive structure to work together ... I would change designation in favour of a weighted-majority system.[203]

A common aspiration, recapitulating comments of those involved in the earlier period, was for 'bread-and-butter' issues to take precedence, perhaps linked to a realignment from orange–green to left–right politics. As one Dublin official put it, 'It clearly would be far better in the North of Ireland if there was no need for power-sharing or minority-veto powers, if it just operated like any normal society, and then the divisions were on social or economic issues rather than on sectarian issues.'[204] A colleague agreed: 'Oh yes, I think religion and politics don't mix. I think that the sort of class-interest politics, the sort of Labour, Liberal and Conservative views of capital and labour, they will come through in the end, the longer [term], that's ten, fifteen, twenty years.'[205]

Another said that 'what might come out of it somewhere along the line is, if not a realignment of right and left politics in Northern Ireland, there'll be certainly a realignment of nationalist and unionist politics within the next five or ten years, and then longer term that might actually move people in class directions'.[206] This view was not, however, universal. A London official, who said he was 'not much of an idealist', did not see this as 'a very realistic proposition'.[207]

Again the reconciliation practitioners were keen advocates. Eamonn Deane of the Holywell Trust made clear his goal 'that we do have politics about real issues and not about sectarianism and about the redistribution of wealth and about people who are less well off, and I suppose what could loosely be called socialist politics'.[208]

Such aspirations were also evident in the 1970s power-sharing experiment. Since then, globalisation, European integration and devolution within European states – belatedly, the UK included – have changed the terms of political trade. Now a new option, a civic cosmopolitanism as described in

Chapter 2, opens up. Ford of Alliance put it this way:

> [O]ne of the things I would say is that in 1921 you were either going to be in the United Kingdom or United Ireland, there was no choice, it was clean-cut, black and white. We've all been in Europe since 1973, the UK is devolving all over the place in a messy, awkward pattern that nobody quite knows where it's going to end … There is no simple pattern and it doesn't seem to matter any longer that there's no simple pattern.[209]

A Belfast official used similar language:

> [W]hat I would like to see would be a fairly fluid arrangement involving the islands, really, and Europe in which all sorts of things were tradeable and inter-changeable. And you might actually have a united Ireland but it would be an entirely different sort of thing than people thought they were getting or thought they were looking at, because there are a lot of ways at the moment in which the border is a line on the map of interest to cartographers, really, and political scientists but for most practical purposes – even with the euro, which is amazing – money flows across it, labour flows across it, people flow across it. And at the same time the whole inter-island thing is so ingrained, there have been such movements over all the years.[210]

A London official picked up on the European dimension particularly. He said:

> I would hope to reach a position where the institutions in Northern Ireland and in Ireland as a whole and in these islands are functioning very well and become so routinised that a lot of the things that have been felt to matter just wither away, rather in the way that when you go from the Vosges to the Black Forest it's sometimes quite difficult, apart from the fact there's a river there somewhere, the Rhine, it's quite difficult to know when you cross the border. Nobody cares a hoot.[211]

FitzGerald trenchantly contended that such a cosmopolitanising trend was essential for Northern Ireland's economic future. Arguing that 'the inward-lookingness of the north is quite extraordinary and the contrast between this outward-looking state and the north is incredible', he complained: 'There is still no sense of being part of Europe at all.'[212]

More positively, Stevens said:

> We have an opportunity because the British/Irish thing is dead and there's a new relationship between Britain and Ireland. We have an opportunity because the Irish State and Irish society has evolved beyond a narrow Catholic nationalism and you have a much more pluralist society in the republic, and we're in a Europe which is not post-national but the EU offers real possibilities to get out of the narrow straitjacket of the nation-state.[213]

Conclusion

Substantial claims were made by British ministers for the achievements of the Belfast agreement, notably that it had 'solved' Northern Ireland's constitutional crisis. Yet, against the backdrop of the loss of intellectual and moral leadership betrayed in the early 1970s, the pursuit of any *substantive* constitutional outcome had become by the late 1990s entirely subordinate to supporting any deal the parties would endorse. The agreement was thus a product of the 'private reason' which accompanies *in camera* discussions, in which participants can bargain rather than deliberate, and can pursue sectarian rather than publicly defensible claims (Chambers, 2004: 405).

Intellectually, whether the arrangements heralded by the agreement would provide for good governance – never mind reconciliation – was left unquestioned. Thus there was to be no discussion, on the critical issue of executive formation, as to whether application of d'Hondt was desirable, given the very wide spectrum of opinion the parties embraced and the concern about the absence of an opposition in the Assembly. These had precisely been the grounds on which Whitelaw's Green Paper had rejected 'PR government'.

Morally, *transformismo* was extended beyond the democratic limits to which it had previously been constrained, seeking to embrace paramilitary organisations in the 'peace process' without their leaders having to embrace universal norms. This came at the expense of a corrosive gap between the 'official rhetoric of transition' (Bean, 2007: 92) and the continued paramilitary sub-culture in working-class neighbourhoods – a gap which it took the McCartney sisters' campaign to bridge.

As Cunningham (2001: 156) recognises, 'the strategy of consociationalism, and particularly in its recent form, is premised on trying to balance the concerns of Nationalist and Unionist blocs and reacting to the relative pressure that they are able to exert in any given period'. Based as it was only on the balance of political forces of the moment, the agreement was thus inherently unstable in its implementation, as the parties sought to shift that balance to their subsequent advantage. There was no incentive for the centrist parties to renew the solidity around the Executive table evidenced in 1974, nor for the anti-system party, SF, to resolve the decommissioning impasse. Governmental failure thus meant polarisation and system collapse.

As a product of mere *Realpolitik*, the Belfast agreement was also more riskily consociationalist than its predecessor (Horowitz, 2001) – in terms of the breadth of the governmental coalition required, set against the (contradictory) strength of the mutual-veto arrangements. The still further negotiations which were to lead eight years later to the St Andrews Agreement meant the latter was more recklessly consociationalist still. Given the historical asymmetry of domination and subordination in Northern Ireland, this provided an untrammelled opportunity for the fundamentalist DUP, having become principal party of government when devolution was restored in 2007, to utilise repeatedly its deadlocking veto. Governmental failure now took the form of chronic sectarian impasse.

The two Northern Ireland party-political representatives willing to be interviewed[214] – no doubt because one represented the only regional liberal party and the other a liberal-socialist voice in the SDLP – defined power-sharing, by contrast, in terms of reconciliation rather than *transformismo*. Ford, the Alliance leader, said: 'If you were to talk about sharing power I think it has to be something significantly more than carving up power.'[215] Similarly, Seán Farren of the SDLP said: 'I think power-sharing is the political expression used for the wider concept of partnership.'[216]

We can now solve the riddle set out at the beginning of this book: why this paradox of peace without reconciliation? The ultimate answer is that the goal was never the reconciliation of a divided society as such, but rather the management of that division in a manner less threatening to order and the State.

Yet the irony of this *Realpolitik* is that it proved not to be realistic. The discussion of the theoretical debates in Chapter 2 and the ex-Yugoslav case studies in Chapter 3 highlighted how the essentialist conception of the world can only lead to a dystopian vision of unending antagonism, however managed. As of mid-2009, the fetid relationship between the now dominant ethnonationalist parties in Northern Ireland and the sense of exclusion experienced by the others, allied to public disillusionment with governmental inertia and a worrying renewal of paramilitary disaffection, indicated that the transformist project had, after three and a half decades, run its course. What might emerge from it is developed in the final chapter.

Notes

1 Author interview, 25 January 2008.
2 Author interview, 19 November 2007.
3 Author interview, 12 December 2007.
4 Author interview, 10 December 2007.
5 Author interview, 26 March 2008.
6 Author interview, 10 December 2007.
7 McGarry and O'Leary (2009b: 370) distort this argument entirely to imply I am referring to paramilitary extremists who manned barricades during the UWC strike.
8 'Leader comment', *Observer* (24 September 2000).
9 Frank Millar, 'Mandelson calls for help to ease pressure on Trimble over RUC', *Irish Times* (26 September 2000).

10 'Back to the agreement', *Irish Times* (24 July 2002).

11 Dan Keenan, 'Nationalist gripes and recession "threat" to peace', *Irish Times* (27 July 2009).

12 Author interview, 8 January 2008.

13 'People and the pact ... our poll results', *Belfast Telegraph* (5 October 1988); 'Your views on Ulster's future', *Belfast Telegraph* (30 January 1990); Denis Coghlan, 'Power-sharing wins highest NI support', *Irish Times* (3 December 1993); William Graham, 'Power-sharing assembly is people's choice', *Irish News* (22 October 1996); 'The News Letter opinion poll', *News Letter* (9 July 1999).

14 See www.ark.ac.uk/nilt/2002/Political_Attitudes/SHAREPWR.html [accessed 17 July 2009].

15 See www.ark.ac.uk/nilt/2003/Political_Attitudes/SHAREPWR.html [accessed 17 July 2009].

16 'Wider ministerial involvement in conference agreed', *Irish Times* (25 May 1989).

17 'Full text of Brooke comments', *Irish Times* (16 August 1989).

18 John Burns, 'Brooke row "no problem"', *Sunday Times* (20 August 1989).

19 'Brooke sees "common ground" for devolution', *Irish Times* (10 January 1990).

20 'Brooke still chasing talks dream', *News Letter* (29 January 1990).

21 Edward Gorman, 'Ulster initiative setback over a choice of words', *The Times* (23 July 1990).

22 'Agreement on a basis for talks is close, says Brooke', *Irish Times* (8 September 1990).

23 NIO news release, 'Speech by the Secretary of State, Rt Hon Peter Brooke MP, in the House of Commons on the renewal of direct rule', 5 July 1990.

24 David McKittrick, 'Dublin in diplomatic wrangle on Ulster talks', *Independent* (5 July 1990).

25 David Hearst, 'Dublin spikes Brooke plan for talks', *Guardian* (6 July 1990).

26 John Foley and John Devine, 'Haughey to stand fast in meeting on North talks', *Irish Independent* (7 July 1990).

27 Stephen Collins, 'Brooke plan in troubled waters', *Irish Press* (1 July 1990).

28 Edward Gorman, 'Ulster initiative setback over a choice of words', *The Times* (23 July 1990).

29 'A basis for formal political talks now exists', *Irish Times* (27 March 1991).

30 Frank Millar and Mark Brennock, 'Optimism as talks venue agreed', *Irish Times* (23 May 1991).

31 Gerry Moriarty, 'NI talks set to begin today', *Irish Times* (17 June 1991).

32 Anne Cadwallader, 'Pressure put on Unionists to accept talks', *Irish Press* (21 May 1991).

33 Mark Brennock, 'NI talks will face deadline', *Irish Times* (10 April 1991).

34 Frank Millar, Denis Coghlan and Gerry Moriarty, 'North leaders agree to start talks on June 17th', *Irish Times* (6 June 1991).

35 Tim Jones, 'Brooke's Ulster initiative on brink of failure', *The Times* (10 May 1991).

36 Mark Brennock, 'Unionists differ on devolution in submissions', *Irish Times* (21 June 1991).

37 Mark Brennock, 'New talks obstacle on timing of Conference', *Irish Times* (20 June 1991).
38 'Still hope for future talks, Brooke says', *Irish Times* (4 July 1991).
39 Martin Cowley, 'Fresh effort for Northern talks pledged by Brooke', *Irish Times* (30 July 1991).
40 William Graham, 'Brooke plan may be spiked by election', *Irish News* (14 September 1991).
41 Colin Brown, 'Brooke initiative fails as parties await election', *Independent* (28 January 1992).
42 'Despair and hope in Ulster', *Independent* (7 February 1992).
43 Frank Millar, 'Fresh round of talks on North will go ahead from tomorrow', *Irish Times* (28 April 1992).
44 Bernard Purcell, 'North's talks: 3 months ultimatum', *Irish Independent* (28 April 1992).
45 Frank Millar, 'European model for North proposed', *Irish Times* (13 May 1992).
46 'Agreeing new political structures: submission by the SDLP to the inter party talks', 11 May 1992. All the talks papers were made available to the author.
47 'Record of a meeting of the structures sub-committee held at Parliament Buildings on 12 May 1992', talks secretariat reference SC/4.
48 'A submission by the Ulster Unionist Party', 11 May 1992.
49 'Record of a meeting of the structures sub-committee at Parliament Buildings on the morning of 13 May', revised reference SC/6.
50 'Record of a plenary meeting held at Parliament Buildings on the afternoon of 19 May 1992', reference PT/15.
51 'Sub-committee report', 10 June 1992.
52 'Summary record of a plenary meeting held in Parliament Buildings on the morning of 11 June 1992' (Talks Secretariat: ref PT/22).
53 Frank Millar, 'The process of mutual discovery is long overdue, says Tanaiste', *Irish Times* (29 July 1992).
54 'Opening statement on behalf of the Irish government', 6 July 1992.
55 'Paper submitted by the Irish government delegation: constitutional issues', 28 August 1992.
56 Donald Macintyre, 'Mayhew favours Bill of Rights for Ulster', *Independent* (28 June 1992).
57 Mark Brennock and Frank Millar, 'NI talks end with no plan to resume', *Irish Times* (11 November 1992).
58 Bernard Purcell, 'Mayhew hope on "horsetrade"', *Irish Independent* (12 November 1992).
59 Gerry Moriartty, 'Pledge from Major on resumption of talks', *Irish Times* (8 April 1993).
60 'As long as there are things to talk about', *Guardian* (8 April 1993).
61 Edward Heath, 'Outflank the IRA bombers', *The Times* (10 June 1993).
62 Edward Gorman, 'Brooke tries to revive initiative', *The Times* (19 November 1990).
63 Edward Gorman, 'Hume wants Irish devolution initiative to be abandoned', *The Times* (8 October 1990).

64 Malachi O'Doherty, Owen Bowcott, Michael Sadlier, Kevin Magee and Kevin Cullen, 'Buried in the rubble?', *Fortnight* 322 (November 1993), pp. 14–19.

65 Joe Carroll and Dick Grogan, 'Taoiseach says Mayhew plan must not interfere with aim of declaration', *Irish Times* (8 February 1994).

66 Stephen Collins, 'Dr Mansergh comes in from political cold', *Irish Press* (5 December 1993).

67 Mansergh worked as an adviser to successive FF taoisigh, before securing election as a party senator and then TD.

68 Author interview, 19 December 2007.

69 Jim Cusack, 'Peace pointless without political solution, NIO says', *Irish Times* (11 November 1993).

70 Geraldine Kennedy, 'Reynolds sees "historic" opportunity', *Irish Times* (8 November 1993).

71 *Ibid.*

72 Author interview, 25 May 2008.

73 Author interview, 25 January 2008.

74 'How the process began', *Sunday Tribune* (26 February 1995).

75 'We must lift our sights, says Spring', *Irish Times* (2 October 1993).

76 Joseph O'Malley, 'NI talks fail to bridge Dublin/London gap', *Sunday Independent* (12 December 1993).

77 Gene McKenna and Bernard Purcell, 'Agreement reached in phone call scramble', *Irish Independent* (15 December 1993).

78 Philip Stephens, 'Joint declaration composed after more than 20 drafts', *Financial Times* (17 December 1993).

79 Stephen Collins, 'How the deal was done', *Sunday Press* (19 December 1993).

80 'Mayhew defines terms of eventual "clarification"', *Irish Times* (21 January 1994).

81 Suzanne Breen, 'Reading republicanism', *Fortnight*, 324 (January 1994).

82 Liam Clarke, 'Roadmap sets out strategy for talks', *Sunday Times* (3 April 1994).

83 Geraldine Kennedy, 'Governments having difficulty framing talks', *Irish Times* (25 May 1994).

84 Anthony Bevins, 'Deadlock over cross-border reforms', *Observer* (11 December 1994).

85 David McKittrick, 'All-party Ulster talks "two years away"', *Independent* (12 September 1994).

86 Dick Grogan, 'Talks future precarious after difficult first day', *Irish Times* (11 June 1996).

87 His young wife, who had miscarried at an early stage in the talks, was pregnant again.

88 Frank Millar, 'Governments aim to kick-start talks', *Irish Times* (7 January 1998).

89 Frank Millar, 'Urgent attempts by governments to agree proposals for political settlement', *Irish Times* (12 January 1998).

90 'Text proposes that Anglo-Irish Agreement would be replaced', *Irish Times* (13 January 1998).

91 Frank Millar, 'Doubts grow over UDP involvement in talks ahead of London

meeting', *Irish Times* (26 January 1998).

92 Frank Millar, 'Unionists allege British change on talks issues', *Irish Times* (12 March 1998).

93 Frank Millar and Geraldine Kennedy, 'Ahern, Blair try to reach common position on North settlement terms', *Irish Times* (2 April 1998).

94 Maol Muire Tynan, 'Governments submit joint paper despite differences on Strand Two', *Irish Times* (6 April 1998).

95 Deaglán de Bréadún, 'Drive for No vote swells ranks of anti-agreement unionists', *Irish Times* (15 May 1998).

96 Author interview, 10 December 2007.

97 Author interview, 8 January 2008.

98 Deaglán de Bréadún, 'Wide gap emerges between parties on structure of new NI assembly', *Irish Times* (1 April 1998).

99 Theresa Judge, 'SDLP strongly opposed to UUP line on assembly', *Irish Times* (1 April 1998).

100 Author interview, 8 January 2008.

101 Author interview, 26 March 2008.

102 Henry McDonald and Patrick Wintour, 'Tortuous trail to Ulster's peace deal', *Observer* (12 April 1998).

103 Author interview 25 February 2008.

104 Author interview, 26 March 2008.

105 Author interview, 25 January 2008.

106 Author interview, 10 December 2007.

107 Author interview, 19 December 2007.

108 Garret FitzGerald, 'Parties faced with unequivocal choice to agree or lose peace', *Irish Times* (3 April 1999).

109 John Mullin, 'Finding way to make executive work', *Guardian* (3 December 1999).

110 See www.scotland.gov.uk/About/strategic-board [accessed 18 July 2009].

111 See www.scotland.gov.uk/About/14944/23089 [accessed 18 July 2009].

112 Author interview, 21 April 2008.

113 'Only trust remains outstanding, Blair tells the politicians', *Irish Times* (16 July 1999).

114 Author interview, 8 January 2008.

115 Author interview, 19 November 2007.

116 Author interview, 9 January 2008.

117 Author interview, 23 May 2008.

118 Author interview, 19 November 2007.

119 Author interview, 1 February 2008.

120 Tim O'Brien, 'Sectarianism in NI "not institutional"', *Irish Times* (30 August 1999).

121 *Dáil Debates*, vol. 489, col. 1036, 21 April 1998.

122 *Ibid.*, col. 1037.

123 Author interview, 8 January 2008.

124 The author was co-initiator of the project with Simon Lee, then Professor of Jurisprudence at Queen's University.

125 Peter Mair, 'Power-dispersing', *Fortnight*, 322 (November 1993).

126 Henry McDonald, Mary Holland and Andy McSmith, 'Trimble victory as Sinn Fein delays', *Observer* (19 April 1998).

127 Theresa Judge, 'Unionist MPs look for No votes at Ulster Hall', *Irish Times* (24 April 1998).

128 Frank Millar, 'Let's shake on it, Mr Adams, *after* the clarity and certainty', *Irish Times* (17 April 2000).

129 Deglán de Bréadún, 'Blair is ready to visit North for talks with Assembly's new leaders', *Irish Times* (2 July 1998).

130 Gerry Moriarty, 'Trimble, Mallon postpone formation of executive', *Irish Times* (15 September 1998).

131 Louise Flanagan, 'Mallon bitter after decommissioning impasse wrecks executive timetable', *Irish Times* (27 October 1998); Noel McAdam, 'Double act who put the focus on getting along', *Belfast Telegraph* (18 February 2002).

132 '"We must not forget how far we have come"', *Irish Times* (2 April 1999).

133 John Mullin, 'Ulster sets out on a new path to peace', *Guardian* (3 July 1999).

134 Clare Murphy, 'Ministers are nominated to executive but hold positions for less than an hour', *Irish Times* (16 July 1999).

135 Frank McNally, 'Deficit in trust and confidence must be addressed, says Ahern', *Irish Times* (16 July 1999).

136 Deglán de Bréadún, 'Direct rule of North ends as new Executive meets', *Irish Times* (3 December 1999).

137 John Mullin, 'Reluctant Mitchell makes return to Belfast', *Guardian* (6 September 1999).

138 Geraldine Kennedy, 'Constitution does not allow for suspension, Ahern says', *Irish Times* (14 February 2000).

139 Peter Murtagh, 'Review will be short and focus on arms issue only, says Mandelson', *Irish Times* (15 February 2000).

140 Frank Millar, 'Blair and Ahern fail to agree on way forward', *Irish Times* (17 February 2000).

141 'Sequence of statements issued by governments and IRA', *Irish Times* (8 May 2000).

142 Gerry Moriarty. 'No alternative to Hillsborough deal, says Mandelson in call for unionist "yes" vote', *Irish Times* (27 May 2000).

143 John Mullin, 'Sinn Fein bans flags on Coronation Day', *Guardian* (3 June 2000).

144 Paul Tanney, '"Uproar" about policing Bill, says SF', *Irish Times* (3 June 2000).

145 Gerry Moriarty and Monika Unsworth, 'Mandelson's proposals on flags anger both sides', *Irish Times* (9 September 2000).

146 Aine Kerr, 'Big jump in number of Irish passports issued for North', *Irish Independent* (25 June 2008). The author is himself an Irish citizen living in Northern Ireland.

147 See www.ark.ac.uk/nilt/2007/Identity/IRBRIT.html [accessed 28 July 2009].

148 Rosie Cowan, 'Ulster deadlock can be broken, insists Blair', *Guardian* (16 July 2001).

149 Clare Murphy, 'Reid says Britain will meet concerns of nationalists', *Irish Times* (23 June 2001).

150 Nicholas Watt, 'Trimble hits back at party critics', *Guardian* (27 October 2000).

151 'Joint declaration by the British and Irish governments', *Irish Times* (2 May 2003).

152 See www.nio.gov.uk/proposals_by_the_british_and_irish_governments_for_a_comprehensive_agreement.pdf [accessed 19 July 2009].

153 Gerry Moriarty, Mark Brennock and Dan Keenan, 'North deal in the balance', *Irish Times* (22 October 2003).

154 'Carrots and manipulation – Mandelson on Blair', *Guardian* (14 March 2007).

155 Author interview, 27 February 2008.

156 'Seamus Mallon', *Belfast Telegraph* (16 April 2005).

157 Owen Bowcott, '"I wouldn't have taken his word for anything"', *Guardian* (14 March 2007).

158 Nicholas Watt, 'Revealed: Blair's offer to meet masked IRA leaders', *Guardian* (17 March 2008).

159 I am indebted to Mary Alice Clancy for this reference.

160 Author interview, 21 April 2008.

161 Chris Thornton, 'Executive under attack over its law making work', *Belfast Telegraph* (18 February 2002).

162 Graham Gudgin, 'How much are we missing the Executive during suspension?', *Belfast Telegraph* (11 November 2002).

163 See www.ark.ac.uk/nilt/1999/Political_Attitudes/ASSMDAY.html [accessed 19 July 2008].

164 Dan Keenan, 'Governments may review agreement more often', *Irish Times* (29 March 2002).

165 'The dustbin of history', *Guardian* (12 January 2006).

166 See www.nio.gov.uk/st_andrews_agreement.pdf [accessed 19 July 2009].

167 John Ware, 'The price of peace', BBC news online (2 March 2008, http://news.bbc.co.uk/1/hi/northern_ireland/7273611.stm [accessed 19 July 2009]). I am again indebted to Mary Alice Clancy for this reference.

168 Stephen Collins, 'Ahern and Blair vow to press ahead', *Irish Times* (7 April 2006).

169 Frank Millar, 'IRA's move from terror to democracy is over, says Blair', *Irish Times* (8 November 2002).

170 *Official Report*, 6 March 2001.

171 Tom McGurk, 'Does Sinn Féin really understand the Republic?', *Sunday Business Post* (26 July 2009).

172 Frank Millar, 'DUP to press for excluding SF from government', *Irish Times* (24 March 2005).

173 Tony McCusker, 'Inside the executive', *Fortnight*, 461 (September 2008).

174 Author interview, 21 January 2008.

175 'Politicians in a parallel province', *Belfast Telegraph* (30 October 2008).

176 'Sinn Fein topping the poll would be a disaster, says DUP', *Belfast Telegraph* (29 May 2009).

177 'Crisis looms for unionism as Sinn Fein tops European poll', *Belfast Telegraph* (8 June 2009).

178 See section 16C(6) of the Northern Ireland (St Andrews Agreement) Act 2006,

available at www.opsi.gov.uk/acts/acts2006/pdf/ukpga_20060053_en.pdf [accessed 5 October 2009].

179 *Newsline 6.30*, BBC Northern Ireland (8 September 2009).
180 Author interview, 11 December 2007.
181 Author interview, 26 February 2008.
182 Author interview, 25 February 2008.
183 Author interview, 19 December 2007.
184 Author interview, 27 November 2007.
185 Author interview, 21 April 2008.
186 Author interview, 25 January 2008.
187 Author interview, 30 January 2008.
188 Author interview, 21 January 2008.
189 Author interview, 23 May 2008.
190 Author interview, 8 January 2008.
191 Author interview, 10 December 2007.
192 Author interview, 8 January 2008.
193 Author interview, 26 February 2008.
194 Northern Ireland Information Service, 'Speech by Secretary of State for Northern Ireland to Institute of Irish Studies, Liverpool', 4 February 2000.
195 Northern Ireland Information Service, 'Speech to the Alliance Party Conference[,] Quality Hotel, Carrickfergus', 8 April 2000.
196 Northern Ireland Information Service, 'Tony Blair: Belfast speech in full', 17 October 2002.
197 Author interview, 30 January 2008.
198 Author interview, 19 December 2007.
199 Author interview, 21 January 2008.
200 Author interview, 27 November 2007.
201 Author interview, 17 January 2008.
202 Author interview, 9 January 2008.
203 Author interview, 23 May 2008.
204 Author interview, 25 February 2008.
205 Author interview, 8 January 2008.
206 Author interview, 21 April 2008.
207 Author interview, 19 November 2007.
208 Author interview, 11 April 2008.
209 Author interview, 7 January 2008.
210 Author interview, 21 January 2008.
211 Author interview, 10 December 2008.
212 Author interview, 27 November 2007.
213 Author interview, 9 January 2008.
214 Repeated interview invitations to leading figures in the UUP and SF, the other key parties to the Belfast agreement, were not reciprocated; the lack of intellectual curiosity among the Northern Ireland 'political class', as against that exhibited by the public officials interviewed, was striking.
215 Author interview, 7 January 2008.
216 Author interview, 23 May 2008.

6

Conclusions and policy implications

Introduction

More than a decade on from the Belfast agreement, the sectarian 'force field' of antagonism in Northern Ireland (Wright, 1987: 286) remained as strong as ever. The agreement certainly did nothing to stem this polarisation, which was exacerbated by the manner of its implementation. This sub-optimal outcome can be traced to a combination of structural weaknesses and the inadequacies of the political class (Wolff, 2005). Structural reforms, linked to a renewal and realignment of politics, are therefore needed to rekindle the sense of common purpose which moved the more idealistic supporters of the agreement in 1998 and which has dissipated in the intervening years.

This needs some conceptual framing. Liberal democracy has acquired global hegemonic status since the end of the Cold War, yet it is an inherently conflicted notion. Its evolution over the last two centuries has been marked, Chantal Mouffe (2000: 4) argues, by persistent tension between the two only contingently related strands of political liberalism and the democratic revolution. But it is incontestable, she affirms, 'that it is legitimate to establish limits to popular sovereignty in the name of liberty'.

International IDEA (2002: 13) similarly identifies the two-sided nature of democracy, which it casts in terms of 'popular control' and 'political equality'. The first element captures the idea of the sovereignty of the people, sometimes described as 'majority rule'. The second addresses the way that rule must be tempered to prevent second-class citizenship, including by what have come to be known as 'minority rights'.

One reason why it has hitherto proved so difficult to establish stable and genuinely shared democratic institutions in Northern Ireland is that these two elements of democracy have not only been in tension in the region but have been directly counterposed, articulated unreflectively by communalist politicians. That is to say, 'political Protestants' have tended to demand that institutions at Stormont maximise the degree of popular control, with an unaddressed elision between 'the public', rhetorically invoked, and the Protestant community. This has given unionism its frequently populist character, accommodating sectarian manifestations of popular Protestantism, such as Orangeism (Bew, Gibbon and Patterson, 1995). By contrast, 'political Catholics' have focused heavily on demanding political equality, even – for example, under the Anglo-Irish Agreement – where this has been unaccountable to the citizens of the polity concerned. This has shaded at the margin into support for or ambivalence towards organisations pursuing equality by undemocratic or even violent means (English, 2003).

Like Mouffe, Norberto Bobbio recognises that the values of liberty and equality that underpin democracy have a contingent relationship. He thus suggests a simple matrix of positions on the political spectrum which parties may adopt, depending on where they stand on each axis: freedom versus authoritarianism, equality versus inequality.

Table 6.1 Equality, liberty and democratic politics

	Equality	Inequality
Freedom	Liberal left	Centre right
Authoritarianism	'Jacobin' left	Far right

Derived from Bobbio (1996b: 78–9)

In Northern Ireland, this typology has obvious referents. Without too much violence to their positions, one can cast the main parties as indicated in Table 6.2. This accords with their affiliations in the European Parliament: the SDLP and the UUP were aligned respectively with the two main centre-left and centre-right groups, respectively the Social Democrats and the Christian Democrats – until the SDLP seat was lost with Hume's retirement in 2004 and the UUP MEP followed the British Conservatives in their much-criticised defection to a more right-wing grouping after the 2009 election. SF is in the same group as the former eastern-bloc Stalinist parties, while the DUP representative is independent but of a character similar to (say) the xenophobic Flemish Interest party in Belgium.

Table 6.2 The Northern Ireland political spectrum

	Equality	Inequality
Freedom	SDLP	Ulster Unionist Party
Authoritarianism	Sinn Féin	Democratic Unionist Party

Cas Mudde (2007: 19) defines such 'populist radical right' parties in Europe by the tropes of 'nativism' (nationalism plus xenophobia), authoritarianism and populism. He not only identifies the DUP as part of this family (*ibid*: 55), however – highlighting in addition its Protestant fundamentalism – but also describes SF as a 'borderline' case outside it. He argues that it shares the authoritarianism and populism of the DUP but, except (importantly) with regard to the British and Protestants, is nationalist yet not xenophobic (*ibid*: 52). For Mudde, and SF's recent trajectory (Bean, 2007) would bear this out, such parties do not have a very fixed position on the conventional socio-economic political agenda. SF was thus willing to endorse an essentially DUP-driven Programme for Government in late 2007 which not only prioritised the economy over society but approached the former in wholly *laisser faire* terms (Wilford and Wilson, 2008b: 23–4).

   This indicates that the electoral polarisation of recent years in Northern Ireland can be captured in terms of a move towards more authoritarian political options *within* each 'community' – that is to say, towards those parties marked by less tolerant dispositions towards the 'other side'. Table 6.3 shows the trend from pre-agreement elections to the Assembly election of March 2007.

Table 6.3 Votes and vote shares in Northern Ireland elections, 1997–2007

Election	DUP		UUP		SDLP		SF	
	No. of votes	%	No. of votes	%	No. of votes	%	No. of votes	%
1997 Westminster	107,348	13.6	258,349	32.7	190,814	24.1	126,921	16.1
1997 council	99,651	15.8	175,036	27.9	130,387	22.6	106,934	16.9
1998 assembly	145,917	18.0	172,225	21.3	177,963	21.9	142,858	17.6
2001 Westminster	181,999	22.5	216,839	26.8	169,865	20.9	175,392	21.7
2001 council	169,477	21.4	181,336	22.9	153,424	19.4	163,269	20.6
2003 assembly	177,944	25.7	156,931	22.7	117,547	16.9	162,758	23.5
2005 Westminster	241,856	33.7	127,314	17.7	125,626	17.5	174,530	24.3
2005 council	208,278	29.6	126,317	18.0	121,991	17.4	163,205	23.2
2007 assembly	207,721	30.1	103,145	14.9	105,164	15.2	180,573	26.2

Data compiled by Rick Wilford

This puts in context the rationalisation, recurrently rehearsed by London and Dublin after the DUP and SF assumed electoral dominance of their respective blocs, that because these parties had 'moderated' they had become viable parties of government – a moderation which was tactical rather than strategic, as Martin Frampton (2009: 187–90) showed in the context of the 'republican movement'. In line with the consistent failure to privilege universal norms over *Realpolitik*, the official position did not recognise the significance of these parties' authoritarian political styles. In June 2008, the homophobic views expressed by the DUP chair of the Assembly Health Committee, Iris Robinson, sent a shockwave around the civilised world (Wilford and Wilson, 2008d: 29–30)[1] and SF began its protracted veto of meetings of the democratically elected Executive (*ibid*: 26–7). In an extreme form, the insensitivity of unionists towards political equality and of nationalists towards popular control had been made manifest – with impasse at worst, inertia at best, the result.

For all the tensions which characterise normal liberal democracies – arguably in themselves necessary if dissent in capitalist societies is to be expressed – they do not routinely dissolve into open antagonism between stereotyped identities. Rather, citizens are treated as individuals, addressed by competing political parties. Moving Northern Ireland beyond sectarian antagonism – the ambition evident among some governing figures in 1974, rediscovered in 2005 with *A Shared Future* and still wistfully evident in several interviews for this book – implies such a normalisation over time. This would entail the decoupling of the two dimensions of liberal democracy from their sectarian associations: popular control would come to be seen in terms of aggregations of individuals into changing political majorities without sectarian restriction and political equality would be cast as the human rights all individuals should enjoy.

Northern Ireland validates Bobbio's (1996a: 90) affirmation of the 'individualistic concept of society'. He points out that 'there is not a single democratic constitution ... which does not presuppose the existence of single individuals who have rights precisely because that is what they are'. This lesson was evident in the ex-Yugoslav comparisons, explored in Chapter 3, where the emphasis on the individual citizen rather than the collectivised 'community' was identified as key to political success. So can these principles of democratic governance offer a roadmap to a more conciliatory future for Northern Ireland?

A project of constitutional tolerance

Power-sharing devolution can comply with the democratic norms of popular control *and* political equality if the focus is on how best to advance the common good through intercultural dialogue. This means abjuring communal domination in favour of genuine partnership and renouncing violence or its threat. The task of constitutional engineering in divided societies is to craft institutions which behave impartially rather than dispensing patronage (Rothstein and Teorell, 2008) – the clientelistic disposition of the DUP in power towards a property developer and party member caused a political scandal after devolution was renewed (Wilford and Wilson, 2008c: 19–20) – and which reward altruistic rather than egoistic behaviour.

Unionism and nationalism may be antagonistic but as individual affiliations 'Britishness' and 'Irishness', still less Protestantism and Catholicism, need not be. In semiological terms (Coward and Ellis, 1977: 28–9), what Northern Ireland's ethnopolitical entrepreneurs achieve is to link a straightforwardly denotative statement, 'X is a Protestant/Catholic by background', into a connotative chain which implies the choice of a British/Irish identity and further of a unionist/nationalist political allegiance – *as if* these were similarly unproblematic rather than contingent. All societies these days are multicultural and it is reasonable to expect all citizens to give allegiance to a public sphere of democratic institutions in Northern Ireland, even while they retain particular cultural identities. This does however entail that such institutions are neutral, so that all can feel equally at ease with them.

The Assembly, government departments and the PSNI perforce recognised this with neutral emblems, which in each case (respectively a flax-flowers logo, a stylistic representation of the Giant's Causeway and a *smorgasbord* of imagery) quickly won public acceptance. A non-partisan flag for Northern Ireland, albeit possibly displayed in the company of both the Union flag and the Tricolour, and/or the European flag, can avoid the otherwise intractable argument which deadlocked the Assembly's ad hoc committee on flags in 2000 (Wilford, 2000: 23) and would command significant support.[2]

There may be an emerging trend, led by 'post-troubles' cohorts, towards rejection of the ideological categories so tainted by division and violence, in line with the argument rehearsed in Chapter 2 as to how quotidian concerns tend to take over from ethnic priorities in normal circumstances. In the 2006 NILT survey, for the first time, more respondents (40 per cent) ticked the 'neither' box than accepted a 'unionist' label or a 'nationalist' identity tag. While significantly more popular among Catholics than Protestants, it attracted a plurality of all age groups up to 54. And among the under-24s it attracted more support (50 per cent) than the other two identities put together.[3] By the 2008 survey, the gap had widened, with 43 per cent of respondents identifying as 'neither', as against 37 per cent 'unionist' (and 19 per cent 'nationalist'), and with now half of the 25–34 cohort also in the 'neither' camp.[4]

A neutral, democratic polity in Northern Ireland must be able to face equally in Irish and British, as well as European, directions. Devolution must not mean *in*volution – as was evident in 2008 in the veto by the DUP environment minister of UK government TV advertising on climate change (Wilford and Wilson, 2009b: 20) – and the region needs to participate fully in larger, up to and including global, networks if it is to keep pace with the wider world, as FitzGerald stressed in the last chapter. In education, integrated schools and the particular arrangements for the student movement in the region show how in the right context Protestants and Catholics – and those who would not be, or define themselves as, either – can face challenging issues without confrontation. By affiliating to the Union of Students in Ireland and the National Union of Students while having a regional structure, the student movement in Northern Ireland, despite tensions on individual campuses, has remained united throughout the 'troubles' and since.[5]

To achieve this status, devolved institutions need to be able to exercise genuine popular control. The Assembly has authority only in those competences 'transferred' under the Northern Ireland Act of 1998. It was envisaged, as under the Government of Ireland Act when this three-way division was conceived, that 'reserved' matters might be transferred, whereas 'excepted' matters would not.[6] Only with the consent of the Northern Ireland Secretary is the Assembly empowered to legislate in the reserved domain and, as an 'ancillary' aspect of a bill, in the excepted arena. This led to the discrepancy identified in the 2001 NILT survey between the institution which was believed by most to have the most say in Northern Ireland, the UK Government, and the institution a large majority believed *should* have the most say, the Assembly.[7]

The threefold categorisation arises (there are only devolved and non-devolved matters in Scotland) mainly because there were powers devolved to the old Stormont Parliament which were assumed by the NIO in 1972 but which could – in a very different light, given current safeguards – be devolved once more were the new arrangements to prove stable and effective. Policing and justice are central and the post-agreement commissions on these matters both envisaged that they would be transferred, as indeed did the St Andrews Agreement. There are others, such as in financial services, which if they were to be devolved would give the Assembly more power and facilitate coordination on a north–south basis if and when so wished (Hadden, 2001). Safeguards in the Northern Ireland Act against Assembly legislation being discriminatory or in contravention of the European Convention on Human Rights or European Community law should of course be retained.

The reserved powers should be transferred, recognising this would not require the Assembly to assume responsibility in all cases in these more onerous arenas. Sometimes the simplest and most progressive thing to do, even in already transferred areas, would be to copy Westminster legislation, rather than ignoring policy innovations developed in Britain's clearer left–right political culture. The Scottish Parliament, while jealous of its autonomy, has used the 'Sewel motion' procedure to achieve this with little fuss (Cairney and Keating, 2004).

There has been remarkably little policy coordination between the Assembly and Holyrood, despite both having primary legislative powers and many similar problems (such as social exclusion and sectarianism). The Scottish First Minister, Alex Salmond, did make this connection in his visit to Stormont shortly after the renewal of devolution in May 2007 and this is a weakness that should be rectified.

Excepted matters include international relations. But these already exclude matters under the purview of the North/South Ministerial Council – in as far as the Assembly and Dáil Eireann chose to act in a collaborative fashion, for example in a European context, they could do so as things stand. Where the Assembly is constrained is in terms of tax-varying powers and the currency arrangements. On the first, it is unlikely the Assembly would ever want to redesign the tax and national-insurance system root and branch, but the same applies to social security, which is currently devolved though parity is conventionally pursued for equal-citizenship reasons. Yet acquiring the capacity to vary rates at the margin, as long as this did not incur unfunded commitments, would introduce more democratic accountability into the debate about public finance in Northern Ireland, show a willingness to address the historically poor 'fiscal effort' (Heald, 2003) which the region has made – failure to appreciate this point underpinned the quixotic attack by the Northern Ireland parties on the Treasury in pursuit of reduced corporation tax for the region (Wilford and Wilson, 2008b) – and allow (if so wished) greater redistribution. There is public support, as the 2000 NILT survey indicated, for the Assembly to acquire tax-varying powers.[8]

The second constraint, vis-à-vis 'legal tender', would prevent the Assembly officially endorsing what is in border areas and large enterprises an informal reality – a dual-currency, sterling–euro zone. Its advocates would claim this would allow business, more supportive of euro membership in Northern Ireland than in Britain, to maximise the potential of cross-border trade and supply chains. The competence of the Assembly should be extended in these two areas also – again, not requiring any consequent policy changes but enabling them if so wished. One Dublin official, asked what he would change of the Belfast agreement, replied: 'The one outstanding issue I would change would be that we would have a single currency on the island of Ireland.'[9]

The ideal constitutional solution would be to accept that, on the one hand, looked at from the standpoint of Northern Ireland as a region of the United Kingdom, there will always be areas that are non-devolved, as with Scotland

and Wales; on the other, from the standpoint of sponsoring reconciliation on the island of Ireland, there could be a recognition by all concerned (it would be hard to see either London or Dublin disagreeing) that the Assembly and the institutions of the Oireachtas could collaborate on *any* matter – including those which are excepted in a UK context – as long as there was agreement between them on how to do so.

The Belfast agreement restricts north–south collaboration to twelve specified policy domains in an annexe, though the main body of the text speaks of 'at least' six implementation bodies and six areas of policy cooperation. The choice was not only arbitrary – the result of the balance of forces as Trimble battled to dilute the north–south agenda in the final days of negotiations (Coakley *et al.*, 2007: 37) – but seems artificial in the light of the more relaxed civic interchange that takes place daily in the business community, the trade union movement, the churches and NGOs and among individuals, for many of whom the border is of no more ideological significance than a line on the map, and a highly permeable one at that. This would realise the aspiration of the agreement, expressed by Laffan and Payne (2001: 11), 'that the institutions and processes that it has set in train may lead to the normalisation of the border'.

This expanded domain of north–south cooperation would also, however, highlight the inadequate accountability in this arena to the Assembly (and the Dáil). The uneven performance of the north–south bodies to date (Coakley *et al.*, 2007) has not been subject to adequate scrutiny and a dedicated Assembly committee is required to pursue this.

On a wider canvas, this broad approach would allow Northern Ireland to punch its weight more effectively on the European stage and, again if democratically so wished, to take a more positive stance on the 'European social model' (Hemerijck, 2002: 173–4), like its devolved counterparts in Scotland and Wales, than that of the two states on these islands. Northern Ireland has, unlike Scotland and Wales, notably failed to join the RegLeg network of European regions with legislative powers, which includes powerful regions like Catalonia. A reinvigorated Civic Forum, organised more coherently than previously on social-partnership lines, and an allied north–south consultative forum would assist civic engagement and policy co-ordination in that regard.

These constitutional arrangements should ease over time the antagonism between unionism and nationalism, in favour of political debate over the nature of the common good. They would do nothing to diminish the equality of UK citizenship enjoyed by Northern Ireland residents – such as the benefits of the rough-and-ready Barnett financial-equalisation formula and access to the more left–right axis of politics in Britain. But they would simultaneously remove all the barriers presented by partition to the residents of the island of Ireland coming together collectively for mutual benefit and in pursuit of the greater goal of reconciliation.

This overall approach would transcend the conventional, 'either-or' approach to Northern Ireland's constitutional status – a product of the competing slogans of 'self-determination'. More attuned to an era of globalisation and interdependence, it allows of a 'both/and' approach, a strategy of *transnationalisation* which is not only more effective in engaging with global actors (for example, through an all-Ireland approach to inward investment)[10] but also allows identities to overlap and lose their relationship of exclusivity (Beck, 2005: 203, 205). Far from being utopian, this is in line with what Beck (2006: 19), in an ironic reference to the former USSR, describes as the '*really existing cosmopolitanization*' of everyday life (original emphasis).

Like the line drawing of the duck that from another angle is a rabbit, this would conclude the endless, irresolvable argument as to whether the Belfast agreement (as amended by its St Andrews successor) is 'really' a unionist duck or a republican rabbit (Aughey, 2005: 102–5). This is therefore a proposal for a durable *settlement* and is more realistic than the hope that antagonism can otherwise indefinitely be frozen, despite political shocks, or that one or other assimilationist 'side' can be allowed constitutionally to prevail without negative consequence. Paradoxically, what would distinguish this approach from *both* conventional 'unionism' and 'nationalism' would be its cosmopolitan engagement with the rest of these islands, rather than an introverted parochialism.

The most likely candidates to advance such an impartial view in recent decades were public servants not captured by the Northern Ireland ethnonationalist protagonists. Remarkably, and tragically ahead of its time, much of this was prefigured in a memorandum to Lynch written by T. K. Whitaker – a significant figure, alongside Lynch's predecessor, Sean Lemass, in the republic's reintegration into the global economy after the disastrous experience of nationalist protectionism (Patterson, 2006). Whitaker, who was originally from the north and who prompted Lemass to meet O'Neill in 1965 – the first such public meeting between the two premiers since 1922 – wrote 'A note on north-south border policy' in November 1968 as new political possibilities, but also new uncertainties, were opening up in the wake of the civil-rights demonstration in Derry in October that year, when marchers were baton-charged by police (Prince, 2007).

Challenging conventional anti-partitionism and mindful that any renewal of republican violence would deepen division, Whitaker argued that modern trends were 'towards liberalisation, towards greater concern with human rights and conditions, towards looser regional political groupings, towards greater tolerance (or indifference) in religious matters'. Insisting that the Irish people 'should not be the prisoners of old ideas, even as to the form that re-unification might take', he described the territorial claim in *Bunreacht na hEireann* as 'unfortunate' and recommended exploration of 'all kinds of pos-sibilities – confederation, external association, condominium, the Benelux Agreement, [and] the political integration principles involved in [the] EEC'. A 'very special formula' might have to be found, he advised.[11]

Similarly, an English official, Norman Dugdale, Permanent Secretary at the Ministry of Health and Social Services, was to suggest in 1973 that the Green Paper of the previous year had dealt with 'symptoms' rather than focusing on the 'underlying reason' for the conflict – which he defined as constitutional antagonism, exacerbated by socio-economic backwardness, 'socio-religious conditioning' and segregated schooling. Dugdale suggested that the conflict could only be resolved by a 'higher synthesis', which neither an 'Irish dimension' nor an 'exclusively UK framework' could pro-vide. He proffered 'a re-jigging of the constitutional relationships between the Republic, Northern Ireland and Great Britain' but recognised that this 'visionary' concept was very much a 'reversal of the historical trend'. He also looked to the emergence of 'a new generation of political figures with no albatrosses on their necks'.[12]

Institutions of governance

To make these 'external' arrangements work, however, the 'internal' govern-ance of Northern Ireland must place a premium on dialogue and deliberation across sectarian boundaries. This can best be done through a requirement to reach cross-communal majorities on executive formation and dissolution. This would cement collective responsibility, allow 'joined-up' govern-ment to be a reality and hold out a model of intercommunal cooperation. Provisions to prevent ethnic domination should not inadvertently entrench communalist politics (for example, by equating Protestant with 'unionist' and Catholic with 'nationalist', as through the designation system), at the expense of new political alignments or at the risk that government may not function at all.

Reflecting ten years on from the Belfast agreement, Mallon urged a loos-ening of the strictures agreed in 1998. He queried the necessity for communal designation as long as rights were otherwise guaranteed, was concerned about the autonomy of individual ministers from the Executive and favoured 'healthier flexibility' in government formation.[13] Speaking in Oxford in September 2008, Mallon's successor as Deputy First Minister, Durkan, sim-ilarly contended that the 'arguably sectarian' system of designation should be replaced in the next Assembly term by a strong bill of rights, and talked about a 'political realignment' more consonant with a 'shared future'.[14]

Contemporaneously, the UUP deputy leader, Danny Kennedy, said it was 'time to move towards a more normal institutional arrangement for cross-community government'. This 'would require parties before entering government to agree the policy agenda they will pursue'.[15] While in office Trimble, the former party leader, admitted that a perverse aspect of the inclusive government established in 1998 was that it 'entrenches a communal approach to politics'.[16]

One option would be to require that, after an Assembly election, a new executive be formed commanding the support of a super-majority of MLAs present and voting – a recurrent undercurrent in the discussion since the 1970s of safeguards against ethnic 'lock-in', as we have seen. This would not be a 'voluntary' coalition to replace the current 'mandatory' one, as Robinson would prefer in the DUP's party interest, but an *agreed* coalition in the *public* interest.

The precise 'weight' of the weighted majority would be a matter for debate, but should not be so large as to have the perverse effect of consigning a veto power to sectarian unionism, as with the 'parallel consent' provisions in the Belfast agreement and, particularly, the St Andrews Agreement. Nor should it be so small that it would encourage unionists to imagine a minimalist *transformismo* and it should certainly not be designed to exclude any particular party. A figure of 65 per cent would appear close to the *via media*.

This would not give any party an automatic right to be in government and so all parties would be incentivised to be conciliatory.[17] Because a government could not be formed entirely out of Protestant or Catholic communalist parties, aspirants to government would be required in particular to be conciliatory to that party or parties *from the other 'community'* with whom they would be partnered and space would open for non-communalist parties.

By the same token, if one party from one 'community' was not willing to make the necessary accommodation, another could scoop the pool as its bargaining position would then be enhanced: without its involvement, government could not be formed and it could therefore demand disproportionate representation in the executive. Equally, a party or parties could take a principled decision in favour of becoming the official Opposition for the Assembly term, or to abstain on the vote to ratify government formation. Such opposition should be formally recognised, in terms of designated time to present Assembly business and resources to support policy development.

These incentives might work backwards to the extent that parties would engage in pre-election pacts, which would offer the electorate a much clearer perspective of the governmental choice(s) they faced. And were sufficient parties to combine (presumably via unholy alliance across the sectarian divide) to prevent a government being formed, and another election to be forced, the parties responsible could not be certain that they would be rewarded by the electorate for their intransigence, or for their dependence on such strange bedfellows. This would also provide an incentive against destructive political behaviour.

Were it to be felt this was setting the bar too high for executive formation by agreement, an alternative would be to establish the convention that, as far as is reasonably practicable, the Executive contain equal numbers of Catholics and Protestants – in the sense that these terms are used as 'objective' indicators of individual 'background' for fair-employment monitoring, rather than assuming 'unionist' or 'nationalist' ideological baggage – while not excluding members of ethnic minorities. This would be a simple device to block ethnic domination and the government thus formed could operate on a lower threshold requirement of 50 per cent, as a 'minimum winning coalition'.

It would be important to stress that this would be a convention, rather than a rigid formula, to avoid inadvertently reinforcing the communalist character of elections to the assembly. If it were perceived that fixed representation for each 'community' in government were guaranteed, the danger would be that parties would only compete for these seats on an intracommunal basis, which would not be a good foundation for subsequent cooperation in government. Belgium has such a 50:50 division of the federal government between Flemings and Walloons and it is certainly no longer any model of intercommunal reconciliation.

Any attempt in this context to construct a purely communal majority in the Assembly in favour of a particular piece of legislation would be met by the break-up of the government, with a 'loss' in the 'blame game' for the party which had gone for the ethnic 'break-out' from partnership in the first place, if the normative framework for the latter had been clearly established and accepted. This in turn would be a prospect from which any party so minded would be likely to recoil.

It would be possible to buttress this arrangement with provisions in the bill of rights, as the Northern Ireland Human Rights Commission (2001, 2004) recommended, to incorporate the Council of Europe Framework Convention for the Protection of National Minorities, alongside other minority rights over and above the European Convention on Human Rights. The framework convention is particularly germane on 'effective participation' and the bill could specify that legislation passed by communal majority in a polarised Assembly (which might in any event contravene some aspect of the ECHR) would automatically be declared *ultra vires*. Keeping such internationally agreed standards to the fore would help resolve the otherwise intractable political debate about what the bill of rights should contain.

Discussion of the sectarian political balance in the Assembly should not obscure the gross imbalance – a ratio of five to one – between men and women among MLAs. This could readily be changed by parties choosing all-women shortlists, a tactic now permitted under UK legislation which led to Wales becoming the first parliament in the world to achieve 50:50 representation by gender at the 2003 Assembly election. The legislation has in effect passed the responsibility to address the gender imbalance from the electorate (who, despite being strongly supportive, can do little about it) to the party 'selectorate' (who can). It is not to suggest a benign essentialism – that women are inherently more 'pacific' than men – to argue, as indicated in Chapter 2, that there are relationships between male domination of politics and a nationalistic political agenda.

For a population of 1.7 million it makes little sense to have an Assembly of 108 members (Scotland has 129 yet three times the population), with ten departments – eleven when policing and justice are devolved – plus the sprawling OFMDFM (Wilford and Wilson, 2003: 102). The Assembly could be reduced in size by cutting the number of seats per STV constituency, though this would favour larger parties. A better approach would be to take the opportunity to introduce a radically new electoral system, more appropriate to a divided society. Currently, there are, effectively, two separate, intracommunal electoral contests, which provide a poor platform for genuine power-sharing.

O'Leary (2001b) defends the use of STV. But he overplays intercommunal transfers in the first assembly election. And he perversely claims that SDLP transfers to SF in 1998 were a sign of moderation; interestingly, in the March 2007 assembly election, SDLP voters reverted to their historical pattern of allocating transfers primarily to Alliance.[18]

The fundamental weakness with STV, and with O'Leary's discussion, is that it is premised on a pre-deliberative conception of democracy: it assumes that elections are merely the aggregation of pre-given preferences, rather than an arena of debate in which citizens respond to contrasting appeals and in which context they may vote tactically. In their critique of the application of the alternative vote (AV) to divided societies, Jon Fraenkel and Bernard Grofman (2006) and John Coakley (2009) simply make the essentialist assumption that transfers will always be intracommunal before they will cross ethnic divides (Horowitz, 2006).

Application of a majoritarian system like AV requires candidates to secure, after transfers, the support of over 50 per cent of electors in their constituency. This stimulates candidates of all parties to make conciliatory and civic-minded appeals, as long as constituencies are heterogeneous (Horowitz, 2002a: 23–5). This was evident to an extent under first past the post in 2005, when the four victorious MPs from the SDLP and UUP all won seats along an axis of heterogeneous constituencies running from South Down, through North Down and South Belfast to Foyle, between the 'orange' and 'green' heartlands respectively to the east and west, with tactical voting (including by Alliance voters) a factor in each case (Wilford and Wilson, 2005b: 37). This showed a decisive willingness among some voters in such a context not just to give a second preference but their *only* vote to a moderate from the 'other side'.

Such incentives to vote-pooling, though real in their centripetal effects (Reilly, 2001), do not represent a magic bullet. They are not in themselves guarantors of interethnic conciliation but should be seen, as argued in Chapter 2, as comprising one tool in a portfolio of policies to heal a divided society. They will not work, as Horowitz (2006) concedes was the case in Fiji in 2001, in conditions where there is effectively a 'one-community, one party' political polarisation, rather than where in each 'community' there is a credible 'communal contender' as well as an 'ethno-nationalist' party (Eide, 1993). Coakley's (2009: 266) hypothetical running of AV for Northern Ireland Assembly elections is questionable, for the reason outlined above, in any particular case. But his trend data raise the genuine worry that the very electoral polarisation since 2003, about which governments in London and Dublin have been so cavalier, could mean that a shift to AV might no longer have the moderating effect, by comparison with STV, which would have been the case in previous years.

Accepting there is a trade-off between the goals of interethnic conciliation and proportional representation would in any event suggest the modification of AV via a top-up of seats allocated to parties to introduce a degree of proportionality. An 'AV+' system was recommended for Westminster by the 1998 review of first past the post conducted by the late Lord Jenkins (Independent Commission on the Voting System, 1998).

Conversely, if it was felt illegitimate to consider any diminution of proportionality, the additional member system would offer another approach which, like AV+, would sustain the idea of linking some representatives to a constituency base (unlike a list electoral system). Any moderating effects of AMS in heterogeneous constituency contests – arising from tactical votes (and pitches) across the sectarian divide – could then in theory be entirely offset by the proportionality associated with the second, party vote, if the most polarised parties ensured their supporters stuck with them on the latter, even at the expense of 'ticket-splitting'. But even if this were so it would still be an improvement on STV.

AMS, which as we have seen was considered in the 1970s and is used in Scotland and Wales, has been advocated by electoral reformers in the republic, to foster a less clientelistic political culture than that encouraged (though not created) by STV (Sinnott, 1999: 117–19), a system 'infrequently used' outside of Ireland (Farrell, 2001: 122). STV favours localistic competition, through the interaction between constituency representatives – including from the same party – rather than a focus on policy matters and the broader public good. AMS also can help realise the goal of gender equality, as predominantly male political elites can be pressurised to place women in high positions on party lists.

These issues associated with the electoral system should all be addressed by an independent commission, operating transparently, to ensure public legitimisation of any change. Reducing the number of government departments, however, would not even require legislative affirmation (the Northern Ireland Act specified a maximum of 10). Around six (seven to include policing and justice), reorganised around policy goals, would be desirable to foster joined-up government. This would not restrict the number of ministers to the same number, as there could be juniors.

As indicated above, the NSMC should have no restrictions placed on its purview or the 'implementation bodies' it might establish, subject to the requirement that decisions are taken on a basis of consensus between north and south and that lines of accountability are clear in both the Dáil and the Assembly. The envisaged reduced number of northern departments should establish north–south units to liaise with those already established in their southern counterparts.

The Joint Ministerial Committee on Devolution, bringing together representatives of the devolved administrations and London, should be put on a more formal and transparent footing, with a view to ensuring a structured exchange of good practice in a context of growing policy divergence (Jeffery, 2005: 26). The JMC oddly emerged in a late-evening announcement in the Lords during the committee stage of the Scotland Bill in October 1999 (Hazell, 2000: 150). The urgency of this became more evident in the wake of the election of a Scottish Nationalist (minority) administration in Edinburgh in 2007 and renewed (English) Conservative interest in the Westminster implications of the 'West Lothian question'.

Currently, not only does the NSMC escape the scrutiny of the Committee for the OFMDFM but also European affairs are inadequately addressed. In 2007, the Oireachtas established a committee to monitor the implementation of the Belfast agreement, which could be used as a vehicle to render the NSMC more effectively accountable. The Assembly is also the only parliament in these islands which lacks a human rights committee. Establishing a committee on 'external' affairs and one on equality and human rights would rectify these failings, ensure the Assembly took an outward-looking perspective and minimise the risk of non-compliance with EU directives and international human-rights requirements.

When power was first transferred in December 1999, the Assembly agreed to establish two standing committees: equality, human rights and community relations; and European affairs. A week later, however, Trimble and Mallon successfully proposed instead an all-embracing Committee of the Centre (now the Committee for the OFMDFM) to monitor their office, with the assumption that the Assembly as a whole would scrutinise external matters (Wilford and Wilson, 2000: 103). As everyone was responsible, in practice no one was responsible.

The biggest challenge for Northern Ireland remains to heal its deep divisions, social as well as communal. The default option for service delivery should be integrated rather than segregated – not only to improve 'community relations' but also to provide efficient, high-quality services accessible to all. The First Minister – whether from a Protestant, Catholic or 'other' background – should be responsible for giving civic leadership, as well as representing Northern Ireland externally in an impartial manner, while the Deputy First Minister should have a specific portfolio. It is a measure of how far Northern Ireland has still to travel that when the First Minister, Robinson, was asked if he should not represent the whole population, rather than the 'unionist community', he did not understand the question.[19]

Making the change

To implement these constitutional changes, new legislation would be required substantially amending the Northern Ireland Act 1998, passed at Westminster to implement the agreement, and the Northern Ireland (St Andrews Agreement) Act 2006, which paved the way for renewed devolution. But the latter broke the official taboo on any tinkering with the Belfast agreement. It would be vital that the changes envisaged did not meet hostility in Dublin, but the generosity of spirit behind the proposals on north–south cooperation should ensure a fair wind from the Government and opposition parties. In any event, the interviews for this book demonstrated a tendency for more nuanced assessment in that quarter than in London of the issues involved.

As this book has also shown, however, the overriding interest of the British State *vis-à-vis* Northern Ireland has been perceived as mental disengagement, driven by a conservative, essentialist conception of the region's 'difference'. After the years of Blairite activism – seemingly driven by the Prime Minister's desire for a place in history as fulfilling Gladstone's mission to 'pacify Ireland' – that conventional approach, euphemistically articulated in the 1970s as 'distancing', has re-emerged.

So the impetus may well have to come from within Northern Ireland. Yet this book has further highlighted the neglected role of NGOs within the region in acting as catalysts for change, particularly the key role played by the trade unions in stemming polarisation and violence. Moreover, the reconciliation practitioners interviewed come from a larger hinterland of organisations which have been important in knitting together what social fabric the region enjoys (Wilson, 2006). And focus groups conducted by the author in late 2008, drawn from voluntary organisations, the trade unions and public servants, detected a strong appetite for 'change' – particularly in the wake of the, to many inspiring, election of Barack Obama as US President.

The 'communal contender' and non-sectarian parties marginalised by the 'peace process' have a clear interest in challenging the domination of their 'ethnonationalist' rivals, as interviews with figures from the UUP, Alliance, SDLP and Greens at that time also evidenced – even if they recognised the 'prisoner's dilemma' which militated against joint action. It is certainly not in their interest that future Assembly elections, like the 2009 European Parliament election, should be defined by an 'arms race' over whether the DUP or SF can top the poll.

Following the advice of FitzGerald, the former Taoiseach, if those more centrist parties were to come together behind a 'platform for change', gelled together by wide civic endorsement, they could plausibly present themselves as a quasi-alternative coalition to the DUP–SF diarchy at the 2011 election and afterwards. The platform could include a commitment by the parties to seek more flexible power-sharing arrangements.

Electoral success would mean that, immediately, these would be the predominant parties in a d'Hondt Executive, vitiating the blocking vetoes installed at St Andrews which have rendered government so inert, and so able to shift the focus from ethnic protagonism to 'bread-and-butter' issues via a substantial Programme for Government. In such a context, it would be very difficult for London, and Dublin, to ignore electorally mandated pressures for reform.

But even if such a platform were not to be the basis for an electoral majority at the next Assembly election, it would at least ensure that a quasi-opposition emerged in the following Assembly term. And this could eventually turn into a quasi-alternative government, even in the absence of formal arrangements for alternation, at a future poll.

Conclusion

This concluding chapter has set out an agenda for structural reform which would not throw out the baby of the Belfast agreement with the sectarian and even paramilitary bathwater with which it has come to be associated. It would preserve the key principles of power-sharing devolution, civic participation, cooperation across jurisdictions, and equality and human rights. But it would reform the constitutional context so as to be more conducive to their realisation. In particular, it holds out the prospect of Northern Ireland becoming a normal, civic society at ease with the various environments – Irish, British and European – in which it finds itself and making the most of that unique positioning.

In sum, what is envisaged here is a settlement, premised on the twin democratic principles of liberty and equality. Within Northern Ireland, this means a power-sharing arrangement which ensures Catholics can never again be subordinated by their minority demographic position but also gives citizens the freedom to choose identities outside communalist straitjackets. Beyond Northern Ireland, it entails a federal relationship with the rest of the UK and a confederal relationship with the rest of Ireland, and a keen engagement with the rest of Europe, allowing everyone resident in Northern Ireland an equal opportunity to exploit wider political networks, as they may freely choose.

This perspective is congruent with universal norms and chimes with the longing of a Northern Ireland public weary of conventional politics as well as violence. It is in tune with a more individualised, globalised and multi-ethnic society. It would establish a political architecture which, far from being utopian, would provide the best possible shell for intercultural dialogue. It thus signposts a route, with practical steps to be taken, from an uneasy peace to a genuine reconciliation.

Notes

1 They evoked a hostile editorial in a respected international science magazine: 'Why homosexuality is not unnatural', *New Scientist* (21 June 2008).
2 See www.ark.ac.uk/nilt/2006/Community_Relations/WHATFLAG.html [accessed 19 July 2009].
3 See www.ark.ac.uk/nilt/2006/Political_Attitudes/UNINATID.html [accessed 23 July 2009].
4 See www.ark.ac.uk/nilt/2008/Political_Attitudes/UNINATID.html [accessed 23 July 2009].
5 See www.nistudents.org/.
6 This breakdown of competences is detailed in schedules to the act.
7 See www.ark.ac.uk/nilt/2001/Political_Attitudes/index.html [accessed 23 July

2009].

8 See www.ark.ac.uk/nilt/2000/Political_Attitudes/ASSMBDO2.html [accessed 23 July 2009].

9 Author interview, 25 February 2008.

10 This has been endorsed by a former head of the Industrial Development Board in Northern Ireland: Alan Gillespie, 'All-island economic marketing agency is way ahead', *Irish Times* (3 October 2007).

11 John Bowman, 'Whitaker advised Lynch to pursue Irish unity peacefully and by seeking unionist agreement', *Irish Times* (1 and 2 January 2001).

12 'Gap "much too wide between planter and Gael" says official', *Irish News* (1 January 2004).

13 Martina Purdy, 'Mallon toasts Good Friday Agreement', *BBC Northern Ireland* (20 March 2008).

14 The text is at www.sdlp.ie/key_speech_item.php?id=7758 [accessed 23 July 2009].

15 Danny Kennedy, 'Crisis in the Executive', *Fortnight*, 461 (September 2008).

16 David White, 'N. Ireland's armed peace', *Financial Times* (13 March 2001).

17 McGarry and O'Leary (2004: 25) present such 'exclusionary' coalitions as threatening to peace. I have already addressed (in Chapter 3) the confusion here between inclusion in the political community and inclusion in government. I also demonstrated (in Chapter 2) that there was no correspondence between the inclusion or otherwise of parties in government in Northern Ireland in the past decade and the incidence of politically-motivated violence, which I have however linked to the effect of perverse 'security' policies which abrogated human rights and the principle of impartiality.

18 This was pointed out by Professor Sydney Elliott in his live analysis for BBC Northern Ireland of the results.

19 Interview on *Hearts and Minds*, BBC Northern Ireland (30 October 2008).

References

State archives

National Archives, Bishop Street, Dublin

Department of Foreign Affairs (DFA)
Department of the Taoiseach (TAOIS)

National Archives, Kew, London

Cabinet Office (CAB)
Foreign and Commonwealth Office (FCO)
Northern Ireland Office (CJ)
Prime Minister's Office (PREM)

Official publications

Council of Europe (2008), *White Paper on Intercultural Dialogue: Living Together as Equals in Dignity* (Strasbourg: Council of Europe), www.coe.int/t/dg4/intercultural/Source/White%20Paper_final_revised_EN.pdf [accessed 16 June 2009]
—— (2005) *Convention on the Prevention of Terrorism* (Strasbourg: Council of Europe), http://conventions.coe.int/Treaty/EN/Treaties/Html/196.htm [accessed 18 July 2009]
—— (2001), *Framework Agreement* [authorised English-language version of Ohrid agreement] (Strasbourg: Council of Europe), www.coe.int/t/e/legal_affairs/legal_co-operation/police_and_internal_security/OHRID%20Agreement%2013august2001.asp [accessed 16 June 2009]
—— (1995), *Framework Convention for the Protection of National Minorities and Explanatory Report* (Strasbourg: Council of Europe), http://conventions.coe.int/Treaty/en/Treaties/Html/157.htm [accessed 16 June 2009]
—— (1992), *European Charter for Regional or Minority Languages* (Strasbourg: Council of Europe), http://conventions.coe.int/treaty/en/Treaties/Html/148.htm [accessed 16 June 2009]
Council of Europe Parliamentary Assembly (2004), Resolution 1384, 'Strengthening of democratic institutions in Bosnia and Herzegovina', http://assembly.coe.int/main.

asp?Link=/documents/adoptedtext/ta04/eres1384.htm [accessed 16 June 2009]

Department of Foreign Affairs (1995), *A New Framework for Agreement* (Dublin: DFA), http://foreignaffairs.gov.ie/home/index.aspx?id=8735 [accessed 16 June 2009]

—— (1993), *Joint Declaration 1993 (Downing St Declaration)* (Dublin: DFA), http://foreignaffairs.gov.ie/home/index.aspx?id=8734 [accessed 16 June 2009]

—— (1985), *The Anglo-Irish Agreement* (Dublin: DFA), http://foreignaffairs.gov.ie/uploads/documents/anglo-irish%20agreement%201985.pdf [accessed 16 June 2009]

European Commission for Democracy Through Law [the Venice Commission] (2005), 'Opinion on the constitutional situation in Bosnia and Herzegovina and the powers of the high representative' (Strasbourg: Council of Europe), www.venice.coe.int/docs/2005/CDL-AD(2005)004-e.pdf [accessed 16 June 2009]

—— (2002), 'Opinion on possible groups of persons to which the Framework Convention for the Protection of National Minorities could be applied in Belgium' (Strasbourg: Council of Europe), www.venice.coe.int/docs/2002/CDL-AD(2002)001-e.asp [accessed 16 June 2009]

Independent Commission on the Voting System (1998), *Report of the Independent Commission on the Voting System* (Cm 4090, London: Stationery Office), www.archive.official-documents.co.uk/document/cm40/4090/4090.htm [accessed 16 June 2009]

The International Body (1996), *Report of the International Body* (Dublin and Belfast: The International Body), http://cain.ulst.ac.uk/events/peace/docs/gm24196.htm [accessed 16 June 2009]

New Ireland Forum (1984), *Report* (Dublin: Stationery Office), http://cain.ulst.ac.uk/issues/politics/nifr.htm#accomm [accessed 16 June 2009]

Northern Ireland Constitutional Convention (1975), *Report* (London: HMSO)

Northern Ireland Executive (2008), *Building a Better Future: Programme for Government 2008–2011* (Belfast: Northern Ireland Executive), www.pfgbudgetni.gov.uk/finalpfg.pdf [accessed 16 June 2009]

—— (2001), *Making a Difference: Programme for Government 2002–2005* (Belfast: Northern Ireland Executive), www.pfgbudgetni.gov.uk/pfgreport0205main1.pdf [accessed 16 June 2009]

—— (2000), *Making a Difference: Programme for Government 2001–2004* (Belfast: Northern Ireland Executive)

Northern Ireland Office (2006), *Agreement at St Andrews* (London: NIO), www.nio.gov.uk/st_andrews_agreement.pdf [accessed 16 June 2009]

—— (1998), *The Agreement: Agreement Reached in the Multi-party Negotiations* (Belfast: NIO), www.nio.gov.uk/agreement.pdf [accessed 16 June 2009]

—— (1979), *The Government of Northern Ireland: A Working Paper for a Conference* (Cmnd 7763, London: HMSO)

—— (1975), *The Government of Northern Ireland: A Society Divided*, discussion paper 3 (London: HMSO)

—— (1974), *The Northern Ireland Constitution* (Cmnd 5675, London: HMSO)

—— (1973), *Northern Ireland Constitutional Proposals* (Cmnd 5259, London: HMSO)

—— (1972), *The Future of Northern Ireland: A Paper for Discussion* (London:

HMSO)

Office of the First Minister and Deputy First Minister (2006), *A Shared Future: First Triennial Action Plan 2006–2009* (Belfast: OFMDFM)

—— (2005), *A Shared Future: Policy and Strategic Framework for Good Relations in Northern Ireland* (Belfast: OFMDFM), www.asharedfutureni.gov.uk/pdf_documents/gprs.pdf [accessed 16 June 2009]

Organisation for Security and Co-operation in Europe (2007), *Bosnia and Herzegovina General Elections 1 October 2006: OSCE/ODIHR Election Observation Mission Final Report* (Warsaw: OSCE), www.osce.org/documents/odihr/2007/02/23206_en.pdf [accessed 16 June 2009]

—— (2003), *Bosnia and Herzegovina General Elections 5 October 2002: Final Report* (Warsaw: OSCE), www.osce.org/documents/odihr/2003/01/1188_en.pdf [accessed 16 June 2009]

US State Department (1995), *The Dayton Peace Accords* (Washington: State Department), www.state.gov/www/regions/eur/bosnia/bosagree.html [accessed 16 June 2009]

Parliamentary records cited

Dáil Debates
Hansard
Official Report (Northern Ireland Assembly)

Media cited

An Phoblacht
Balkan Crisis Report/Balkan Insight
BBC Northern Ireland
Belfast Telegraph
CNN
The Economist
Financial Times
Fortnight
Guardian
Independent
Irish Independent
Irish News
Irish Press (no longer published)
Irish Times
Jerusalem Post
New York Times
News Letter
Observer (Irish edition)
Spectator
Sunday Independent
Sunday Press (no longer published)
Sunday Times (Irish edition)

References

Sunday Tribune
The Times
Washington Post

Unpublished theses

Finlayson, Alan (1996), 'Political Ideology and the Mythic Discourse of Nationalism' (Queen's University Belfast)

Russell, David (2004), 'Constitutional Design in Multi-communal Societies: A Comparative Study of Lebanon and Northern Ireland' (University of York)

Books, articles and papers

Acheson, Nicholas and Carl Milofsky (2008), 'Peace building and participation in Northern Ireland: local social movements and the policy process since the "Good Friday" agreement', *Ethnopolitics*, 7:1, 63–80

Akenson, Donald Harman (1988), *Small Differences: Irish Catholics and Irish Protestants 1815–1922* (Dublin: Gill and Macmillan)

Al-Azmeh, Aziz (2008), 'Afterword', in Aziz Al-Azmeh and Effie Fokas (eds), *Islam in Europe: Diversity, Identity and Influence* (Cambridge: Cambridge University Press), 208–15

Allen, Tim and John Eade (1999), 'Understanding ethnicity', in Allen and Eade (eds), *Divided Europeans: Understanding Ethnicities in Conflict* (The Hague: Kluwer Law International), 11–40

Alonso, Rogelio (2007), *The IRA and Armed Struggle* (London: Routledge)

Amnesty International (2009), *Israel/Gaza–Operation 'Cast Lead': 22 Days of Death and Destruction* (London: AI), www.amnesty.org/en/library/asset/MDE15/015/2009/en/8f299083–9a74–4853–860f–0563725e633a/mde150152009en.pdf [accessed 26 July 2009]

— (1994), *Political Killings in Northern Ireland* (London: Amnesty International)

Anderson, Benedict (1983), *Imagined Communities* (London: Verso)

Anderson, Don (1994), *14 May Days: The Inside Story of the Loyalist Strike of 1974* (Dublin: Gill and Macmillan)

Ashe, Fidelma (2006), 'Gendering the Holy Cross dispute: women and nationalism in Northern Ireland', *Political Studies*, 54:1, 147–64

Aughey, Arthur (2005), *The Politics of Northern Ireland: Beyond the Belfast Agreement* (London: Routledge)

Bakke, Kristin M., Xun Cao, John O'Loughlin and Michael D. Ward (2009), 'Social distance in Bosnia-Herzegovina and the North Caucasus region of Russia: inter and intra-ethnic attitudes and identities', *Nations and Nationalism*, 15:2, 227–53

Bardon, Jonathan (1992), *A History of Ulster* (Belfast: Blackstaff Press)

Barry, Brian (2001), *Culture and Equality: An Egalitarian Critique of Multiculturalism* (Cambridge: Polity Press)

—— (1975), 'The consociational model and its dangers', *European Journal of Political Research*, 3, 393–412

Bauer, Otto (2000 [1906]), *The Question of Nationalities and Social Democracy* (Minneapolis: University of Minnesota Press)

Bauman, Zygmunt (2004), *Identity* (Cambridge, Polity Press)

—— (2002), 'Cultural variety or variety of cultures?', in Siniša Malešević and Mark Haugaard (eds), *Making Sense of Collectivity* (London: Pluto Press), 167–80

—— (2001), *Community* (Cambridge, Polity Press)

Bean, Kevin (2007), *The New Politics of Sinn Féin* (Liverpool: Liverpool University Press)

Beck, Ulrich (2009), *World at Risk* (Cambridge: Polity Press)

—— (2006), *The Cosmopolitan Vision* (Cambridge: Polity Press)

—— (2005), *Power in a Global Age* (Cambridge: Polity Press)

—— (1997), *The Reinvention of Politics: Rethinking Modernity in the Global Social Order* (Cambridge, Polity Press)

Beck, Ulrich and Edgar Grande (2007), *Cosmopolitan Europe* (Cambridge, Polity Press)

Belloni, Roberto (2007), *State Building and International Intervention in Bosnia* (London: Routledge)

Belmont, Katharine, Scott Mainwaring and Andrew Reynolds (2002), 'Introduction: institutional design, conflict management, and democracy', in Andrew Reynolds (ed.), *The Architecture of Democracy: Constitutional Design, Conflict Management, and Democracy* (Oxford: Oxford University Press), 1–11

Benhabib, Seyla (2002a), *The Claims of Culture: Equality and Diversity in the Global Era* (Princeton, NJ: Princeton University Press)

—— (2002b), 'Transformations of citizenship: the case of contemporary Europe', *Government and Opposition*, 37:4, 439–65

Bennett, Tony (2001), *Differing Diversities: Cultural Policy and Cultural Diversity* (Strasbourg: Council of Europe)

Benton, Ted and Ian Craib (2001), *Philosophy of Social Science: The Philosophical Foundations of Social Thought* (Basingstoke: Palgrave)

Bew, Paul, Peter Gibbon and Henry Patterson (1995), *Northern Ireland 1921–1994: Political Forces and Social Classes* (London: Serif)

Bew, Paul and Gordon Gillespie (1999 [1993]), *Northern Ireland: A Chronology of the Troubles 1968–1999* (Dublin: Gill and Macmillan)

Bew, Paul and Henry Patterson (1985), *The British State and the Ulster Crisis: From Wilson to Thatcher* (London: Verso)

Bhaskar, Roy (1975), *A Realist Theory of Science* (Leeds: Leeds Books)

Biagini, Eugenio (2007), *British Democracy and Irish Nationalism 1876–1906* (Cambridge: Cambridge University Press)

Bideleux, Robert and Ian Jeffries (1998), *A History of Eastern Europe: Crisis and Change* (London: Routledge)

Bieber, Florian (2008), 'After Dayton, Dayton? The Evolution of an unpopular peace', in Marc Weller and Stefan Wolff (eds), *International State-Building after Violent Conflict: Bosnia Ten Years after Dayton* (London: Routledge), 14–30

—— (2006), *Post-War Bosnia: Ethnicity, Inequality and Public Sector Governance* (Basingstoke: Palgrave)

—— (2005), 'Partial implementation, partial success: the case of Macedonia', in Ian O'Flynn and David Russell (eds), *Power Sharing: New Challenges for Divided Societies* (London: Pluto Press), 107–22

Bjørgo, Tore (2005), 'Conclusions', in Tore Bjørgo (ed.), *Root Causes of Terrorism: Myths, Reality and Ways Forward* (London, Routledge), 256–64

Bloomer, Fiona and Peter Weinreich (2003), 'Cross-community relations projects and interdependent identities', in Owen Hargie and David Dickson (eds), *Researching the Troubles: Social Science Perspectives on the Northern Ireland Conflict* (Edinburgh: Mainstream), 141–61

Bloomfield, David (1998), *Political Dialogue in Northern Ireland: The Brooke Initiative 1989–92* (Basingstoke: Macmillan)

Bloomfield, Ken (2007), *A Tragedy of Errors: The Government and Misgovernment of Northern Ireland* (Liverpool: Liverpool University Press)

—— (1994), *Stormont in Crisis: A Memoir* (Belfast: Blackstaff Press)

Blumi, Isa (2003), 'Ethnic borders in a democratic society in Kosova: the UN's identity card', in Florian Bieber and Židas Daskalovski (eds), *Understanding the War in Kosovo* (London: Frank Cass), 217–36

Bobbio, Norberto (1996a), *The Age of Rights* (Cambridge: Polity Press)

—— (1996b) *Left and Right: The Significance of a Political Distinction* (Cambridge: Polity Press)

Bogaards, Matthijs (2000), 'The uneasy relationship between empirical and normative types in consociational theory', *Journal of Theoretical Politics*, 12:4, 395–423

—— (1998), 'The favourable factors for consociational democracy: a review', *European Journal of Political Research*, 33, 475–96

Bogdanor, Vernon (1999), *Devolution in the United Kingdom* (Oxford: Oxford University Press)

Borooah, Vani K., Patrick McKee, Norma Heaton and Gráinne Collins (1995), 'Catholic–Protestant income differences in Northern Ireland', *Review of Income and Wealth*, 41:1, 41–56

Borooah, Vani K. and John Mangan, 'Love thy neighbour: how much bigotry is there in western countries', *Kyklos*, 60:3, 295–317

Bose, Sumantra (2003), *Kashmir: Roots of Conflict, Paths to Peace* (Cambridge, MA: Harvard University Press)

—— (2002), *Bosnia After Dayton: Nationalist Partition and International Intervention* (London: Hurst & Co)

Boyle, Kevin and Tom Hadden (1994), *Northern Ireland: The Choice* (London: Penguin)

—— (1985), *Ireland: A Positive Proposal* (Harmondsworth: Penguin)

Boyle, Kevin, Tom Hadden and Paddy Hillyard (1980), *Ten Years on in Northern Ireland: The Legal Control of Political Violence* (London: Cobden Trust)

—— (1975), *Law and the State: The Case of Northern Ireland* (London: Martin Robertson and Co)

Bracewell, Wendy (2000), 'Rape in Kosovo: masculinity and Serbian nationalism', *Nations and Nationalism*, 6:4, 563–90

Brass, Paul R. (1991), *Ethnicity and Nationalism: Theory and Comparison* (London: Sage)

Breuilly, John (1982), *Nationalism and the State* (Manchester: Manchester University Press)

British Council Ireland (2005), *Britain & Ireland: Lives Entwined* (Dublin: British

Council Ireland)

Brown, Rupert and Myles Hewstone (2005), 'An integrative theory of intergroup contact', *Advances in Experimental Social Psychology*, 37, 255–343

Brubaker, Rogers (2004), *Ethnicity Without Groups* (Cambridge, MA: Harvard University Press)

—— (2002), 'Ethnicity without groups', *Archives Européenes de Sociologie*, 43:2, 163–89

—— (1996), *Nationalism Reframed: Nationhood and the National Question in the New Europe* (Cambridge: Cambridge University Press)

Bruton, John (2006), 'A personal perspective on Ireland's relationship with Britain', in British Council Ireland, *Britain and Ireland: Lives Entwined II* (Dublin: British Council Ireland), 13–32

Buckland, Patrick (1979), *The Factory of Grievances: Devolved Government in Northern Ireland 1921–1939* (Dublin: Gill and Macmillan)

Byrne, Jonny, Ulf Hansson and John Bell (2006), *Shared Living: Mixed Residential Communities in Northern Ireland* (Belfast: Institute for Conflict Research)

Cairney, Paul and Michael Keating (2004), 'Sewel motions in the Scottish Parliament', *Scottish Affairs*, 47, 115–34

Calhoun, Craig (2002), 'The class consciousness of frequent travelers: towards a critique of actually existing cosmopolitanism', *South Atlantic Quarterly*, 101:4, 869–97

Calic, Marie-Janine (2003), 'Explaining ethnic violence in Bosnia-Herzegovina', in Farimah Daftery and Stefan Troebst (eds), *Radical Ethnic Movements in Contemporary Europe* (New York: Berghahn Books), 105–30

Callaghan, James (1973), *A House Divided* (London: Collins)

Cartritte, Britt (2002), 'Contemporary ethnopolitical identity and the future of the Belgian state', *Nationalism and Ethnic Politics*, 8:3, 43–71

Cassese, Antonio (1995), *Self-determination of Peoples: A Legal Reappraisal* (Cambridge: Cambridge University Press)

Castells, Manuel (1996), *The Rise of the Network Society* (Oxford: Blackwell)

Chambers, Simone (2004), 'Behind closed doors: publicity, secrecy and the quality of deliberation', *Journal of Political Philosophy*, 12:4, 389–410

Chandler, David (2000 [1999]), *Bosnia: Faking Democracy After Dayton* (London: Pluto Press)

Chryssochoou, Xenia (2004a), *Cultural Diversity: Its Social Psychology* (Oxford: Blackwell)

—— (2004b), 'Living together on what grounds? Defining the common project and the value-competences to achieve it', in Council of Europe, *Joint Youth and Culture Initiative: Expert Group Meeting – 'Building dialogue on what values?'* (Strasbourg: Council of Europe), 53–9

Cinalli, Manlio (2005), 'Below and beyond power sharing: relational structures across institutions and civil society', in Ian O'Flynn and David Russell (eds), *Power Sharing: New Challenges for Divided Societies* (London: Pluto Press), 172–87

Civic Forum (2002), *A Regional Strategy for Social Inclusion* (Belfast: Civic Forum)

Coakley, John (2009), 'The political consequences of the electoral system in Northern Ireland', *Irish Political Studies*, 24:3, 253–84

References

Coakley, John, Brian Ó Caoindealbháin and Robin Wilson (2007), 'Institutional cooperation: the north-south implementation bodies', in John Coakley and Liam O'Dowd (eds), *Crossing the Border: New Relationships between Northern Ireland and the Republic of Ireland* (Dublin: Irish Academic Press), 31–60

Coleman, Stephen and Jay G. Blumler (2009), *The Internet and Democratic Citizenship: Theory, Practice and Policy* (Cambridge: Cambridge University Press)

Community Relations Council (2008), *Towards Sustainable Security: Interface Barriers and the Legacy of Segregation in Belfast* (Belfast: Community Relations Council), http://www.nicrc.org.uk/filestore/documents/iwg-publication.pdf [accessed 16 June 2009]

Conces, Rory (2005), 'A Sisyphean tale: the pathology of ethnic nationalism and the pedagogy of forging humane democracies in the Balkans', *Studies in East European Thought*, 57, 139–84

Connor, Walker (1994), *Ethnonationalism: The Quest for Understanding* (Princeton, NJ: Princeton University Press)

Costa, Pietro (2004), 'From national to European citizenship: a historical comparison', in Richard Bellamy, Dario Castiglione and Emilio Santoro (eds), *Lineages of European Citizenship: Rights, Belonging and Participation in Eleven Nation-States* (Basingstoke, Palgrave), 207–26

Cowan, Jane K., Marie-Bénédicte Dembour and Richard A. Wilson (2001), 'Introduction', in Cowan, Dembour and Wilson (eds), *Culture and Rights: Anthropological Perspectives* (Cambridge: Cambridge University Press), 1–26

Coward, Rosalind and John Ellis (1977), *Language and Materialism: Developments in Semiology and the Theory of the Subject* (London: Routledge and Kegan Paul)

Cradden, Terry (1993), *Trade Unionism, Socialism and Partition* (Belfast: December Publications)

Crossman, Richard (1977), *The Diaries of a Cabinet Minister: Volume III, 1968–70* (London: Hamish Hamilton and Jonathan Cape)

Cunningham, Michael (2001), *British Government Policy in Northern Ireland 1969–2000* (Manchester: Manchester University Press)

Daftery, Farimah (2001), 'Testing Macedonia', European Centre for Minorities Issues brief 4 (Flensburg: European Centre for Minority Issues), www. ecmi.de/download/brief_4.pdf [accessed 16 June 2009]

Daskalovski, Zhidas (2004), 'Democratic consolidation and the "stateness" problem: the case of Macedonia', *Global Review of Ethnopolitics*, 3:2, 52–66

Dawson, Graham (2007), *Making Peace with the Past? Memory, Trauma and the Irish Troubles* (Manchester: Manchester University Press)

Delanty, Gerard (1995), *Inventing Europe: Idea, Identity, Reality* (Basingstoke: Macmillan)

Delanty, Gerard and Patrick O'Mahony (2002), *Nationalism and Social Theory* (London: Sage)

Deschouwer, Kris (2005), 'The unintended consequences of consociational federalism: the case of Belgium', in Ian O'Flynn and David Russell (eds), *Power Sharing: New Challenges for Divided Societies* (London: Pluto Press), 92–106

Devlin, Paddy (1993), *Straight Left: An Autobiography* (Belfast: Blackstaff Press)

De Winter, Lieven, Marc Swyngedouw and Patrick Dumont (2006), 'Party system(s) and electoral behaviour in Belgium: from stability to Balkanisation', *West European Politics*, 29:5, 933–56

De Zwart, Frank (2005), 'The dilemma of recognition: administrative categories and cultural diversity', *Theory and Society*, 34:2, 137–69

Dixon, Paul (2001), *Northern Ireland: The Politics of War and Peace* (Basingstoke: Palgrave)

—— (1997), 'Paths to peace in Northern Ireland (I): civil society and consociational approaches', *Democratization*, 4:2, 1–27

Disdarević, Srđan (2004), 'The unfinished state?', in Christophe Solioz and Tobias K. Vogel (eds), *Dayton and Beyond: Perspectives on the Future of Bosnia and Herzegovina* (Baden-Baden: Nomos), 37–44

Donia, Robert J. and John V. A. Fine Jr (1994), *Bosnia and Hercegovina: A Tradition Betrayed* (London: Hurst & Co)

Donoughue, Bernard (2005), *Downing Street Diary: With Harold Wilson in No. 10* (London: Jonathan Cape)

— (1987), *Prime Minister: The Conduct of Policy under Harold Wilson and James Callaghan* (London: Jonathan Cape)

Dowds, Lizanne (2009), 'Public attitudes and identity', in Rick Wilford and Robin Wilson (eds), *Northern Ireland Devolution Monitoring Report: May 2009* (London: University College), www.ucl.ac.uk/constitution-unit/files/research/devolution/dmr/NI_May09.pdf [accessed 17 July 2009], 29–30

Driver, Stephen and Luke Martell (1998), *New Labour: Politics After Thatcherism* (Cambridge: Polity Press)

Dryzek, John S. (2005), 'Deliberative democracy in divided societies: alternatives to agonism and analgesia', *Political Theory*, 33, 218–42

Duffy, Terence and James Dingley (1999), 'Northern Ireland and the UK since the Good Friday Agreement', *Representation*, 36:1, 39–52

Durkheim, Emile (1972), *Selected Writings*, edited with an introduction by Anthony Giddens (Cambridge: Cambridge University Press)

Edwards, Michael (2004), *Civil Society* (Cambridge: Polity Press)

Edwards, Owen Dudley (1970), *The Sins of our Fathers* (Dublin: Gill and Macmillan)

Eide, Asbjørn (1993), *New Approaches to Minority Protection* (London: Minority Rights Group International)

Elliott, Sydney (2001), 'The people's verdict', in Robin Wilson (ed.), *Agreeing to Disagree? A Guide to the Northern Ireland Assembly* (London: Stationery Office), 129–37

Elliott, Sydney and W. D. Flackes (1999 [1980]), *Northern Ireland: A Political Directory 1968–1999* (Belfast: Blackstaff Press)

English, Richard (2003), *Armed Struggle: A History of the IRA* (London: Macmillan)

Eriksen, Thomas Hylland (1993) *Ethnicity and Nationalism: Anthropological Perspectives* (London: Pluto Press)

Erk, Jan and Lawrence Anderson (2009), 'The paradox of federalism: does self-rule accommodate or exacerbate ethnic divisions?', *Regional and Federal Studies*, 19:2, 191–202

European Stability Initiative (2002), 'The other Macedonian conflict', European Stability Initiative discussion paper (Berlin: ESI), www.esiweb.org/pdf/esi_

document_id_32.pdf [accessed 16 June 2009]

—— (2001), *Democracy, Security and the Future of the Stability Pact for South Eastern Europe* (Berlin: ESI), www.esiweb.org/pdf/esi_document_id_15.pdf [accessed 16 June 2009]

Fallend, Franz (2004), 'Are right-wing populism and government participation incompatible? The case of the Freedom Party of Austria', *Representation*, 40:2, 115–30

Farrell, David M. (2001), *Electoral Systems: A Comparative Introduction* (Basingstoke: Palgrave)

Farrington, Christopher (2007), 'Party competition in ethnically divided societies: empirically testing the existence of centrifugal dynamics', paper delivered at Queen's University Belfast conference, 'Northern Ireland Beyond Crises: Is it Working?', 6 December 2007

Faulkner, Brian (1978), *Memoirs of a Statesman* (London: Weidenfield and Nicholson)

Fearon, James D. and David D. Laitin (2000), 'Violence and the social construction of ethnic identity', *International Organization*, 54:4, 845–77

Fisk, Robert (1975), *The Point of No Return: The Strike which Broke the British in Ulster* (London: Andre Deutsch)

FitzGerald, Garret (2006), 'The 1974–5 threat of a British withdrawal from Northern Ireland', *Irish Studies in International Affairs*, 17, 141–50

—— (1992), *All in a Life* (Dublin: Gill and Macmillan)

—— (1972), *Towards a New Ireland* (London: Charles Knight & Co)

Foundation on Inter-Ethnic Relations (1999) *The Lund Recommendations on the Effective Participation of National Minorities in Public Life & Explanatory Note* (The Hague: Foundation on Inter-Ethnic Relations)

—— (1998), *The Oslo Recommendations Regarding the Linguistic Rights of National Minorities in Public Life & Explanatory Note* (The Hague: FI-ER)

—— (1996), *The Hague Recommendations Regarding the Education Rights of National Minorities in Public Life & Explanatory Note* (The Hague: FI-ER)

Fraenkel, Jon and Bernard Grofman (2006), 'Does the alternative vote foster moderation in ethnically divided societies? The case of Fiji', *Comparative Political Studies*, 39:5, 623–51

Frampton, Martin (2009), *The Long March: The Political Strategy of Sinn Féin, 1981–2007* (Basingstoke: Palgrave)

Frost, Catherine (2006), 'Is post-nationalism or liberal-culturalism behind the transformation of Irish nationalism?', *Irish Political Studies*, 21:3, 277–95

Gallagher, Tom (2003), *The Balkans After the Cold War: From Tyranny to Tragedy* (London: Routledge)

Garvin, Tom (2005 [1987]), *Nationalist Revolutionaries in Ireland 1858–1928* (Dublin: Gill and Macmillan)

— (1996), *1922: The Birth of Irish Democracy* (Dublin: Gill and Macmillan)

Geary, Patrick J. (2003), *The Myth of Nations: The Medieval Origins of Europe* (Princeton, NJ: Princeton University Press)

Gellner, Ernest (1993), 'Nationalism and the development of European societies', in Jyrki Iivonen (ed.), *The Future of the Nation State in Europe* (Aldershot: Edward Elgar)

—— (1983), *Nations and Nationalism* (Oxford: Blackwell)

Ghai, Yash Pal (2002), 'Constitutional asymmetries: communal representation, federalism, and cultural autonomy', in Andrew Reynolds (ed.), *The Architecture of Democracy: Constitutional Design, Conflict Management, and Democracy* (Oxford: Oxford University Press), 141–70

—— (2001), *Public Participation and Minorities* (London: Minority Rights Group International)

Gibbon, Peter (1977), 'Some basic problems of the contemporary situation', *Socialist Register*, 14, 81–7

Giddens, Anthony (1994), *Beyond Left and Right: The Future of Radical Politics* (Cambridge: Polity Press)

Gilligan, Chris (2007), 'The Irish question and the concept "identity" in the 1980s', *Nations and Nationalism*, 13:4, 599–617

Glenny, Misha (1999), *The Balkans 1804–1999: Nationalism, War and the Great Powers* (London: Granta Books)

Gow, James (2008),'The ICTY, war crimes enforcement and Dayton: the ghost in the machine', in Marc Weller and Stefan Wolff (eds), *International State-Building after Violent Conflict: Bosnia Ten Years after Dayton* (London: Routledge), 47–63

Gramsci, Antonio (1971), *Selections from the Prison Notebooks of Antonio Gramsci*, edited and translated by Quintin Hoare and Geoffrey Nowell Smith (London: Lawrence and Wishart)

Greer, Scott L. (2004), *Territorial Politics and Health Policy* (Manchester: Manchester University Press)

Guelke, Adrian (2003), 'Civil society and the Northern Irish peace process', *Voluntas*, 14:1, 61–78

—— (2000), '"Comparatively peaceful": South Africa, the Middle East and Northern Ireland', in Michael Cox, Adrian Guelke and Fiona Stephen (eds), *A Farewell to Arms? From 'Long War' to Long Peace in Northern Ireland* (Manchester: Manchester University Press), 223–33

Guibernau, Montserrat (2004), 'Anthony D. Smith on nations and national identity: a critical assessment', *Nations and Nationalism*, 10:1/2, 125–41

Habermas, Jürgen (2004), 'Religious tolerance – the pacemaker for cultural rights', *Philosophy*, 79, 5–18

—— (2001), 'Why Europe needs a constitution', *New Left Review*, 11, 5–26

Hadden, Tom (2001), 'Devolved and retained powers', in Robin Wilson (ed.), *Agreeing to Disagree? A Guide to the Northern Ireland Assembly* (London: Stationery Office)

Hadden, Tom and Kevin Boyle (1989), *The Anglo-Irish Agreement: Commentary, Text and Official Review* (London: Sweet & Maxwell)

Haines, Joe (1977), *The Politics of Power* (London: Jonathan Cape)

Hall, John A. (2002), 'A disagreement about difference', in Siniša Malešević and Mark Haugaard (eds), *Making Sense of Collectivity: Ethnicity, Nationalism and Globalization* (London: Pluto), 181–94

Hall, Stuart (2003), 'New Labour's double shuffle', *Soundings*, 24, 10–24

—— (1996a), 'New ethnicities', in David Morley and Kuan-Hsing Chen (eds), *Critical Dialogues in Cultural Studies* (London: Routledge), 441–9

—— (1996b), 'Gramsci's relevance for the study of race and ethnicity', in David Morley and Kuan-Hsing Chen (eds), *Critical Dialogues in Cultural Studies* (London: Routledge), 411–40

Halliday, Fred (2001), *The World at 2000: Perils and Promises* (Basingstoke: Palgrave)

Halpern, Sue (1986), 'The disorderly universe of consociational democracy', *West European Politics*, 9:2, 181–97

Hannum, Hurst (1992), *Autonomy, Sovereignty and Self-determination: The Accommodation of Conflicting Rights* (Philadelphia, PA: University of Pennsylvania Press)

Hargie, Owen, David Dickson and Seanenne Nelson (2003), 'Cross-community communication and relationships in the workplace: a case study of a large Northern Ireland organisation', in Owen Hargie and David Dickson (eds), *Researching the Troubles: Social Science Perspectives on the Northern Ireland Conflict* (Edinburgh: Mainstream), 183–207

Hayes, Maurice (1995), *Minority Verdict: Experiences of a Catholic Civil Servant* (Belfast: Blackstaff Press)

Hayes, Bernadette C. and Ian McAllister (1999), 'Ethnonationalism, public opinion and the Good Friday Agreement', in Joseph Ruane and Jennifer Todd (eds), *After the Good Friday Agreement* (Dublin: University College Dublin Press), 30–48

Hayward, Katy (2009), *Irish Nationalism and European Integration: The Official Redefinition of the Island of Ireland* (Manchester: Manchester University Press)

—— (2006), 'Reiterating national identities: the European Union conception of conflict resolution in Northern Ireland', *Cooperation and Conflict*, 41:3, 261–84

Hazell, Robert (2003), 'Conclusion: the devolution scorecard as the devolved assemblies head for the polls', in Robert Hazell (ed.), *The State of the Nations 2003: The Third Year of Devolution in the United Kingdom* (Exeter: Imprint Academic), 285–302

—— (2000), 'Intergovernmental relations: Whitehall rules OK?', in Robert Hazell (ed.), *The State and the Nations: The First Year of Devolution in the United Kingdom* (Thorverton, Imprint Academic), 149–82

Heald, David (2003), *Funding the Northern Ireland Assembly: Assessing the Options*, Northern Ireland Economic Council research monograph 10 (Belfast: Northern Ireland Economic Council) [incorporated into the Economic Research Institute of Northern Ireland], www.erini.ac.uk/Publications/PDF/Healdfinalpaper2.pdf [accessed 16 June 2009]

Heath, Edward (1998), *The Course of My Life: My Autobiography* (London: Hodder and Stoughton)

Heidelberg Institute on International Conflict Research (2008), *Conflict Barometer 2008* Heidelberg: Heidelberg Institute on International Conflict Research), www.hiik.de/en/konfliktbarometer/pdf/ConflictBarometer_2008.pdf [accessed 16 June 2009]

Held, David (2004), *Global Covenant: The Social Democratic Alternative to the Washington Consensus* (Cambridge: Polity Press)

—— (2003), 'From executive to cosmopolitan multilateralism', in David Held and Mathias Koenig-Archibugi (eds), *Taming Globalization: Frontiers of Governance*

(Cambridge: Polity Press), 160–86

Held, David, Anthony McGrew, David Goldblatt and Jonathan Perraton (1999), *Global Transformations: Politics, Economics and Culture* (Cambridge: Polity Press)

Helsinki Watch (1991), *Human Rights in Northern Ireland* (New York: Human Rights Watch)

Hemerijck, Anton (2002), 'The self-transformation of the European social model(s)', in Gøsta Esping-Andersen, with Duncan Gallie, Anton Hemerijck and John Myles, *Why We Need a New Welfare State* (Oxford: Oxford University Press), 173–213

Hennessy, Peter (1989), *Whitehall* (London: Secker and Warburg)

Hennessey, Tom and Robin Wilson (1997), *With All Due Respect: Pluralism and Parity of Esteem* (Belfast: Democratic Dialogue), http://cain.ulst.ac.uk/dd/report7/ddreport7.pdf [accessed 16 June 2009]

Heskin, Ken (1980), *Northern Ireland: A Psychological Analysis* (Dublin: Gill and Macmillan)

Hillyard, Paddy, Grace Kelly, Eithne McLaughlin, Demi Patsios and Mike Tomlinson (2003), *Bare Necessities: Poverty and Social Exclusion in Northern Ireland – Key Findings* (Belfast: Democratic Dialogue), http://cain.ulst.ac.uk/dd/report16/ddreport16.pdf [accessed 16 June 2009]

Hirst, Paul (2002), 'Renewing democracy through associations', *Political Quarterly*, 73:4, 409–21

Hobsbawm, Eric (1994), *The Age of Extremes: The Short Twentieth Century 1914–1991* (London: Michael Joseph)

—— (1990), *Nations and Nationalism since 1780: Programme, Myth, Reality* (Cambridge: Cambridge University Press)

Hollinger, David A. (2005 [1995]), *Postethnic America: Beyond Multiculturalism* (New York: Basic Books)

Horowitz, Donald L. (2006), 'Strategy takes a holiday: Fraenkel and Grofman on the alternative vote', *Comparative Political Studies*, 39:5, 652–62

—— (2003), 'Electoral systems: a primer for decision makers', *Journal of Democracy*, 14:4, 115–27

—— (2002a) 'Constitutional design: proposals versus processes', in Andrew Reynolds (ed.), *The Architecture of Democracy: Constitutional Design, Conflict Management, and Democracy* (Oxford: Oxford University Press), 15–36

—— (2002b), 'Eating leftovers: making peace from scraps off the negotiating table', in Günther Baechler and Andreas Wenger (eds), *Conflict and Cooperation: The Individual Between Ideal and Reality* (Zürich: Neue Zürcher Zeitung), 293–309

—— (2002c), 'Explaining the Northern Ireland agreement: the sources of an unlikely constitutional consensus', *British Journal of Political Science*, 32, 193–220

—— (2001), 'The Northern Ireland agreement: clear, consociational, and risky', in John McGarry (ed.), *Northern Ireland and the Divided World: The Northern Ireland Conflict and the Good Friday Agreement in Comparative Perspective* (Oxford: Oxford University Press), 89–108

—— (1994), 'Democracy in divided societies', in Larry Diamond and Marc F. Plattner (eds), *Nationalism, Ethnic Conflict, and Democracy* (Baltimore, MD: Johns Hopkins University Press), 35–55

—— (1985), *Ethnic Groups in Conflict* (Berkeley, CA: University of California Press)

References

Hughes, James (2009), 'Paying for peace: comparing the EU's role in the conflicts in Northern Ireland and Kosovo', *Ethnopolitics*, 8:3–4, 287–306

Ignatieff, Michael (1999), *The Warrior's Honor: Ethnic War and the Modern Conscience* (London: Vintage)

—— (1994), *Blood and Belonging: Journeys into the New Nationalism* (New York: Farrar, Straus and Giroux)

Ilievski, Zoran and Dane Taleski (2009), 'Was the EU's role in conflict management in Macedonia a success?', *Ethnopolitics*, 8:3–4, 355–67

Independent Commission on Policing for Northern Ireland [the Patten report] (1999), *A New Beginning: Policing in Northern Ireland*, www.nio.gov.uk/a_new_beginning_in_policing_in_northern_ireland.pdf [accessed 16 June 2009]

International Commission on the Balkans (2005), *The Balkans in Europe's Future* (Sofia: Commission Secretariat), http://cls-sofia.org/uploads/files/Projects%20files/Intern ational%20Commission%20on%20the%20Balkans.pdf [accessed 16 June 2009]

International Crisis Group (2007), *Ensuring Bosnia's Future: A New International Engagement Strategy* (Brussels: International Crisis Group), www.crisisgroup. org/home/index.cfm?id=4655&l=1 [accessed 16 June 2009]

International IDEA (2002), *Handbook on Democracy Assessment* (The Hague: Kluwer Law International)

Janev, Goran (2003), 'Kosovo independence and Macedonian stability: is there any alternative to the nationalistic discourse?', in Florian Bieber and Židas Daskalovski (eds), *Understanding the War in Kosovo* (London: Frank Cass), 302–20

Jarman, Neil (2008), 'Security and segregation: interface barriers in Belfast', *Shared Space* [journal of the Community Relations Council], 6, 21–33

—— (2004), *Demography, Development and Disorder: Changing Patterns in Interface Areas* (Belfast: Institute for Conflict Research), www.conflictresearch.org.uk/doc-uments/Interface_Paper.pdf [accessed 16 June 2009]

Jenne, Erin K. (2009), 'The paradox of ethnic partition: lessons from *de facto* partition in Bosnia and Kosovo', *Regional and Federal Studies*, 19:2, 273–89

Jeffery, Charlie (2005), 'Devolution and divergence: public attitudes and institutional logics', in John Adams and Katie Schmuecker (eds), *Devolution in Practice 2006* (London: Institute for Public Policy Research), 10–28

Joppke, Christian and Steven Lukes (1999), 'Introduction: multicultural questions', in Joppke and Lukes (eds), *Multicultural Questions* (Oxford: Oxford University Press), 1–24

Kaldor, Mary (2004), 'Nations and globalisation', *Nations and Nationalism*, 10:1&2, 161–77

—— (1999), *New and Old Wars: Organized Violence in a Global Era* (Cambridge: Polity Press)

Katunaric, Vjeran (2003), *Peace Enclaves/Cradles: Final Report – Main Findings and Policy Proposals* (Strasbourg: Council of Europe), http://www.coe.int/t/dg4/cultureheritage/Source/Completed/Dialogue/DGIV_CULT_PREV_PE(2003)4_Katunaric_E.PDF [accessed 16 June 2009]

Kaufman, Stuart J. (2006), 'Escaping the symbolic politics trap: reconciliation initiatives and conflict resolution in ethnic wars', *Journal of Peace Research*, 43:2, 201–18

—— (2001), *Modern Hatreds: The Symbolic Politics of Ethnic War* (Ithaca, NY: Cornell University Press)

Kausch, Kristina and Isaías Barreñada (2005), 'Alliance of Civilizations: international security and cosmopolitan democracy – seminar conclusions', FRIDE working paper 13 (Madrid: Fundación para las Relaciones Internacionales y el Diálogo Exterior), www.fride.org/publicacion/136/la-alianza-de-civilizaciones-seguridad-internacional-y-democracia-cosmopolita [accessed 16 June 2009]

Keane, John (2003), *Global Civil Society?* (Cambridge: Cambridge University Press)

—— (1998), *Civil Society: Old Images, New Visions* (Cambridge: Polity Press)

Kellner, Peter and Christopher Hitchens (1976), *Callaghan: The Road to Number 10* (London: Cassell)

Khan, Yasmin (2007), *The Great Partition: The Making of India and Pakistan* (New Haven, CT: Yale University Press)

King, Cecil (1975), *The Cecil King Diary 1970–4* (London: Jonathan Cape)

Koppa, Maria-Eleni (2001), 'Ethnic Albanians in the Former Yugoslav Republic of Macedonia: between nationality and citizenship', *Nationalism and Ethnic Politics*, 7:4, 37–65

Kornprobst, Markus (2005), 'Episteme, nation-builders and national identity: the re-construction of Irishness', *Nations and Nationalism*, 11:3, 403–21

Kuhn, Thomas S. (1962), *The Structure of Scientific Revolutions* (Chicago: University of Chicago Press)

Kwok-Bun, Chan (2002), 'Both sides now: culture contact, hybridization, and cosmopol-itanism', in Steven Vertovec and Robin Cohen (eds), *Conceiving Cosmopolitanism: Theory, Context, and Practice* (Oxford: Oxford University Press), 191–208

Kymlicka, Will (1995), 'Introduction', in Kymlicka (ed.), *The Rights of Minority Cultures* (Oxford: Oxford University Press), 1–27

Laclau, Ernesto (1996), *Emancipation(s)* (London: Verso)

—— (1994), 'Introduction', in Ernesto Laclau (ed.), *The Making of Political Identities* (London: Verso), 1–8

Laclau, Ernesto and Chantal Mouffe (1985), *Hegemony and Socialist Strategy* (London: Verso)

Lægaard, Sune (2008), 'Moderate secularism and multicultural equality', *Politics*, 28:3, 160–8

Laffan, Brigid and Jane O'Mahony (2008), *Ireland and the European Union* (Basingstoke: Palgrave)

Laffan, Brigid and Diane Payne (2001), *Creating Living Institutions: EU Cross-border Cooperation After the Good Friday Agreement* (Armagh: Centre for Cross-Border Studies), www.crossborder.ie/pubs/creatingliving.pdf [accessed 16 June 2009]

Laver, Michael (2000), 'Coalitions in Northern Ireland: preliminary thoughts', paper delivered at a Democratic Dialogue round table, Europa Hotel Belfast, September 2000, on the prospective Programme for Government of the devolved administration

Lijphart, Arend (2004), 'Constitutional design for divided societies', *Journal of Democracy*, 15:2, 96–109

—— (2002), 'The wave of power-sharing democracy', in Andrew Reynolds (ed.), *The Architecture of Democracy: Constitutional Design, Conflict Management, and*

References

Democracy (Oxford: Oxford University Press), 37–54

—— (2001), 'Constructivism and consociational theory', *Newsletter of the American Political Science Association Organized Section in Comparative Politics*, 12:1, 11–13

—— (2000), 'Definitions, evidence, and policy: a response to Matthijs Bogaards' critique', *Journal of Theoretical Politics*, 12:4, 425–31

—— (1977), *Democracy in Plural Societies* (New Haven, CT: Yale University Press)

Longley, Edna (2001), 'Multi-Culturalism and Northern Ireland', in Edna Longley and Declan Kiberd, *Multi-Culturalism: The View from the Two Irelands* (Cork: Cork University Press)

Lustick, Ian S. (1997), 'Lijphart, Lakatos and consociationalism', *World Politics*, 50:1, 88–117

Lutz, Karin Gilland and Christopher Farrington (2006), 'Alternative Ulster? Political parties and the non-constitutional policy space in Northern Ireland', *Political Studies*, 54:4, 715–42

Maalouf, Amin (2000), *On Identity* (London: Harvill Press)

McGarry, John and Brendan O'Leary (2009a), 'Power shared after the deaths of thousands', in Rupert Taylor (ed.), *Consociational Theory: McGarry and O'Leary and the Northern Ireland Conflict* (London: Routledge), 15–84

—— (2009b), 'Under friendly and less-friendly fire', in Rupert Taylor (ed.), *Consociational Theory: McGarry and O'Leary and the Northern Ireland Conflict* (London: Routledge), 333–88

—— (2004), 'Introduction', in McGarry and O'Leary (eds), *The Northern Ireland Conflict: Consociational Engagements* (Oxford: Oxford University Press), 1–61

MacGinty, Roger (2003), 'Constitutional referendums and ethnonational conflict: Northern Ireland', *Nationalism and Ethnic Politics*, 9:2, 1–22

McGrattan, Cillian (2007), 'Change and continuity in contemporary Irish nationalism: path-dependency and the hidden politics of policy entrenchment', paper delivered at Queen's University Belfast Conference, 'Beyond the Nation?: Critical Reflections on Nations and Nationalism in Uncertain Times', September 2007

McGregor, Patrick and Patricia McKee (1995), 'A widening gap?', in Paul Teague and Robin Wilson (eds), *Social Exclusion, Social Inclusion* (Belfast: Democratic Dialogue), http://cain.ulst.ac.uk/dd/report2/ddreport2.pdf [accessed 16 June 2009], 39–44

McKeown, Ciaran (1984), *The Passion of Peace* (Belfast: Blackstaff Press)

Mair, Peter (2006), 'Ruling the void? The hollowing of western democracy', *New Left Review*, 42, 25–51

Malcolm, Noel (1996), 'Bosnia deconstructed', *Prospect*, January, 8–10

Malešević, Siniša (2004), '"Divine *ethnies*" and "sacred nations": Anthony D. Smith and the Neo-Durkheimian theory of nationalism', *Nationalism and Ethnic Politics*, 10:4, 561–93

—— (2002), 'Identity: conceptual, operational and historical critique', in Siniša Malešević and Mark Haugaard (eds), *Making Sense of Collectivity: Ethnicity, Nationalism and Globalisation* (London: Pluto Press), 195–215

Mandelson, Peter (2000), 'Make Votes Count lecture, 28 June 2000', www.unlockdemocracy.org.uk/charter88archive/press/0006_mandelson.html [accessed

214

16 June 2009]

Marx, Karl (1973), *Grundrisse: Introduction to the Critique of Political Economy* (Harmondsworth, Penguin Books)

Marx, Karl and Friedrich Engels (1968), *Karl Marx and Friedrich Engels: Selected Works* (London: Lawrence and Wishart)

Maudling, Reginald (1978), *Memoirs* (London: Sidgwick and Jackson)

Mazower, Mark (2004), *Salonica, City of Ghosts: Christians, Muslims and Jews 1430–1950* (London: Harper Collins)

—— (1998), *Dark Continent: Europe's Twentieth Century* (London: Penguin Books)

Mepham, David (2005), 'Social justice in a shrinking world', in Nick Pearce and Will Paxton (eds), *Social Justice: Building a Fairer Britain* (London: Politico's Publishing), 133–57

Miley, Thomas Jeffrey (2007), 'Against the thesis of the "civic nation": the case of Catalonia in contemporary Spain', *Nationalism and Ethnic Politics*, 13:1, 1–37

Mitchell, George (1999), *Making Peace* (London: William Heinemann)

Mitchell, James (2004), 'Understanding Stormont–London relations', paper presented to Political Studies Association British and comparative territorial politics specialist group conference, Queen's University Belfast, January 2004, www.devolution. ac.uk/pdfdata/Mitchell_Stormont_London_paper.pdf [accessed 16 June 2009]

Moloney, Ed (2002), *A Secret History of the IRA* (London: Allen Lane)

Moore, Carolyn (2008), 'A Europe of the regions vs. the regions in Europe: reflections on regional engagement in Brussels', *Regional and Federal Studies*, 18:5, 517–35

Moreno, Luis, Ana Arriba and Araceli Serrano (1998), 'Multiple identities in decentralized Spain', *Regional and Federal Studies*, 8:3, 65–88

Morison, John and Stephen Livingstone (1995), *Reshaping Public Power: Northern Ireland and the British Constitutional Crisis* (London: Sweet & Maxwell)

Mostov, Julie (2007), 'Soft borders and transnational citizens', in Seyla Benhabib, Ian Shapiro and Danilo Petranović (eds), *Identities, Affiliations, and Allegiances* (Cambridge: Cambridge University Press), 136–58

Mouffe, Chantal (2000), *The Democratic Paradox* (London: Verso)

—— (1993), *The Return of the Political* (London: Verso)

Mowlam, Mo (2002), *Momentum: The Struggle for Peace, Politics and the People* (London: Hodder and Stoughton)

Moynihan, Daniel Patrick (1993), *Pandaemonium: Ethnicity in International Politics* (Oxford: Oxford University Press)

Mudde, Cas (2007), *Populist Radical Right Parties in Europe* (Cambridge: Cambridge University Press)

Mulaj, Klejda (2005), 'On Bosnia's borders and ethnic cleansing: internal and external factors', *Nationalism and Ethnic Politics*, 11:1, 1–24

New Ulster Movement (1971), *The Reform of Stormont*, http://cain.ulst.ac.uk/othelem/ organ/num/num71a.htm [accessed 16 June 2009]

Nic Craith, Máiréad (2002), *Plural Identities – Singular Narratives: The Case of Northern Ireland* (New York: Berghahn Books)

Northern Ireland Human Rights Commission (2008), *A Bill of Rights for Northern Ireland: Advice to the Secretary of State for Northern Ireland* (Belfast: Northern Ireland

Human Rights Commission), www.nihrc.org/dms/data/NIHRC/attachments/ dd/files/51/A_Bill_of_Rights_for_Northern_Ireland_(December_2008).pdf [accessed 16 June 2009]

—— (2004), *Progressing a Bill of Rights for Northern Ireland: An Update* (Belfast: Northern Ireland Human Rights Commission), http://nihrc.org/dms/data/NIHRC/ attachments/dd/files/52/BOR_Progress_Report_Apr04.pdf [accessed 16 June 2009]

—— (2001), *Making a Bill of Rights for Northern Ireland: A Consultation by the Northern Ireland Human Rights Commission* (Belfast: NIHRC), http://nihrc. org/dms/data/NIHRC/attachments/dd/files/52/BoR_consultation.pdf [accessed 16 June 2009]

Noutcheva, Gergana, Nathalie Tocci, Bruno Coppieters, Tamara Kovziridze, Michael Emerson and Michael Huysseune (2004), 'Europeanization and secessionist conflicts: concepts and theories', *Journal on Ethnopolitics and Minority Issues in Europe*, www.ecmi.de/jemie/download/1–2004Chapter1.pdf [accessed 16 June 2009]

Nowak, Manfred (2004), 'Has Dayton failed?', in Christopher Solioz and Tobias K. Vogel (eds), *Dayton and Beyond: Perspectives on the Future of Bosnia and Herzegovina* (Baden-Baden: Nomos), 45–58

Nutley, Sandra and Jeff Web (2000), 'Evidence and the policy process', in Huw Davies, Sandra Nutley and Peter Smith (eds), *What Works? Evidence-based Policy and Practice in Public Services* (Bristol: The Policy Press), 13–41

Oberschall, Anthony and L. Kendall Palmer (2005), 'The failure of moderate politics: the case of Northern Ireland', in Ian O'Flynn and David Russell (eds), *Power Sharing: New Challenges for Divided Societies* (London: Pluto Press), 77–91

O'Donnell, Catherine (2007), *Fianna Fáil, Irish Republicanism and the Northern Ireland Troubles 1968–2005* (Dublin: Irish Academic Press)

O'Duffy, Brendan (2007), *British–Irish Relations and Northern Ireland: From Violent Politics to Conflict Regulation* (Dublin: Irish Academic Press)

O'Flynn, Ian (2006), *Deliberative Democracy and Divided Societies* (Edinburgh: Edinburgh University Press)

O'Halloran, Clare (1987), *Partition and the Limits of Irish Nationalism* (Dublin: Gill and Macmillan)

Okin, Susan Moller (1999), *Is Multiculturalism Bad for Women?* (Princeton, NJ: Princeton University Press)

O'Leary, Brendan (2006), 'Foreword: the realism of power-sharing', in Michael Kerr, *Conflict and Coexistence in Northern Ireland and Lebanon* (Dublin: Irish Academic Press), xvii–xxxv

—— (2004a), 'The limits to coercive consociationalism in Northern Ireland', in John McGarry and Brendan O'Leary (eds), *The Northern Ireland Conflict: Consociational Engagements* (Oxford: Oxford University Press), 97–131

—— (2004b), 'The nature of the agreement', in McGarry and O'Leary (eds), *The Northern Ireland Conflict: Consociational Engagements*, 260–93

—— (2001a), 'The character of the 1998 agreement: results and prospects', in Rick Wilford (ed.), *Aspects of the Belfast Agreement* (Oxford: Oxford University Press), 49–83

—— (2001b), 'Comparative political science and the British-Irish Agreement', in John McGarry (ed.), *Northern Ireland and the Divided World: The Northern Ireland Conflict and the Good Friday Agreement in Comparative Perspective* (Oxford: Oxford University Press), 53–88

O'Leary, Cornelius, Sydney Elliott and R. A. Wilford (1988), *The Northern Ireland Assembly: A Constitutional Experiment* (London: Hurst & Co)

Oxford Research International (2007), *The Silent Majority Speaks: Snapshots of Today and Visions of the Future of the Bosnia Herzegovina* (New York: United Nations Development Programme), www.undp.ba/index.aspx?PID=7&RID=413 [accessed 16 June 2009]

Özkırımlı, Umut (2005), *Contemporary Debates on Nationalism: A Critical Engagement* (Basingstoke: Palgrave)

—— (2000), *Theories of Nationalism: A Critical Introduction* (London: Macmillan)

Paintin, Katie (2009), *States of Conflict: A Case Study on Conflict Prevention in Macedonia* (London: Institute for Public Policy Research)

Papisca, Antonio (2007), 'Citizenship and citizenships *ad omnes includendos*: a human rights approach', in Léonce Bekemans, Maria Karasinska-Fendler, Marco Mascia, Antonio Papisca, Constantine A. Stephanou and Peter G. Xuereb (eds), *Intercultural Dialogue and Citizenship: Translating Values into Actions – A Common Project for Europeans and Their Partners* (Venice: Marsilio), 457–80

Pappalardo, Adriano (1981), 'The conditions for consociational democracy: a logical and empirical critique', *European Journal of Political Research*, 9, 365–90

Patterson, Henry (2006), *Ireland Since 1939: The Persistence of Conflict* (Dublin: Penguin Ireland)

Patterson, Henry and Eric Kaufmann (2007), *Unionism and Orangeism in Northern Ireland Since 1945: The Decline of the Loyal Family* (Manchester: Manchester University Press)

Pollak, Andy (1993), *A Citizens' Inquiry: The Opsahl Report on Northern Ireland* (Dublin: Lilliput)

Powell, Jonathan (2008), *Great Hatred, Little Room: Making Peace in Northern Ireland* (London: Bodley Head)

Prince, Simon (2007), *Northern Ireland's '68: Civil Rights, Global Revolt and the Origins of the Troubles* (Dublin: Irish Academic Press)

Prior, Jim (1986), *A Balance of Power* (London: Hamish Hamilton)

Purdie, Bob (1990), *Politics in the Streets: The Origins of the Civil Rights Movement in Northern Ireland* (Belfast: Blackstaff Press)

Rees, Merlyn (1985), *Northern Ireland: A Personal Perspective* (London: Methuen)

Reilly, Benjamin (2001), *Democracy in Divided Societies: Electoral Engineering for Conflict Management* (Cambridge: Cambridge University Press)

Reiss, Mitchell B. (2008), 'The troubles we've seen', *American Interest*, www.the-american-interest.com/ai2/article-bd.cfm?Id=454&MId=20 [accessed 16 June 2009]

Rellstab, Ursula (2001), *Transversal Study: Cultural Policy and Cultural Diversity – National Report: Switzerland* (Strasbourg: Council of Europe), www.coe.int/t/dg4/cultureheritage/Completed/Diversity/CCCULT_2001_7_EN.PDF [accessed 16 June 2009]

References

Richter Malabotta, Melita (2005), 'Managing cultural transitions: multiculturalism, interculturalism and minority policies', in Nada Švob-Đokić (ed.), *The Emerging Creative Industries in Southeastern Europe* (Zagreb: Institute for International Relations), 113–25

Robins, Keith (2006), *The Challenge of Transcultural Diversities: Cultural Policy and Cultural Diversity* (Strasbourg: Council of Europe)

Rothstein, Bo (2005), *Social Traps and the Problem of Trust* (Cambridge: Cambridge University Press)

Rothstein, Bo and Jan Teorell (2008), 'What is quality of government? A theory of impartial government institutions', *Governance*, 21:2, 165–90

Roxburgh, Angus (2002), *Preachers of Hate: The Rise of the Far Right* (London: Gibson Square Books)

Salecl, Renata (1994), 'The crisis of identity and the struggle for new hegemony in the former Yugoslavia', in Ernesto Laclau (ed.), *The Making of Political Identities* (London: Verso), 205–32

Sartori, Giovanni (1997 [1994]), *Comparative Constitutional Engineering: An Inquiry into Structures, Incentives and* Outcomes (Basingstoke: Macmillan)

Sayer, Andrew (2000), *Realism and Social Science* (London: Sage)

Schmidt, Vivien A. (2006), *Democracy in Europe: The EU and National Polities* (Oxford: Oxford University Press)

Sebastián, Sofia (2008a), 'The stabilisation and association process: are EU inducements failing in the Western Balkans?', FRIDE working paper 53 (Madrid: Fundación para las Relaciones Internacionales y el Diálogo Exterior), www.fride. org/publication/356/the-stabilisation-and-association-process-are-eu-inducements-failing-in-the-western-balkans [accessed 16 June 2009]

—— (2008b), 'Elections in Bosnia and Herzegovina', FRIDE democracy backgrounder 17 (Madrid: Fundación para las Relaciones Internacionales y el Diálogo Exterior), www.fride.org/publication/492/elections-in-bosnia-and-herzegovina [accessed 16 June 2009]

—— (2007), 'Leaving Dayton behind: constitutional reform in Bosnia and Herzegovina', FRIDE working paper 46 (Madrid: Fundación para las Relaciones Internacionales y el Diálogo Exterior), www.fride.org/publication/291/leaving-dayton-behind-constitutional-reform-in-bosnia-and-herzegovina [accessed 16 June 2009]

Sen, Amartya (2006), *Identity and Violence: The Illusion of Destiny* (New York: W. W. Norton)

Shani, Ornit (2007), *Communalism, Caste and Hindu Nationalism: The Violence in Gujarat* (Cambridge: Cambridge University Press)

Sharp, Alan (1996), 'The genie that would not go back into the bottle', in Seamus Dunn and T. G. Fraser (eds), *Europe and Ethnicity: World War I and Contemporary Ethnic Conflict* (London: Routledge), 10–29

Shirlow, Peter and Brendan Murtagh (2006), *Belfast: Segregation, Violence and the City* (London: Pluto Press)

Silber, Laura and Allan Little (1995), *The Death of Yugoslavia* (London: Penguin Books)

Silke, Andrew (2005), 'Fire of Iolaus: the role of state countermeasures in causing terrorism and what needs to be done', in Tore Bjørgo (ed.), *Root Causes of Terrorism:*

Myths, Reality and Ways Forward (London: Routledge), 241–55

Sinnott, Richard (1999 [1992]), 'The electoral system', in John Coakley and Michael Gallagher (eds), *Politics in the Republic of Ireland: Third Edition* (London: Routledge), 9–126

Sisk, Timothy D. (2004), 'Peacemaking in civil wars: obstacles, options and opportunities', in Ulrich Schneckener and Stefan Wolff (eds), *Managing and Settling Ethnic Conflicts* (London: Hurst & Co), 248–70

—— (1996), *Power Sharing and International Mediation in Ethnic Conflicts* (Washington, DC: United States Institute of Peace)

Sluga, Glenda (2005), 'What is national self-determination? Nationality and psychology during the apogee of nationalism', *Nations and Nationalism*, 11:1, 1–20

Smith, Anthony D. (2009), *Ethno-symbolism and Nationalism: A Cultural Approach* (London: Routledge)

—— (1998), *Nationalism and Modernism: A Critical Survey of Recent Theories of Nations and Nationalism* (London: Routledge)

—— (1986), *The Ethnic Origins of Nations* (Oxford: Blackwell)

—— (1983), *Theories of Nationalism* (London: Duckworth)

Smith, M. L. R. (1999), 'The intellectual internment of a conflict: the forgotten war in Northern Ireland', *International Affairs*, 75:1, 77–97

Sniderman, Paul M. and Louk Hagendoorn (2007), *When Ways of Life Collide: Multiculturalism and its Discontents in the Netherlands* (Princeton, NJ: Princeton University Press)

Solioz, Christopher and Tobias K. Vogel (2004), 'Introduction', in Solioz and Vogel (eds), *Dayton and Beyond: Perspectives on the Future of Bosnia and Herzegovina* (Baden-Baden: Nomos), 15–21

Sørensen, Georg (1999), 'Sovereignty: change and continuity in a fundamental institution', *Political Studies*, 47, 590–604

Spinner-Halev, Jeff (1999), 'Cultural pluralism and partial citizenship', in Christian Joppke and Steven Lukes (eds), *Multicultural Questions* (Oxford: Oxford University Press), 65–86

Stanbridge, Karen (2005), 'Nationalism, international factors and the "Irish question" in the era of the First World War', *Nations and Nationalism*, 11:1, 21–42

Stalker, John (1988), *Stalker* (London: Harrap)

Taylor, Charles (1994), *Multiculturalism: Examining the Politics of Recognition* (Princeton, NJ: Princeton University Press)

Taylor, Peter (1980), *Beating the Terrorists? Interrogation in Omagh, Gough and Castlereagh* (Harmondsworth: Penguin Books)

Taylor, Rupert (ed.) (2009), *Consociational Theory: McGarry and O'Leary and the Northern Ireland Conflict* (London: Routledge)

—— (2001), 'Northern Ireland: consociation or social transformation?', in John McGarry (ed.), *Northern Ireland and the Divided World: Post-Agreement Northern Ireland in Comparative Perspective* (Oxford: Oxford University Press), 37–52

Thatcher, Margaret (1995 [1993]), *The Downing Street Years* (London: Harper Collins Publishers)

Thompson, Mark (1994), *Forging War: The Media in Serbia, Croatia and Bosnia-Hercegovina* (London: Article 19)

References

Townshend, Charles (2005), *Easter 1916: The Irish Rebellion* (London: Allen Lane)

Toynbee, Polly and David Walker (2001), *Did Things Get Better? An Audit of Labour's Successes and Failures* (London: Penguin Books)

Trägårdh, Lars (2007), 'Democratic governance and the creation of social capital in Sweden: the discreet charm of governmental commissions', in Trägårdh (ed.), *State and Civil Society in Northern Europe: The Swedish Model Reconsidered* (New York: Berghahn Books), 254–70

Trench, Alan (ed.) (2004), *Has Devolution Made a Difference? The State of the Nations 2004* (Exeter: Imprint Academic)

Urban, Mark (1992), *Big Boys' Rules: The SAS and the Struggle Against the IRA* (London: Faber and Faber)

Van Schendelen, M. P. C. M. (1984), 'The views of Arend Lijphart and collected criticisms', in Van Schendelen (ed.), *Consociationalism, Pillarization and Conflict Management in the low Countries* (Amsterdam: Uitgeverij Boom), 19–55

Varshney, Ashutosh (2002), *Ethnic Conflict and Civic Life: Hindus and Muslims in India* (New Haven, CT: Yale University Press)

Vertovec, Steven and Robin Cohen (2002), 'Introduction: conceiving cosmopolitanism', in Vertovec and Cohen (eds), *Conceiving Cosmopolitanism: Theory, Context, and Practice* (Oxford: Oxford University Press), 1–22

Vincent, Andrew (2002), *Nationalism and Particularity* (Cambridge: Cambridge University Press)

Volkan, Vamik (1997), *Blood Lines: From Ethnic Pride to Ethnic Terrorism* (Boulder, CO: Westview Press)

Walker, Graham (2004), *A History of the Ulster Unionist Party: Protest, Pragmatism and Pessimism* (Manchester: Manchester University Press)

—— (1985), *The Politics of Frustration: Harry Midgley and the Failure of Labour in Northern Ireland* (Manchester: Manchester University Press)

Whitelaw, William (1989), *The Whitelaw Memoirs* (London: Aurum Press)

Whyte, John (1990), *Interpreting Northern Ireland* (Oxford: Clarendon Press)

Wikan, Unni (2002), *Generous Betrayal: Politics of Culture in the New Europe* (Chicago: University of Chicago Press)

Wilford, Rick (2006), 'Joining up is hard to do: the devolved Northern Ireland Executive 1999–2002', inaugural professorial lecture, Queen's University Belfast, 26 October 2006

—— (2000), 'The assembly', in Rick Wilford and Robin Wilson (eds), *Northern Ireland Devolution Monitoring Report: November 2000* (London: University College), http://www.ucl.ac.uk/constitution-unit/files/research/devolution/dmr/ninov00.pdf [accessed 16 June 2009], 17–27

—— (1992), 'Inverting consociationalism? Policy, pluralism and the post-modern', in Brigid Hadfield (ed.), *Northern Ireland: Politics and the Constitution* (Buckingham: Open University Press), 29–46

—— (ed.) (2001), *Aspects of the Belfast Agreement* (Oxford: Oxford University Press)

Wilford, Rick and Robin Wilson (2008a), 'Northern Ireland: devolution once again', in Alan Trench (ed.), *The State of the Nations 2008* (Exeter: Imprint Academic Press), 87–122

—— (2005), 'Northern Ireland: while you take the high road …', in Alan Trench (ed.), *The Dynamics of Devolution: The State of the Nations 2005* (Exeter: Imprint Academic Press), 63–90

—— (2004), 'Northern Ireland: renascent?', in Alan Trench (ed.), *Has Devolution Made a Difference? The State of the Nations 2004* (Exeter: Imprint Academic Press), 79–120

—— (2003), 'Northern Ireland: valedictory?', in Robert Hazell (ed.), *The State of the Nations 2003: The Third Year of Devolution in the United Kingdom* (Exeter: Imprint Academic Press), 79–118

—— (2000), 'A "bare knuckle ride": Northern Ireland', in Robert Hazell (ed.), *The State and the Nations: The First Year of Devolution in the United Kingdom* (Thorverton, Imprint Academic), 79–115

—— (eds) (2009a), *Northern Ireland Devolution Monitoring Report: January 2009* (London: University College), http://www.ucl.ac.uk/constitution-unit/files/research/devolution/dmr/NI_Jan09.pdf [accessed 16 June 2009]

—— (eds) (2009b), *Northern Ireland Devolution Monitoring Report: May 2009* (London: University College), www.ucl.ac.uk/constitution-unit/files/research/devolution/dmr/NI_May09.pdf [accessed 17 July 2009]

—— (eds) (2008b), *Northern Ireland Devolution Monitoring Report: January 2008* (London: University College), www.ucl.ac.uk/constitution-unit/files/research/devolution/dmr/NI_Jan08.pdf [accessed 16 June 2009]

—— (eds) (2008c), *Northern Ireland Devolution Monitoring Report: May 2008* (London: University College), www.ucl.ac.uk/constitution-unit/research/devolution/MonReps/NI_May08.pdf [accessed 16 June 2009]

—— (eds) (2008d), *Northern Ireland Devolution Monitoring Report: September 2008* (London: University College), www.ucl.ac.uk/constitution-unit/research/devolution/MonReps/NI_Sept08.pdf [accessed 16 June 2009]

—— (eds) (2007a), *Northern Ireland Devolution Monitoring Report: January 2007* (London: University College), www.ucl.ac.uk/constitution-unit/research/devolution/MonReps/NI_Jan07.pdf [accessed 16 June 2009]

—— (eds) (2007b), *Northern Ireland Devolution Monitoring Report: April 2007* (London: University College), www.ucl.ac.uk/constitution-unit/research/devolution/MonReps/NI_April07.pdf [accessed 16 June 2009]

—— (eds) (2007c), *Northern Ireland Devolution Monitoring Report: September 2007* (London: University College), www.ucl.ac.uk/constitution-unit/research/devolution/MonReps/NI_Sept07.pdf [accessed 16 June 2009]

—— (eds) (2006), *Northern Ireland Devolution Monitoring Report: January 2006* (London: University College), www.ucl.ac.uk/constitution-unit/research/devolution/Monitoring%20Reports/Jan06/NI%20Jan06.pdf [accessed 16 June 2009]

—— (eds) (2005a), *Northern Ireland Devolution Monitoring Report: April 2005* (London: University College), www.ucl.ac.uk/constitution-unit/files/research/devolution/dmr/ni_april_2005.pdf [accessed 16 June 2009]

—— (eds) (2005b), *Northern Ireland Devolution Monitoring Report: July 2005* (London: University College), www.ucl.ac.uk/constitution-unit/files/research/devolution/dmr/ni_july_2005.pdf [accessed 16 June 2009]

References

—— (eds) (2001), *Northern Ireland Devolution Monitoring Report: November 2001* (London: University College), www.ucl.ac.uk/constitution-unit/files/research/devolution/dmr/ninov01.pdf [accessed 16 June 2009]

Wilford, Rick, Robin Wilson and Kathleen Claussen (2007), *Power to the People? Assessing Democracy in Northern Ireland* (Dublin: TASC at New Island)

Wilkinson, Richard G. (2005), *The Impact of Inequality: How to Make Sick Societies Healthier* (London, Routledge)

Wilkinson, Richard and Kate Pickett (2009), *The Spirit Level: Why More Equal Societies Almost Always Do Better* (London: Allen Lane)

Wilkinson, Steven I. (2004), *Votes and Violence: Electoral Competition and Ethnic Riots in India* (Cambridge: Cambridge University Press)

Wilson, Harold (1979), *Final Term: The Labour Government 1974–1976* (London: Weidenfeld and Nicholson)

—— (1971), *The Labour Government 1964–70* (London: Weidenfeld and Nicholson)

Wilson, Robin (2007), *A Shared Today: Belfast's Ballynafeigh Neighbourhood* (Belfast: Ballynafeigh Community Development Association)

—— (2006), *What Works for Reconciliation* (Belfast: Democratic Dialogue), http://cain.ulst.ac.uk/dd/report19/ddreport19.pdf [accessed 16 June 2009]

—— (2001), 'The politics of contemporary ethno-nationalist conflicts', *Nations and Nationalism*, 7:3, 365–84

—— (1985), 'Imperialism in crisis: the "Irish dimension"', in Mary Langan and Bill Schwarz (eds), *Crises in the British State 1880–1930* (London: Hutchinson), 151–78

Wolff, Stefan (2007), 'Conflict resolution between power sharing and power dividing, or beyond?', *Political Studies Review*, 5:3, 377–93

—— (2006), *Ethnic Conflict: A Global Perspective* (Oxford: Oxford University Press)

—— (2005), 'Between stability and collapse: internal and external dynamics of post-agreement institution building in Northern Ireland', in Sid Noel (ed.), *From Power Sharing to Democracy: Post-conflict Institutions in Ethnically Divided Societies* (Montreal and Kingston: McGill-Queen's University Press), 44–66

—— (2004), 'Managing and settling ethnic conflicts', in Ulrich Schneckener and Stefan Wolff (eds), *Managing and Settling Ethnic Conflicts* (London: Hurst & Co), 1–17

—— (2002), 'Introduction: from Sunningdale to Belfast, 1973–98', in Jörg Neuheiser and Stefan Wolff (eds), *Peace at Last? The Impact of the Good Friday Agreement on Northern Ireland* (Oxford: Berghahn Books), 1–24

Woodward, Susan L. (1995), *Balkan Tragedy: Chaos and Dissolution After the Cold War* (Washington, DC: The Brookings Institution)

Wright, Frank (1987), *Northern Ireland: A Comparative Analysis* (Dublin: Gill and Macmillan)

Yuval-Davis, Nira (1998), 'Gender and nation', in Rick Wilford and Robert L. Miller (eds), *Women, Ethnicity and Nationalism: The Politics of Transition* (London: Routledge), 23–35

Zahar, Marie-Joelle (2005), 'The dichotomy of international mediation and leader intransigence', in Ian O'Flynn and David Russell (eds), *Power Sharing: New Challenges for Divided Societies* (London: Pluto Press), 123–37

Index

Note: 'n' after a page reference indicates the number of a note on that page.